LINGVIS: Visual Analytics for Linguistics

I0879743

CSLI Lecture Notes
Number 220

LingVis

Visual Analytics for Linguistics

edited by

Miriam Butt, Annette Hauti–Janisz & Verena Lyding

CSLI Publications
Center for the Study of
Language and Information
Stanford, California

Copyright © 2020
CSLI Publications
Center for the Study of Language and Information
Leland Stanford Junior University
Printed in the United States
24 23 22 21 20   1 2 3 4 5

Library of Congress Cataloging-in-Publication Data

Names: Butt, Miriam, 1966- editor. | Hautli-Janisz, Annette, editor. | Lyding, Verena, editor.

Title: LingVis : visual analytics for linguistics / edited by Miriam Butt, Annette Hautli-Janisz, Verena Lyding.

Description: Stanford, California : CSLI Publications, Center for the Study of Language and Information, [2019] | Series: CSLI lecture notes ; no. 220 | Includes bibliographical references and index.

Identifiers: LCCN 2018051797 (print) | LCCN 2018052968 (ebook)
| ISBN 9781684000357 (Electronic) | ISBN 1684000351 (Electronic)
| ISBN 9781684000340 (hardback) | ISBN 1684000343 (hardback)
| ISBN 9781684000333 (paperback) ISBN 1684000335 (paperback)

Subjects: LCSH: Information visualization. | Visual analytics. | Linguistics.
| BISAC: LANGUAGE ARTS & DISCIPLINES / Linguistics / General.

Classification: LCC QA76.9.I52 (ebook) | LCC QA76.9.I52 L56 2019 (print)
| DDC 001.4/226–dc23

LC record available at `https://lccn.loc.gov/2018051797`

CIP

∞ The acid-free paper used in this book meets the minimum requirements of the American National Standard for Information Sciences—Permanence of Paper for Printed Library Materials, ANSI Z39.48-1984.

CSLI Publications is located on the campus of Stanford University.

Visit our web site at
`http://cslipublications.stanford.edu/`
for comments on this and other titles, as well as for changes and corrections by the author and publisher.

Contents

Contributors

ALEJANDRO BENITO-SANTOS: Department of Computer Science and Automatics, Universidad de Salamanca, abenito@usal.es

ANDRÉ BLESSING: Institut für Maschinelle Sprachverarbeitung, Universität Stuttgart, Pfaffenwaldring 5b, D-70569 Stuttgart, andre.blessing@ims.uni-stuttgart.de

MIRIAM BUTT: Department of Linguistics, University of Konstanz, D-78457 Konstanz, miriam.butt@uni-konstanz.de

FANNY CHEVALIER: Department of Computer and Mathematical Sciences at Scarborough, University of Toronto, fanny@dgp.toronto.edu

CHRISTOPHER COLLINS: University of Ontario Institute of Technology, Oshawa, ON, Canada, christopher.collins@uoit.ca

AMELIE DORN: Österreichische Akademie der Wissenschaften, amelie.dorn@oeaw.ac.at

THOMAS ERTL: Institute for Visualization and Interactive Systems (VIS) & Visualisation Research Centre (VISUS), Universität Stuttgart, Universitätsstrasse 38, D-70569 Stuttgart, thomas.ertl@vis.uni-stuttgart.de

MENNATALLAH EL-ASSADY: Department of Computer and Information Science, University of Konstanz, D-78457 Konstanz, mennatallah.el-assady@uni-konstanz.de

DIRK GEERAERTS: Quantitative Lexicology and Variational Linguistics, Katholieke Universiteit Leuven, PO Box 03308, B-3000 Leuven, dirk.geeraerts@kuleuven.be

ANNETTE HAUTLI-JANISZ: Department of Linguistics, University of Konstanz, D-78457 Konstanz, annette.hautli@uni-konstanz.de

MARTI HEARST: School of Information, University of California, Berkeley, USA, hearst@berkeley.edu

KRIS HEYLEN: Quantitative Lexicology and Variational Linguistics, Katholieke Universiteit Leuven, PO Box 03308, B-3000 Leuven, kris.heylen@kuleuven.be

MARKUS JOHN: Institute for Visualization and Interactive Systems (VIS), Universität Stuttgart, Universitätsstrasse 38, D-70569 Stuttgart, markus.john@vis.uni-stuttgart.de

DANIEL A. KEIM: Department of Computer and Information Science, University of Konstanz, D-78457 Konstanz, keim@uni-konstanz.de

STEFFEN KOCH: Institute for Visualization and Interactive Systems (VIS), Universität Stuttgart, Universitätsstrasse 38, D-70569 Stuttgart, steffen.koch@vis.uni-stuttgart.de

JONAS KUHN: Institut für Maschinelle Sprachverarbeitung, Universität Stuttgart, Pfaffenwaldring 5b, D-70569 Stuttgart, jonas.kuhn@ims.uni-stuttgart.de

ANTONIO LOSADA: Department of Computer Science and Automatics, Universidad de Salamanca, alosada@usal.es

VERENA LYDING: Institute for Applied Linguistics, Eurac Research, I-39100 Bolzano, verena.lyding@eurac.edu

PAUL MEURER: University Library, University of Bergen, paul.meurer@uib.no

CHRISTIAN ROHRDANTZ: Vidatics GmbH, D-78467 Konstanz, christian.rohrdantz@vidatics.de

VICTORIA ROSÉN: Department of Linguistic, Literary and Aesthetic Studies, University of Bergen, Postboks 7805, 5020 Bergen, victoria.rosen@uib.no

CHRISTIN SCHÄTZLE: Department of Linguistics, University of Konstanz, D-78457 Konstanz, christin.schaetzle@uni-konstanz.de

KOENRAAD DE SMEDT: Department of Linguistic, Literary and Aesthetic Studies, University of Bergen, Postboks 7805, 5020 Bergen, desmedt@uib.no

DIRK SPEELMAN: Quantitative Lexicology and Variational Linguistics, Katholieke Universiteit Leuven, PO Box 03308, B-3000 Leuven, dirk.speelman@kuleuven.be

ANDREAS STOFFEL: Department of Computer and Information Science, University of Konstanz, D-78457 Konstanz, andreas.stoffel@uni-konstanz.de

ROBERTO THERÓN: Department of Computer Science and Automatics, Universidad de Salamanca, theron@usal.es

EVELINE WANDL-VOGT: Österreichische Akademie der Wissenschaften, eveline.wandl-vogt@oeaw.ac.at

THOMAS WIELFAERT: Quantitative Lexicology and Variational Linguistics, Katholieke Universiteit Leuven, PO Box 03308, B-3000 Leuven, thomas.wielfaert@kuleuven.be

JIAN ZHAO: University of Waterloo, 200 University Ave W, Waterloo, ON N2L 3G1 Canada, jianzhao@uwaterloo.ca

Preface and Acknowledgements

This volume represents a new area of research within the CSLI Publications portfolio: Visual Analytics for Linguistics (LingVis). LingVis brings together research insights from Information Visualization, Visual Analytics, Computational, Historical and Formal Linguistics to push forward new ways of visualizing language structure and linguistic features. Work within this new interdisciplinary field began emerging in the last decade and is becoming established as a new subfield within linguistics. We are very grateful to CSLI Publications for supporting our endeavor to bring together a landmark collection of some of the earliest work in the field, showcasing the opportunities visualizations offer for linguistic problems on the one hand, and the challenges in data representation and modelling that linguistics presents for Visual Analytics and Information Visualization on the other hand.

We would like to thank all of our contributors, especially those who had papers ready on time and waited patiently for the volume to be completed.

In editing this volume, we received extensive help from a number of sources. First of all, no volume would be complete without the work of anonymous reviewers, whom we have to thank for their thorough work. Secondly, Susanne Trissler of *Texte von Format. Das Konstanzer Wissenschaftslektorat* edited and proofread the final version of the volume. Finally, we would like to thank Dana Kendra Peters and Sarah Weaver of CSLI Publications, and in particular, Dikran Karagueuzian for his enduring vision of what CSLI Publications should be and could be and for making things happen.

1

Introduction

MIRIAM BUTT, ANNETTE HAUTLI-JANISZ AND VERENA LYDING

This volume collects pioneering work in the emerging field of Visual Analytics for Linguistics, *LingVis* for short. LingVis is motivated by the growing need within linguistic research of dealing with large amounts of (partly unstructured) high dimensional data. The interactive and explorative access to data via Visual Analytics provides exciting and innovative ways forward for meeting the needs of linguistics in the digital data age. In turn, the multidimensional nature and complexity of linguistic data provides challenges for research within Visual Analytics as the data type and research questions are interestingly different from the more dominant applications in the natural sciences, economics or politics.

Since the first ACL 2008 Tutorial on the topic, namely *Interactive Visualization for Computational Linguistics* by Christopher Collins, Gerald Penn and Sheelagh Carpendale and the 2009 ESSLLI course *Linguistic Information Visualization* by Gerald Penn and Sheelagh Carpendale,[1] the field has expanded. Several workshops and tutorials have taken up the topic, the most prominent among them the 2014 Herrenhäuser conference on Visual Linguistics,[2] tutorials at KONVENS 2016 and DGfS 2018, the VisLR workshop series at LREC 2014, 2016 and 2018[3] and the workshop series on Visualization for the Digital

[1] `http://esslli2009.labri.fr/course_82.html`
[2] `http://www.visual-linguistics.net/symposium/index_en.html`
[3] `https://typo.uni-konstanz.de/vislr/`

Visual Analytics for Linguistics (LingVis).
edited by Miriam Butt, Annette Hautli-Janisz and Verena Lyding.
Copyright © 2020, CSLI Publications.

Humanities (Vis4DH) co-located with the IEEE VIS Conference from 2016 to 2019.[4]

Visual Analytics as described by Keim et al. (2009) brings together Information Visualization, Visual Data Analysis, and Visual Data Mining. The main objective of this line of research is to provide a tight coupling between automatic data mining models and interactive information visualizations to gain knowledge from data while harvesting the user knowledge and feedback through human interaction. Following Shneiderman's mantra of "overview first, zoom and filter, then details-on-demand" (Shneiderman 1996), Visual Analytics provides sophisticated visual representations for complex data that combine ease of access to the underlying data with powerful methods of sorting through data and identifying, visualizing and exploring patterns via just a few clicks. This entails breaking down the multidimensionality of the data into intuitive and distinctive visual variables such as position, color, shape, size or saturation and determining optimal visual arrangements so that centrally relevant patterns stand out distinctly and so that users are provided with an at-a-glance overview of the data, while simultaneously having easy access to the individual data points underlying the patterns being identified.

Given that ever more digital data is becoming available for linguistic study and Natural Language Processing (NLP), the need for fast and efficient algorithms that allow for the quick exploration and analysis of different types of data has increased. In linguistics and NLP, the most typical data sets encompass speech data, raw text or corpora (some perhaps transcribed). The latter have typically been annotated either manually, automatically or semi-automatically with different types of information and to various degrees of complexity (McEnery and Hardie 2012).

Since the first forays into LingVis, researchers have gathered experience in terms of which types of linguistic problems are particularly amenable to LingVis approaches and whether and which types of visualizations are more suitable than others for different types of linguistic data and questions. The volume provides a representative picture of the field's current state of the art, presenting some of the earliest work that has been done and including newer approaches to a range of linguistic areas that include historical linguistics, discourse and text analysis, treebanks and syntactic structures, lexical semantics and dictionary construction. Several of these areas fall into the rapidly developing area of *Digital Humanities*, whereby linguistic or NLP assisted analysis of

[4]`http://www.vis4dh.org`

texts plays an important role in disciplines such as literature or political science, and of course, linguistics, particularly historical linguistics which is heavily text- and manuscript based.

Marti Hearst's paper on *TileBars: Visualization of Term Distribution Information in Full Text Information Access* was first published in 1995. We have included a reprint of the original publication as the first paper in this collected volume since Hearst's paper has achieved the status of a classic and foundational piece of work in the field. Newer LingVis works are often referred back to this paper by reviewers and asked to compare and contrast. Marti Hearst suggested the use of TileBars in the context of information retrieval. TileBars allowed for the visual representation of various parameters which could be computed over documents, such as relative document length, query term frequency and query term distribution with respect to the document and to other documents in the collection. The patterns in a column of TileBars represent these parameters and can be quickly scanned and deciphered, aiding users in making judgments about the potential relevance of the retrieved documents. The TileBars visualization also allowed for simultaneous access of the underlying text, thus conforming to Shneiderman's mantra and representing one of the earliest works in LingVis.

We follow this paper by work on *Tree Visualization Techniques for Discourse Analysis* by **Jian Zhao, Fanny Chevalier and Christopher Collins**. As detailed above, Christopher Collins was one of the first practitioners of LingVis. His 2010 dissertation was the first thesis to be written in the area (under the supervision of Sheelagh Carpendale and Gerald Penn) and he co-taught the very first tutorial on the topic in 2008. The contribution chosen for the volume with co-authors Zhao and Chevalier represents newer work and illustrates how visualization techniques can be applied in the area of discourse parsing. In this paper, the authors revisit and extend earlier work on DAViewer with a focus on the design of the representations for discourse parsing. DAViewer is an interactive visualization system for assisting computational linguists by augmenting the manual analysis process to explore, compare, evaluate, and annotate the results of discourse parsers in order to inspire the development of improved parsing algorithms. The interface is built around a table of discourse tree visualizations, interactively coordinated with other visualization components including the texts under analysis and detailed information about selected objects. They introduce a set of design rationales for supporting discourse parsing, which are used to assess the benefits and drawbacks of three discourse tree representations: node-link, space-filling, and matrix.

The paper by **Paul Meurer, Victoria Rosén and Koenraad de Smedt** is also concerned with assisting computational linguists in their annotational and analytic work by designing and providing suitable interactive visualizations. However, the focus here lies within the realm of syntax rather than discourse analysis and their paper *Interactive Visualizations in INESS* presents several innovative features of effective visualizations for syntactic tasks surrounding the creation and inspection of treebanks. INESS (Infrastructure for the Exploration of Syntax and Semantics) is a treebanking infrastructure, which offers access to treebanks of different types, such as LFG (Lexical-Functional Grammar), HPSG (Head-driven Phrase Structure Grammar), dependency grammar, phrase structure grammar (constituency) and Universal Dependencies. The authors focus on the visual presentation and inspection of complex syntactic analyses, including interactive visualizations that combine multiple levels of syntactic description and represent the relations between them.

Miriam Butt and Daniel Keim together with Frans Plank began a collaboration in 2008, comparatively early on in the history of LingVis. The initial collaboration was made possible via university-internal funding designed to foster collaboration across disciplines, which in this case involved computer science, and general and computational linguistics. The collaboration has since grown to span several different types of projects, funded by several different third parties. The next two papers included in this volume present a subset of the joint work over the years. **Annette Hautli-Janisz, Christian Rohrdantz, Christin Schätzle, Andreas Stoffel, Miriam Butt and Daniel A. Keim** present LingVis approaches for historical linguistics that span early initial work as well as newer, treebank-based research in their paper on *Visual Analytics in Diachronic Linguistic Investigations.* Hautli-Janisz et al. discuss two approaches to using Visual Analytics in diachronic linguistic research with a particular focus on developing a generalized design space for diachronic visualizations. By defining a generalized design space, they aim to propose a general guideline for the question how the type of data and related research questions should inform the design of the visual analysis system. As examples, they situate two exploratory and interactive visual analysis systems with respect to the design decisions inherent in the presented framework. The first visualization uses English newspaper data to track the semantic change of English verbs by looking at the contexts these verbs appear in (using a by now outdated LDA approach to calculate semantic similarity). The second, more recent example tracks syntactic change in Icelandic by investigating the determining factors for two well-known phenomena in the history of Icelandic: V1 (verb first) word order and dative subjects.

In their paper, *Discourse Maps – Feature Encoding for the Analysis of Verbatim Conversation Transcripts*, **Mennatallah El-Assady and Annette Hautli-Janisz** present a dynamic visualization for the comparison of discourse patterns between speakers or speaker parties. This further example of a LingVis collaboration at the University of Konstanz pairs shallow text mining with a linguistically informed extraction of morphological, syntactic, semantic and pragmatic features that indicate and model relevant aspects of political discourse. The overall application is geared towards identifying and analyzing deliberative political discourse, which are mapped onto a glyph-based representation. They present a use case, where Discourse Maps are used to analyze a real debate scenario, namely the high-profile S21 public arbitration process in Germany. Components of the system are now available for interactive use via server-based applications on `lingvis.io`. This work was initially inspired by efforts to boost work within the digital humanities and social sciences and crucially included a collaboration with political science.

Another collaboration within the area of digital humanities is represented by **André Blessing, Markus John, Steffen Koch, Thomas Ertl and Jonas Kuhn** through their paper *Reflected Text Analytics through Interactive Visualization.* Blessing et al. present a discussion on cross-disciplinary methodology for the question of how techniques from NLP and Visual Analytics can be best exploited to help address research questions in the digital humanities. The authors focus on specific challenges for computational processing and visual analysis in the domain of digital humanities. They observed two issues to be prevalent: text data that often is small, specialized and heterogenous in nature, and an oftentimes hermeneutic approach to analysis, which implies that no concrete analytical target might be specified upfront, but analyses rather follow an extended process of exploration and refinement of the analytical categories ultimately applied. The authors discuss these observations in a programmatic way and presents concrete examples of tool combinations from NLP and Visual Analytics that have been beneficial for various digital humanities projects they have worked on collaboratively over the years.

A different type of digital humanities project is discussed by **Alejandro Benito, Antonio Losada, Roberto Therón, Eveline Wandl-Vogt and Amelie Dorn** in *An Interactive Visualization of the Historical Dictionary of Bavarian Dialects in Austria.* Benito et al. discuss the goals, motivations and other particularities of a visual exploratory analysis tool for historical dictionaries of the Bavarian dialects in Austria. They present a web-based tool which aims at serving the purpose of exploring the interrelationships of lemmas in a dictionary. By means of building on computational analyses of the input data and the application of data visualization techniques, the tool supports the not necessarily technical or academic user in carrying out spatio-temporal analysis, fast full-text search and social network analysis. As an input data set the authors employ the digitized version of the Historical Dictionary of Bavarian Dialects in Austria (*Wörterbuch der bairischen Mundarten in Österreich* or WBÖ), an initiative started in 1963 which compiles more than five million paper slips collected during the years 1911–1998 in different areas of current Austria, the Czech Republic, Hungary and northern Italy. The paper provides an excellent example of how modern LingVis methods can support and extend the traditional field of lexicography.

The final paper in the volume is also concerned with word meanings and how they develop over time. In their paper *Visual Analystics for Parameter Tuning of Semantic Vector Space Models*, **Thomas Wielfaert, Kris Heylen, Dirk Speelman and Dirk Geeraerts** leverage modern statistical methods for the calculation of the semantic (dis)similarity of words and propose a tool to facilitate the parameter optimization of Distributional Semantic Models by visual means. The tool implements a Visual Analytics approach which allows for the interactive exploration and comparison of how differently parametrized models affect the semantic similarity between specific items or groups of items with specific properties. By visualizing semantic similarity matrices directly and by supporting their manual evaluation, the tool complements automated statistical measures which exist to evaluate each single model. This is relevant since the automatically computed scores are neither capable of telling the researcher what is going on from a linguistic point of view, nor do they provide a realistic option to look at the data points and analyze the errors in the context of the model that is being investigated.

In sum, this volume has endeavored to collect both representative and pioneering work in the area of LingVis – Visualizations for Linguistic work. As can be seen, the papers span quite a number of different subdisciplines from information retrieval to core syntax, lexical semantics, lexicography, historical linguistics and discourse and text analysis. The visualizations proposed include graphs, pixel-based approaches, glyph visualizations and a variety of other methods for the representation of high-dimensional linguistic data in two-dimensional space by utilizing color, size and shape in addition to spatial relations.

References

Keim, Daniel A., Florian Mansmann, Andreas Stoffel, and Hartmut Ziegler. 2009. Visual Analytics. In L. Liu and M. T. Özsu, eds., *Encyclopedia of Database Systems*, pages 3341–3346. Boston, MA: Springer.

McEnery, Tony and Andrew Hardie. 2012. *Corpus Linguistics: Method, Theory and Practice*. Cambridge: Cambridge University Press.

Shneiderman, Ben. 1996. The eyes have it: A task by data type taxonomy for information visualizations. In *Proceedings of the IEEE Symposium on Visual Languages*, pages 336–343.

2

TileBars: Visualization of Term Distribution Information in Full Text Information Access

MARTI HEARST

Abstract[1]

The field of information retrieval has traditionally focused on textbases consisting of titles and abstracts. As a consequence, many underlying assumptions must be altered for retrieval from full-length text collections. This paper argues for making use of text structure when retrieving from full text documents, and presents a visualization paradigm, called TileBars, that demonstrates the usefulness of explicit term distribution information in Boolean-type queries. TileBars simultaneously and compactly indicate relative document length, query term frequency, and query term distribution. The patterns in a column of TileBars can be quickly scanned and deciphered, aiding users in making judgments about the potential relevance of the retrieved documents.

2.1 Introduction

Information access systems have traditionally focused on retrieval of documents consisting of titles and abstracts. As a consequence, the underlying assumptions of such systems are not necessarily appropriate

[1]This paper is a reprint of the original paper that appeared in 1995 in the *Proceedings of the SIGCHI Conference on Human Factors in Computing Systems*, pages 59–66. New York: ACM Press/Addison-Wesley Publishing Co.

Visual Analytics for Linguistics (LingVis).
edited by Miriam Butt, Annette Hautli-Janisz and Verena Lyding.
Copyright © 2020, CSLI Publications.

for full text documents, which are becoming available online in ever-increasing quantities. Context and structure should play an important role in information access from full text document collections. A critical structural aspect of a full-length text is the pattern of distributions of the terms that comprise it. When a system retrieves a document in response to a query, it is important to indicate not only how strong the match is (e.g., how many terms from the query are present in the document), but also how frequent each term is, how each term is distributed in the text and where the terms overlap within the document. This information is especially important in long texts, since it is less clear how the terms in the query contribute to the ranking of a long text than a short abstract. The need for this kind of distributional information has not been emphasized in the past, perhaps in part because researchers had not focused on long texts.

To address these issues, I introduce a new display paradigm called *TileBars* which allows users to simultaneously view the relative length of the retrieved documents, the relative frequency of the query terms, and their distributional properties with respect to the document and each other. TileBars seem to be a useful analytical tool for understanding the results of Boolean-type queries, and preliminary work indicates they are useful for determining document relevance when applied to sample queries from a standard full text test collection. This approach to visualization of the role of the query terms within the retrieved documents may also help explain why standard information retrieval measures succeed or fail for a given query.

2.2 Background: Standard Information Retrieval

The purpose of information retrieval is to help users effectively access large collections of objects with the goal of satisfying the users' stated information needs (Croft and Turtle 1992).[2] The most common approaches to text retrieval are Boolean term specification and similarity search. I use the term "similarity search" as an umbrella term covering the vector space model (Salton 1989), probabilistic models (Cooper et al. 1994, Fuhr and Buckley 1993) and any other approach which attempts to find the documents that are most similar to a query or to one another based solely or primarily on the terms they contain.

Similarity search, in effect, ranks documents according to how close, in a multidimensional term space, combinations of the documents' terms are to combinations of the terms in the query. The closer two

[2]This paper will focus on collections of textual information only, although other media types apply as well.

documents are to one another in the term space, the more topics they are presumed to have in common. This is a reasonable framework when comparing short documents, since the goal is often to discover which pairs of documents are most alike. For example, a query against a set of medical abstracts which contains terms for the name of a disease, its symptoms, and possible treatments is best matched against an abstract with as similar a constitution as possible. In similarity search, the best overall matches are not necessarily the ones in which the largest percentage of the query terms are found, however. For example, given a query of T terms, the vector space model permits a document that contains only a subset S of the query terms to be ranked relatively high if these terms occur infrequently in the corpus as a whole but frequently in the document.

In Boolean retrieval a query is stated in terms of disjunctions, conjunctions, and negations among sets of documents that contain particular words and phrases. Documents are retrieved whose contents satisfy the conditions of the Boolean statement. The users can have more control over what terms actually appear in the retrieved documents than they do with similarity search. In its basic form, Boolean search does not produce a ranking order, although ranking criteria as used in similarity search are often applied to the results of the Boolean search (Fox and Koll 1988).

2.2.1 The Problem with Ranking

There is great concern in the information retrieval literature about how to rank the results of Boolean and similarity searches. I contend that this concern is misplaced. Once a manageable subset of the thousands of available documents has been found, then the issue becomes a matter of providing the user with information that is informative and compact enough that it can be interpreted swiftly.[3] As discussed in the next subsection, there are many different ways in which a long text can be "similar" to the query that issued it, and so a system should supply the user with a way to understand the relationship between the retrieved documents and the query.

Furthermore, the standard approach to document ranking is opaque; users are unable to see what role their query terms played in the ranking

[3]As further evidence for this viewpoint, Noreault et al. (1981) performed an experiment on bibliographic records in which they tried every combination of 37 weighting formulas working in conjunction with 64 combining formulas on Boolean queries. They found that the choice of scheme made almost no difference: the best combinations got about 20% better than random ordering, and no one scheme stood out above the rest. These results imply that small changes to weighting formulas don't have much of an effect.

of the retrieved documents. An ordered list of titles and probabilities is under-informative. The link between the query terms, the similarity comparison, and the contents of the texts in the dataset is too underspecified to assume that a single indicator of relevance can be assigned.

Instead, the representation of the retrieval results should present as many attributes of the texts and their relationship to the queries as possible, and present the information in a compact, coherent and accurate manner. Accurate in this case means a true reflection of the relationship between the query and the documents.

Consider for example what happens when one performs a keyword search using WAIS (Kahle and Medlar 1991). If the search completes, it results in a list of document titles and relevance rankings. The rankings are based on the query terms in some capacity, but it is unclear what role the terms play or what the reasons behind the rankings are. The length of the document is indicated by a number, which although interpretable, is not easily read from the display. Figure 1 represents the results of a search on *image* and *network* on a database of conference announcements. The user cannot determine to what extent either term is discussed in the document or what role the terms play with respect to one another. If the user prefers a dense discussion of images and would be happy with only a tangential reference to networking, there is no way to express this preference.

```
image network

This is a searchable index.  Enter search keywords: [          ]

Index conf.announce contains the following 164 items relevar
'image network'.  The first figure for each entry is its rel
score, the second the number of lines in the item.

* 1000 1190 /ftp/pub/conf.announce/jenc5
* 886 125 /ftp/pub/conf.announce/image.processing.conf
* 800 334 /ftp/pub/conf.announce/image.analysis.symposium
* 743 303 /ftp/pub/conf.announce/sans-III
* 543 376 /ftp/pub/conf.announce/atnac.94
* 486 133 /ftp/pub/conf.announce/sid
* 486 125 /ftp/pub/conf.announce/qes2
* 457 138 /ftp/pub/conf.announce/europen.forum.94
* 429 378 /ftp/pub/conf.announce/mva.94
* 429 785 /ftp/pub/conf.announce/openview.conf
* 429 104 /ftp/pub/conf.announce/high.performance.networkinc
* 400 217 /ftp/pub/conf.announce/nonlinear.signal.workshop
* 429 378 /ftp/pub/conf.announce/vision.interface.94
* 429 785 /ftp/pub/conf.announce/inet.94
* 429 104 /ftp/pub/conf.announce/icmcs.94
* 400 217 /ftp/pub/conf.announce/internetworking.94
* 371 220 /ftp/pub/conf.announce/iss.95
* 371 168 /ftp/pub/conf.announce/qes1
* 343 152 /ftp/pub/conf.announce/conti.94
* 343 247 /ftp/pub/conf.announce/elvira
```

FIGURE 1 A sketch of the results of a WAIS search on *image* and *network* on a dataset of conference announcements.

Attempts to place this kind of expressiveness into keyword based system are usually flawed in that the users find it difficult to guess how to weight the terms. If the guess is off by a little they may miss documents that might be relevant, especially because the role the weights play in the computation is far from transparent. Furthermore, the user may be willing to look at documents that are not extremely focused on one term, so long as the references to the other terms are more than passing ones. Finally, the specification of such information is complicated and time-consuming.

2.2.2 The Importance of Document Structure

A problem with applying similarity search to full-length text documents is that the structure of full text is quite different from that of abstracts. Abstracts are compact and information-dense. Most of the (uncommon) terms in an abstract are salient for retrieval purposes because they act as placeholders for multiple occurrences of those terms in the original text, and because generally these terms pertain to the most important topics in the text. Consequently, if the text is of any sizeable length, it will contain many subtopic discussions that are never mentioned in its abstract, if one exists. On the other hand, an expository text may be viewed as a sequence of subtopics set against a "backdrop" of one or two main topics. A long text is often comprised of many different subtopics which may be related to one another and to the backdrop in many different ways. The main topics of a text are discussed in its abstract, if one exists, but subtopics usually are not mentioned. Therefore, instead of querying against the entire content of a document, a user should be able to issue a query about a coherent subpart, or subtopic, of a full-length document, and that subtopic should be specifiable with respect to the document's main topic(s).

Figure 2 illustrates some of the possible distributional relationships between two terms in the main topic/subtopic framework. An information access system should be aware of each of the possible relationships and make judgments as to relevance based in part on this information. Thus a document with a main topic of "cold fusion" and a subtopic of "funding" would be recognizable even if the two terms do not overlap perfectly. The reverse situation would be recognized as well: documents with a main topic of "funding policies" with subtopics on "cold fusion" should exhibit similar characteristics.

The idea of the main topic/subtopic dichotomy can be generalized as follows: different distributions of term occurrences have different semantics; that is, they imply different things about the role of the terms in the text. The possible distribution relations that can hold between two sets of terms, and predictions about the usefulness of each

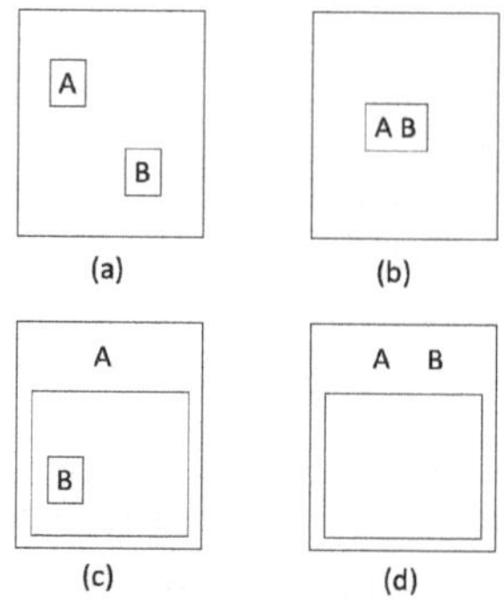

FIGURE 2 Possible relationships between two terms in a full text. (a) The distribution is disjoint, (b) co-occurring locally, (c) term A is discussed globally throughout the text, B is only discussed locally, (d) both A and B are discussed globally throughout the text.

distribution type, are enumerated and explained in Hearst (1994a).

2.2.3 TextTiling: Automatic Discovery of Document Structure

To determine the kind of document structure described above, I have developed an algorithm, called *TextTiling*, that partitions expository texts into multi-paragraph segments that reflect their subtopic structure (Hearst 1994b). (Since the segments are adjacent and non-overlapping, they are called TextTiles.) The algorithm detects subtopic boundaries by analyzing the term repetition patterns within the text. The main idea is that terms that describe a subtopic will co-occur locally, and a switch to a new subtopic will be signaled by the ending of co-occurrence of one set of terms and the beginning of the co-occurrence of a different set of terms. In texts in which this assumption is valid, the central problem is determining where one set of terms ends and the next begins. The algorithm is domain-independent, and is fully implemented. The results of TextTiling are difficult to evaluate; comparisons to human judgments show the results are imperfect, as is often the case in fuzzy natural language processing tasks, but serviceable for their application to the task described below.

2.3 TileBars

This section presents one solution to the problems described in the previous subsections. The approach is synthesized in reaction to three hypotheses:

- Long texts differ from abstracts and short texts in that, along with term frequency, term distribution information is important for determining relevance.
- The relationship between the retrieved documents and the terms of the query should be presented to the user in a compact, coherent, and accurate manner (as opposed to the single-point of information provided by a ranking).
- Passage-based retrieval should be set up to provide the user with the context in which the passage was retrieved, both within the document, and with respect to the query.

Figure 3 shows an example of a new representational paradigm, called TileBars, which provides a compact and informative iconic representation of the documents' contents with respect to the query terms. TileBars allow users to make informed decisions about not only which documents to view, but also which passages of those documents, based on the distributional behavior of the query terms in the documents. As mentioned above, the goal is to simultaneously indicate:

1. The relative length of the document,
2. The frequency of the term sets in the document, and
3. The distribution of the term sets with respect to the document and to each other.

Each large rectangle indicates a document, and each square within the document represents a TextTile. The darker the tile, the more frequent the term (white indicates 0, black indicates 8 or more instances, the frequencies of all the terms within a term set are added together). Since the bars for each set of query terms are lined up one next to the other, this produces a representation that simultaneously and compactly indicates relative document length, query term frequency, and query term distribution. The representation exploits the natural pattern-recognition capabilities of the human perceptual system (Mackinlay 1986); the patterns in a column of TileBars can be quickly scanned and deciphered.

Term overlap and term distribution are both easy to compute and can be displayed in a manner in which both attributes together create easily recognized patterns. For example, overall darkness indicates a text in which both term sets are discussed in detail. When both

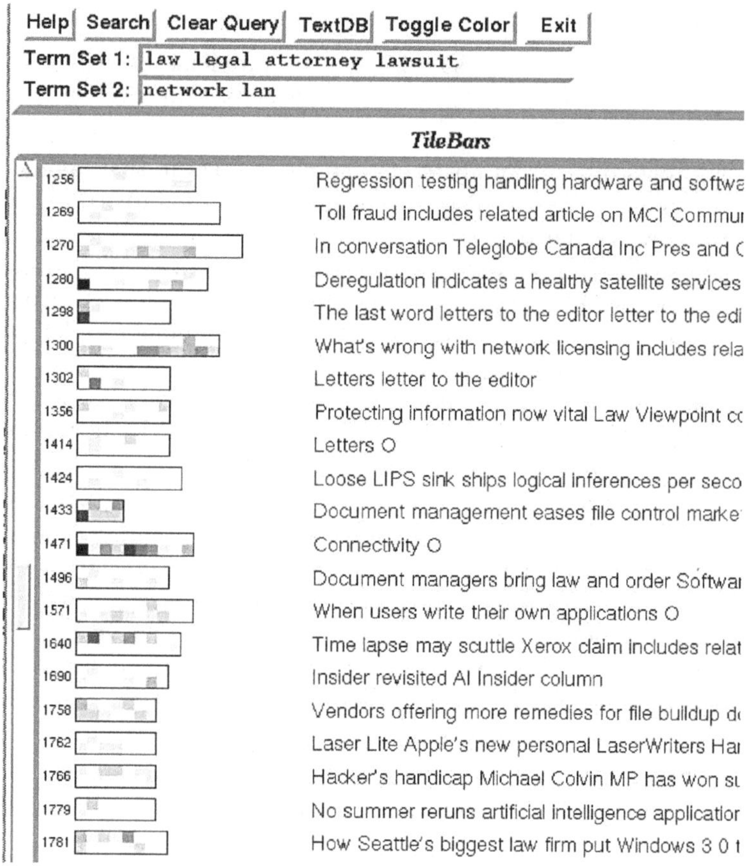

FIGURE 3 The TileBar display paradigm. Rectangles correspond to documents, squares correspond to text segments, the darkness of a square indicates the frequency of terms in the segment from the corresponding Term Set. Titles and the initial words of a document appear next to its TileBar.

term sets are discussed simultaneously, their corresponding tiles blend together to cause a prominent block to appear. Scattered discussions have lightly colored tiles and large areas of white space.

TileBars make use of the following visualization properties (extracted from Senay and Ignatius 1990):

- A variation in position, size, value [gray scale saturation], or texture is ordered [ordinal] that is, it imposes an order which is universal and immediately perceptible. (Bertin 1983)

- If shading is used, make sure differences in shading line up with the values being represented. The lightest ("unfilled") regions represent "less", and darkest ("most filled") regions represent "more". (Kosslyn et al. 1983)
- Because they do have a natural visual hierarchy, varying shades of gray show varying quantities better than color. (Tufte 1983)

Note that the stacking of the terms in the query-specification portion of the document is reflected in the stacking of the tiling information in the TileBar: the top row indicates the frequencies of terms from Term Set 1 and the bottom row corresponds to Term Set 2. Thus the issue of how to specify the keyterms becomes a matter of what information to request in the interface. There is an implicit OR among the terms within a term set and an implicit AND between the term sets. Retrieved documents must have at least K hits from each term set, where K is an adjustable parameter.

TileBars allow users to be aware of what part of the document they are about to view before viewing it. To see what the document is about overall, they can simply mouse-click on the part of the representation that symbolizes the beginning of the document. Alternatively, they may go directly to a segment in the middle of the text in which terms from both term sets overlap, knowing in advance how far down in the document the passage occurs.

The TileBar representation allows for grouping by distribution pattern. Each pattern type occupies its own window in the display and users can indicate preferences by virtue of which windows they use. Thus there is no single correct ranking strategy: in some cases the user might want documents in which the terms overlap throughout; in other cases isolated passages might be appropriate. A variation of the interface organizes the retrieval results according to the distribution pattern type.

2.3.1 Networks and the Law

Figure 3 shows some of the TileBars produced for the query on the term sets (*law legal attorney lawsuit*) AND (*network lan*) on the ZIFF collection (Harman 1993). (ZIFF is comprised mainly of commercial computer news.) In response to this query one might expect documents about computer networks used in law firms, lawsuits involving illegal use of networks, and patent battles among network vendors. Since retrieval is on a collection of commercial computer texts, most instances of the word *network* will refer to the computer network sense, with exceptions for neural networks and perhaps some references to computer science theory and telephone systems. Since *legal* is an adjective, it can be used as a modifier in a variety of situations, but a strong showing of hits in its term set should indicate a legitimate legal discussion.

In the figure, the results have not been sorted in any manner other than document ID number. It is instructive to compare what the bars imply about the content of the texts with what actually appears in the texts. Document 1433 stands out because it appears to discuss both term sets in some detail. Documents 1300 and 1471 are also prominent because of a strong showing of the network term set. Document 1758 also has well-distributed instances of both term sets, although with less frequency than in document 1433. Legal terms have a strong distributional showing in 1640, 1766, 1781 as well. There are also several documents with very few occurrences of either term, although in some cases terms are more locally concentrated than in others. Most of the other documents look uninteresting due to their lack of overlap or infrequency of term occurrences.

Looking now at the actual documents we can determine the accuracy of the inferences drawn from the TileBars. Clicking on the first tile of document 1433 brings up a window containing the contents of the document, centered on the first tile. The search terms are highlighted with two different colors, distinguished by term set membership, and the tile boundaries are indicated by ruled lines and tile numbers. The document describes in detail the use of a network within a legal office.

Looking at document 1300, the intersection between the term sets can be viewed directly by clicking on the appropriate tile. From the TileBar we know in advance that the tile to be shown appears about three quarters of the way through the document. Clicking here reveals a discussion of legal ramifications of licensing software when distributing it over the network. Document 1471 has only the barest instance of legal terms and so it is not expected to contain a discussion of interest — most likely a passing reference to an application. Indeed, the term is used as part of a hypothetical question in an advice column describing how to configure LANs. Note that a document like this would have been ranked highly by a mechanism that only takes into account term frequency.

The remaining documents with strong distributions of legal terms, 1758, 1640, 1766, 1781, discuss a documentation management system on a networked PC system in a legal office, a lawsuit between software providers, computer crime, and another discussion of a law firm using a new networked software system, respectively. Only the latter has overlap with networking terms. Interestingly, the solitary mention of networking at the end of 1766 lists it as a computer crime problem to be worried about in the near future. This is an example of the suggestive nature of the positional information inherent in the representation.

Finally, looking at the seemingly isolated discussion of document 1298 we see a letter-to-the-editor about the lack of liability and property law in the area of computer networking. This letter is one of several letters-to-the-editor; hence its isolated nature. This is an example of a perhaps useful instance of isolated, but strongly overlapping, term occurrences. In this example, one might wonder why one legal term continues on into the next tile. This is a result of the tiling algorithm being slightly off in the boundary determination in this case.

As mentioned above, the remaining documents appear uninteresting since there is little overlap among the terms and within each tile the terms occur only once or twice. We can confirm this suspicion with a couple of examples. Document 1270 has one instance of a legal term; it is a passing reference to the former profession of an interview subject. Document 1356 discusses a court's legal decision about intellectual property rights on information. Tile 3 provides a list of ways to protect confidential information, one item of which is to avoid storing confidential information on a LAN. So in this case the reference to networks is only in passing.

Note that the conjunction of information about how much of each term set is present with how much the hits from each term set overlap provide indicate different kinds of information, which cannot be discerned from a ranking.

2.3.2 Computer-aided Medical Diagnosis

Figures 4 and 5 show the results of a query on three term sets in a version of the interface that allows the user to restrict which documents are displayed according to several constraints: minimum number of hits for each term set, minimum distribution (the percentage of tiles containing at least one hit), and minimum adjacent overlap span. In this example the user is interested in documents that discuss computer-aided techniques for medical diagnosis, and the query is a conjunction of three term sets: (*patient medicine medical*) AND (*test scan cure diagnosis*) AND (*software program*). In Figure 4 the user has indicated that the document must contain a substantive discussion of the diagnosis terms, and that overlap among all three term sets must occur at least once within the span of three adjacent tiles. Note that this looser restriction yields some documents about computer-aided diagnosis with only passing references to medicine, which may indeed meet the user's information need. In Figure 5, the user has emphasized the importance of the medical terms as well by specifying that displayed documents must have hits in at least 30% of their tiles. Judging from the titles displayed, this restriction was indeed useful in isolating documents of interest. Placing such constraints may cause relevant documents to be discarded, but an interface like this allows the user some control over the ever-present trade-off between showing only relevant documents and showing all relevant documents.

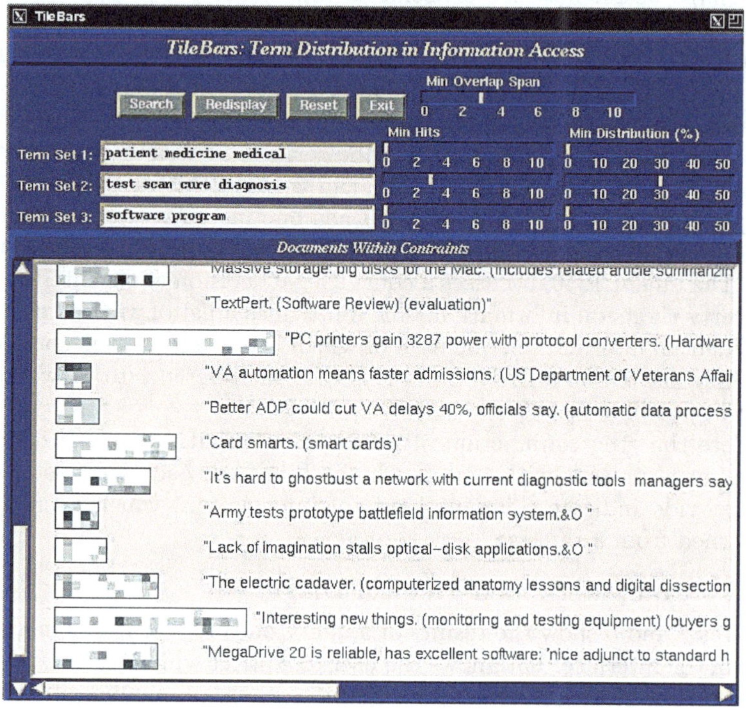

FIGURE 4 TileBar search on (*patient medicine medical* AND *test scan cure diagnosis* AND *software program*) with some distribution constaints.

2.3.3 Implementation Notes

The current implementation of the information access method underlying the TileBar display makes use of ≈ 132,000 documents of the ZIFF portion of the TREC/TIPSTER corpus (Harman 1993). The interface uses the Tcl/TK X11-based toolkit (Ousterhout 1991) and the search engine uses TDB (Cutting et al. 1991), implemented in Common Lisp. The use of TextTiles is not critical to the implementation; paragraphs or other segmentation units could be substituted, although this could

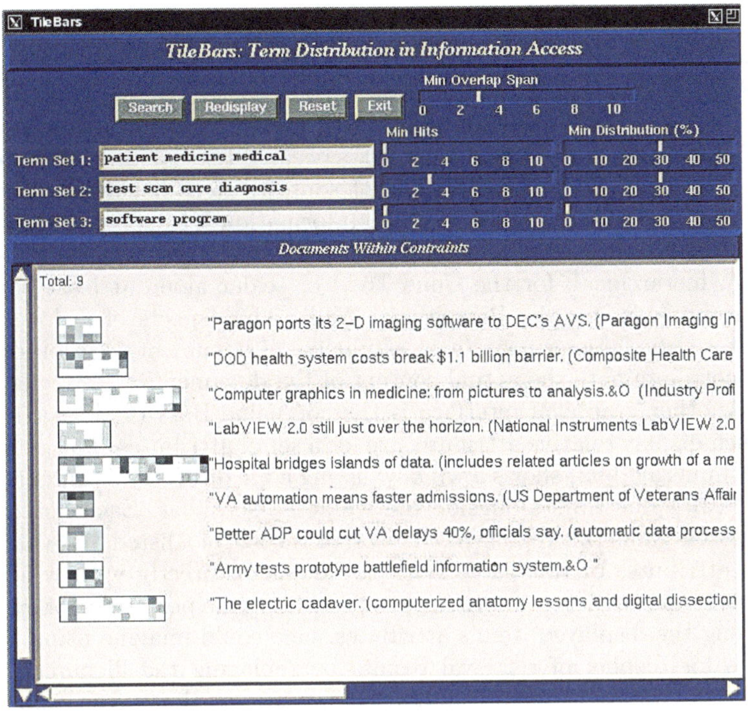

FIGURE 5 TileBar search on (*patient medicine medical* AND *test scan cure diagnosis* AND *software program*) with stricter distribution constaints.

result in units of less helpful granularity. Note that TextTiling is run in advance for the entire collection and the resulting indices stored for later use; therefore although the time for retrieval is greater than for a standard Boolean full-text query, it is not significantly so. Performance issues for indexing with passages are discussed in, for example, Moffat et al. (1994).

2.4 Related Work

As mentioned above, most information access systems have not grappled with how to display retrieval results from long texts specifically. Hypertext systems address issues related to display of contents of individual documents but are less concerned with display of contents of a large number of documents in response to a query. The Superbook system (Egan et al. 1989) shows where the hits from a query are in terms of the structure of a single, large, hierarchically structured document, but does not handle multiple documents simultaneously, nor does it show the terms of a multi-term query separately, nor does it display the frequencies graphically.

In general, document content information is difficult to display using existing graphical interface techniques because textual information does not conform to the expectations of sophisticated display paradigms, such as the techniques seen in the Information Visualizer (Robertson et al. 1993). These techniques either require the input to be structured (e.g., hierarchical, for the Cone Tree) or scalar along at least one dimension (e.g., for the Perspective Wall). The aspects of a document that satisfy these criteria (e.g., a timeline of document creation dates) do not illuminate the actual content of the documents.

Another graphical interface is that of Value Bars (Chimera 1992), which display relative attribute size for a set of attributes. The example in Chimera (1992) shows a window listing a file directory's contents and vertical Value Bars alongside the window's scrollbar. Each horizontal slice of a Value Bar represents the size or the age of a listed file, although the attributes of the Value Bars do not align directly with window's contents nor with one another, thus precluding the perception of overlap among the displayed item's attributes. One could imagine using Value Bars for display of retrieval results by replacing the filenames with titles of retrieved documents and having the attributes correspond to the number of hits for term sets. However, the display would still not indicate term overlap or term distribution. Similar remarks apply to the Read Wear interface (Hill et al. 1992).

Turning now to information retrieval systems, the simplest approach to displaying retrieval results is, of course, to list the titles or first lines of the retrieved documents and their ranks, and many systems do this. Existing systems that do more can be characterized as performing one of two functions: (1) displaying the retrieved documents according to their overall similarity to a query or other retrieved documents, and/or (2) displaying the retrieved documents in terms of keywords or attributes pre-selected by the user. Neither of these approaches address the issues of term distribution, frequency, and overlap that TileBars do. For reasons argued above, systems of type (1) are problematic, especially with respect to full-text collections.

Systems of type (2) show the relation of the contents of texts to user-selected attributes; these include VIBE (Korfhage 1991), the InfoCrystal (Spoerri 1993), the Cube of Contents (Arents and Bogaerts 1993), and the system of Aboud et al. (1993). These systems require users to select the classifications around which the display is organized. The goal of VIBE (Korfhage 1991) is to display the contents of the en-

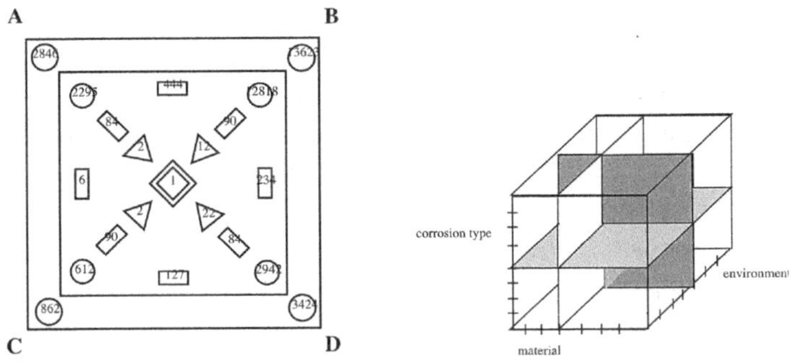

(a) (b)

FIGURE 6 Sketches of (a) the InfoCrystal (b) the Cube of Contents.

tire document collection in a meaningful way. The InfoCrystal (Spoerri 1993) is a sophisticated interface which allows visualization of all possible relations among N user-specified "concepts" (or Boolean keywords). The InfoCrystal displays, in a clever extension of the Venn-diagram paradigm, the number of documents retrieved that have each possible subset of the N concepts. Figure 6(a) shows a sketch of what the InfoCrystal might display as the result of a query against four keywords or Boolean phrases, labeled A, B, C, and D. The diamond in the center indicates that one document was discovered that contains all four keywords. The triangle marked with "12" indicates that twelve documents were found containing attributes A, B, and D, and so on. The Information Crystal does not indicate information about the distribution or frequency of occurrence of the query terms within the document. Thus it is perhaps more appropriate for titles and abstracts than for full text. The Cube of Contents (Arents and Bogaerts 1993) helps the user build a query by selecting values for up to three mutually exclusive attributes (Figure 6-b). This assumes a text pre-labeled with relevant information and an understanding of domain-dependent structural information for the document set. Again, frequency and distribution information could not be indicated easily in this framework.

2.5 Conclusions and Future Work

I have introduced a new display device, called TileBars, that visualizes explicit term distribution information in a full text information access system. The representation simultaneously and compactly indicates relative document length, query term frequency, and query term distribution. The patterns in a column of TileBars can be quickly scanned and deciphered, aiding users in making fast judgments about the potential relevance of the retrieved documents. TileBars can be sorted or filtered according to their distribution patterns and term frequencies, aiding the users' evaluation task still more. An in-depth description of an example helped show the semantic affects of various term distribution patterns. The TileBar representation should extend easily to representing media types other than text.

In the future user studies should be run to determine how users interpret the meaning of the term distributions and how they may be used in relevance feedback. It may be useful to determine in what situations the users' expectations are not met, in hopes of identifying what additional information will help prevent misconceptions. Another kind of evaluation is currently underway (Hearst 1995), exploring the effects of term distribution in the TREC/TIPSTER test collection (Harman 1993) on individual queries. Associated with the documents in the TIPSTER collection are a set of queries and human-assigned relevance judgments. In the past two years there has been a spate of research on passage retrieval in this collection, but the results are mixed and difficult to interpret. The main trend seems to be that some combination of scores from the full document with scores from the highest scoring passage or segment yields a small improvement over the baseline of using the full document alone. The work reported in Hearst (1995) attempts to determine how term distribution and overlap affects retrieval results in this task, and in the process provides an argument for the use of a TileBar-like display. Preliminary results indicate that scores can be improved by taking individual term distribution preferences for individual queries into account.

Information access mechanisms should not be thought of as retrieval in isolation. Cutting et al. (1990) advocate a text access paradigm that "weaves together interface, presentation and search in a mutually reinforcing fashion"; this viewpoint is adopted here as well. For example, the user might send the contents of the a TileBar window to an interface like Scatter/Gather (Cutting et al. 1993) which can cluster the document subset, and display their main topics. The user could then select a subset of the clusters to be sent back to the TileBar session. This kind of integration will be attempted in future work.

Acknowledgements

This paper has benefited from the comments of Jan Pedersen and six anonymous reviewers. I would also like to thank Robert Wilensky for supporting this line of research and Marc Teitelbaum for help in an earlier implementation.

References

Aboud, M., Claude Chrisment, R. Razouk, Florence Sèdes, and C. Soulé-Dupuy. 1993. Querying a hypertext information retrieval system by the use of classification. *Information Processing and Management* 29(3):387–396.

Arents, Hans C. and Walter F. L. Bogaerts. 1993. Concept-based retrieval of hypermedia information – from term indexing to semantic hyperindexing. *Information Processing and Management* 29(3):373–386.

Bertin, Jacques. 1983. *Semiology of Graphics.* Translated by William J. Berg. Madison, WI: The University of Wisconsin Press.

Chimera, Richard. 1992. Value bars: An information visualization and navigation tool for multi-attribute listings. In *Proceedings of the SIGCHI Conference on Human Factors in Computing Systems*, pages 293–294.

Cooper, William S., Fredric C. Gey, and Aitoa Chen. 1994. Probabilistic retrieval in the TIPSTER collections: An application of staged logistic regression. In D. Harman, ed., *Proceedings of the Second Text Retrieval Conference TREC-2*, pages 57–66. National Institute of Standards and Technology Special Publication 500-215.

Croft, W. Bruce and Howard R. Turtle. 1992. Text retrieval and inference. In P. S. Jacobs, ed., *Text-Based Intelligent Systems: Current Research and Practice in Information Extraction and Retrieval*, pages 127–156. Hillsdale, NJ: Lawrence Erlbaum Associates.

Cutting, Douglass R., David Karger, and Jan Pedersen. 1993. Constant interaction-time Scatter/Gather browsing of very large document collections. In *Proceedings of the 16th Annual International ACM/SIGIR Conference on Research and Development in Information Retrieval*, pages 126–135.

Cutting, Douglass R., Jan O. Pedersen, and Per-Kristian Halvorsen. 1991. An object-oriented architecture for text retrieval. In *Conference Proceedings of RIAO'91, Intelligent Text and Image Handling*, pages 285–298. Also available as Xerox PARC Technical Report SSL-90-83.

Cutting, Douglass R., Jan O. Pedersen, Per-Kristian Halvorsen, and Meg Withgott. 1990. Information theater versus information refinery. In P. S. Jacobs, ed., *AAAI Spring Symposium on Text-based Intelligent Systems.*

Egan, Dennis E., Joel R. Remde, Louis M. Gomez, Thomas K. Landauer, Jennifer Eberhardt, and Carol C. Lochbaum. 1989. Formative design evaluation of SuperBook. *ACM Transaction on Information Systems* 7(1):30–57.

Fox, Edward A. and Matthew B. Koll. 1988. Practical enhanced Boolean retrieval: Experiences with the SMART and SIRE systems. *Information Processing and Management* 24(3):257–267.

Fuhr, Norbert and Chris Buckley. 1993. Optimizing document indexing and search term weighting based on probabilistic models. In D. Harman, ed., *The First Text Retrieval Conference (TREC-1)*, pages 89–100. National Institute of Standards and Technology Special Publication 500-207.

Harman, Donna. 1993. Overview of the first Text REtrieval Conference. In *Proceedings of the 16th Annual International ACM/SIGIR Conference on Research and Development in Information Retrieval*, pages 36–48.

Hearst, Marti A. 1994a. *Context and Structure in Automated Full-Text Information Access*. Ph.D. thesis, University of California at Berkeley. (Computer Science Division Technical Report UCB/CSD-94/836).

Hearst, Marti A. 1994b. Multi-paragraph segmentation of expository text. In *Proceedings of the 32nd Annual Meeting of the Association for Computational Linguistics*, pages 9–16.

Hearst, Marti A. 1995. An investigation of term distribution effects on individual queries. Tech. Rep. ISTL-QCA-1994-12-06, Xerox PARC.

Hill, William C., James D. Hollan, Dave Wroblewski, and Tim McCandless. 1992. Edit wear and read wear. In *Proceedings of the SIGCHI Conference on Human Factors in Computing Systems*, pages 3–9.

Kahle, Brewster and Art Medlar. 1991. An information system for corporate users: Wide area information servers. Tech. Rep. TMC199, Thinking Machines Corporation.

Korfhage, Robert R. 1991. To see or not to see – is that the query? In *Proceedings of the 14th Annual International ACM/SIGIR Conference on Research and Development in Information Retrieval*, pages 134–141.

Kosslyn, S., S. Pinker, W. Simcox, and L. Parkin. 1983. *Understanding Charts and Graphs: A Project in Applied Cognitive Science*. National Institute of Education. ED 1.310/2:238687.

Mackinlay, Jock. 1986. Automating the design of graphical presentations of relational information. *ACM Transactions on Graphics* 5(2):110–141.

Moffat, Alistair, Ron Sacks-Davis, Ross Wilkinson, and Justin Zobel. 1994. Retrieval of partial documents. In D. Harman, ed., *Proceedings of the Second Text Retrieval Conference TREC-2*, pages 181–190. National Institute of Standards and Technology Special Publication 500-215.

Noreault, Terry, Michael McGill, and Matthew B. Koll. 1981. A performance evaluation of similarity measures, document term weighting schemes and representations in a Boolean environment. In R. N. Oddy, S. E. Robertson, C. J. van Rijsbergen, and P. W. Williams, eds., *Information Retrieval Research*, pages 57–76. London: Butterworths.

Ousterhout, John. 1991. An X11 toolkit based on the Tcl language. In *Proceedings of the Winter 1991 USENIX Conference*, pages 105–115.

Robertson, George C., Stuart K. Card, and Jock D. Mackinlay. 1993. Information visualization using 3D interactive animation. *Communications of the ACM* 36(4):56–71.

Salton, Gerard. 1989. *Automatic text processing: the transformation, analysis, and retrieval of information by computer*. Reading, MA: Addison-Wesley.

Senay, Hikmet and Eve Ignatius. 1990. Rules and principles of scientific data visualization. Tech. Rep. GWU-IIST-90-13, Institute for Information Science and Technology, The George Washington University.

Spoerri, Anselm. 1993. InfoCrystal: A visual tool for information retrieval & management. In *Proceedings of the Second International Conference on Information Knowledge and Management*, pages 11–20.

Tufte, Edward. 1983. *The Visual Display of Quantitative Information*. Chelshire, CT: Graphics Press.

3

Designing Tree Visualization Techniques for Discourse Analysis

JIAN ZHAO, FANNY CHEVALIER AND CHRISTOPHER COLLINS

Abstract

A discourse parser is a natural language processing system which can represent the organization of a document based on a rhetorical structure tree — one of the key data structures enabling applications such as text summarization, question answering and dialogue generation. Computational linguists currently rely on manually exploring and comparing the discourse structures to get intuitions for improving parsing algorithms. In this paper, we revisit our earlier work on DAViewer, an interactive visualization system for assisting computational linguists to explore, compare, evaluate, and annotate the results of discourse parsers. We present an investigation of the rationales guiding design decisions for discourse analysis and compare three alternative representations of discourse parse trees. We report the results of an expert review of these design alternatives for the task of comparing discourse parsing algorithms.

3.1 Introduction

Natural Language Processing (NLP) is a vitally important area of computer science research — the results of research in this field are quickly put to wide use in systems such as text categorization, automatic translation, topic extraction, speech recognition, and summarization. The

Visual Analytics for Linguistics (LingVis).
edited by Miriam Butt, Annette Hautli-Janisz and Verena Lyding.
Copyright © 2020, CSLI Publications.

subfield of automated discourse analysis aims to analyze the semantic structure and relationships within a text document. Discourse parsers offer promise for automated evaluation of text coherence, for example, as used in automated measurements of the quality of writing (Feng et al. 2014). While parsing a sentence for its grammatical structure (syntatic parsing) may be familiar to many readers, discourse parsing crosses sentence boundaries, extracting relationships within an entire document. These discourse structures are the foundation of many text-based algorithms such as certain types of summarization (Marcu 1999), question answering (Chai and Jin 2004) and dialog generation (Prendinger et al. 2007). Yet, accurate discourse analysis remains a challenge due to the complex and nuanced nature of language, and research in this area is still very active. In this paper we explore alternative designs for the discourse tree visualization in DAViewer, an interactive visualization tool for computational linguists to visually explore, compare, evaluate, and annotate automatically generated discourse structures with the aim of improving the underlying parsing algorithms (Zhao et al. 2012).

Discourse analysis in the NLP community has been heavily influenced by the Rhetorical Structure Theory (RST) framework (Mann and Thompson 1988), with later developments in segmented discourse relation theory (Lascarides and Asher 2007) and shallow discourse parsing (Prasad et al. 2010) having growing impact. In this work we focus on classical RST-style discourse parsing. While new techniques in machine learning are reducing the need for manual analysis (e.g., Ghosh et al. 2011), many robust RST-style discourse parsers rely on a corpus — a large collection of human labeled documents — as a reference (called a *gold standard*) for training and evaluating algorithms. Several techniques have been proposed to make discourse parsers under the RST framework, which represents the organization of text as a tree structure after dividing it into non-overlapping text chunks (Figure 1a). While such an abstracted representation offers a helpful support for analysis, there are no adequate visual exploration tools to assist NLP researchers in discourse studies: in practice, researchers display or print out static representations of the discourse tree structures in the form of indented text chunks (Figure 1b). This makes the exploration and comparison process tedious, and particularly inefficient for the task of comparing the outputs of several variations of an algorithm.

Our visualization system, DAViewer is designed as an interactive tool to augment the manual analysis process, supporting the verification of hypotheses and discovery of insights about existing parsers in order to inspire the development of improved parsing algorithms. As reported in our previous publication, we developed DAViewer using a

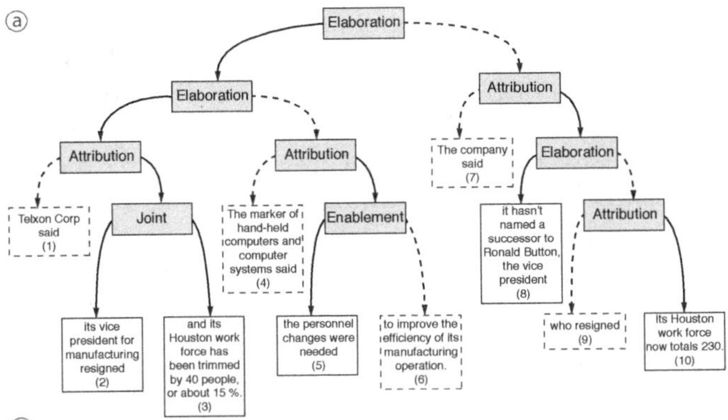

ⓑ

```
(Elaboration[N][S]
    (Elaboration[N][S]
        (Attribution[S][N]
            'Telxon Corp. said'
            (Joint[N][N]
                'its vice president for manufacturing resigned'
                'and its Houston work force has been trimmed by 40 people, or about 15%.'))
            (Attribution[S][N]
                'The maker of hand-held computers and computer systems said'
                (Enablement[N][S]
                    'the personnel changes were needed'
                    'to improve the efficiency of its manufacturing operation.')))
            (Attribution[S][N]
                'The company said'
                (Elaboration[N][S]
                    "it hasn't named a successor to Ronald Bufton, the vice president"
                    (Attribution[S][N]
                        'who resigned.'
                        'Its Houston work force now totals 230.'))))
```

FIGURE 1 Example of a typical discourse tree structure: (a) node-link representation of the hierarchical binary tree and (b) indented text format.

user-centered process, starting by the identification of the particular domain problems and challenges from which we derived design requirements for the visualization tool (Zhao et al. 2012). In close collaboration with computational linguistics experts at every stage of the development, we implemented and iteratively refined a functional prototype to address our target users' needs. The resulting interface is built around a table of discourse tree visualizations, interactively coordinated with other visualization components including the texts under analysis and detailed information about selected objects. DAViewer is designed in such a way that computational linguists can actively integrate the visual exploration of intermediate results into their research process and use these results to further develop and refine robust algorithms in discourse studies. We conducted a formative study with a domain expert over a period of four weeks and found that our tool dramatically sped up some comparison and analysis tasks which were otherwise difficult to carry out. We also collected use case scenarios thus far unsupported using the traditional workflow. Our domain expert continued to use the tool for her research after the end of our study.

In this chapter we revisit and extend this work on DAViewer with a focus on the design of the representations for discourse parsing. We introduce a set of design rationales for supporting discourse parsing, which we use to assess the benefits and drawbacks of three discourse tree representations: node-link, space-filling, and matrix. We report on an expert review conducted by an NLP researcher in discourse analysis in which she assessed the tree designs for the task of comparing discourse parse trees.

3.2 Background

Our work combines computational linguistics and visualization. This section provides relevant background in these areas of research.

3.2.1 Discourse Analysis

In this work we focus on RST-style discourse parsing, in which the discourse structure is a binary tree[1] built from non-overlapping text chunks called elementary discourse units (EDUs). The EDUs are segmented from the document and serve as the leaves of the discourse tree. The discourse parsing algorithm successively combines EDUs to create internal nodes, each of which corresponds to a rhetorical relation between its branches (e.g., Attribution, Cause, etc.). Hernault et al. (2010) describe the 18 relations which are used in the parsers tested in this research, and are widely used by the NLP community. Under each relation, the children can be either *nucleus* or *satellite*. With respect to the parent relation, the text associated with a nucleus branch is considered more prominent or important than the text associated with a satellite branch.

There are two ways to combine the segmentation and parsing algorithms. They can be coupled, so that the segmentation of the text into EDUs and the creation of the parse tree are interdependent and co-optimized. Or, the segmentation can take place in a separate, initial step, and the parsing algorithm is then forced to build the tree from these EDUs. The second (decoupled) method is more common and is used in this work. By forcing the EDUs to be the same across parsing algorithms, it allows for easier structural comparison of the trees generated by different parsers.

A popular corpus used in this area of research is the RST Discourse Treebank (RST-DT) (Carlson et al. 2001), which consists of 385 documents transcribed from the *Wall Street Journal* and annotated under

[1]While the original tree is not necessarily binary, a widely accepted practice in NLP consists of converting an n-ary tree into a binary tree (Hernault et al. 2010).

the RST framework. Figure 1a shows a typical rendering of a discourse tree, generated over the text of an article, with rhetorical relations shown in gray-filled boxes, and EDUs depicted with white boxes labeled with sequence numbers (i.e., the EDU's position as it appears in the text). Solid or dashed lines indicate whether the branch (or EDU) is nucleus or satellite respectively.

Several attempts have been made to develop discourse parsers using the RST framework. Many discourse parsers rely on a bottom-up approach for the tree building, i.e., linking EDUs and internal nodes with a parent relation, level by level until encountering the top root node. The HILDA discourse parser (duVerle and Prendinger 2009), further improved by Feng and Hirst (2012), is an instantiation of this approach to parsing, and is used in this work. Our external expert is working to improve parsing built with the HILDA parser as a starting point.

Despite the efforts of computational linguists, the generation of highly accurate discourse structures over a text document remains an open research question in NLP. In order to get a better understanding of the flaws and strengths of existing and newly created algorithms, the common practice consists of a close analysis of the discourse trees generated by different parsers: the comparison of a generated tree with the gold standard reveals how the obtained result differs from the optimal solution; and the comparison between generated trees helps analysts identify the impact of tuned parameters of the same algorithm, or differing performances of multiple algorithms. In particular, linguists are interested in answering the following questions regarding algorithm performance on a particular discourse:

Q1 At a given intermediate level in the discourse tree, is the text separated into meaningful groups (chunks)? Do the nucleus branches capture the prominent content of the text?

Q2 Where are the errors in the generated discourse tree? Do errors at low levels propagate to upper levels of the tree structure?

Q3 What are the structural and relational differences between branches generated by two parsing algorithms over the same EDUs?

And more globally, regarding performance on the entire corpus:

Q4 Does the algorithm generate common parsing structures (or errors) across all the documents in the corpus?

Q5 How consistently does each algorithm perform across documents in the corpus? Which types of documents are more problematic?

With the lack of efficient analytics systems to address their needs, linguists struggle to answer such questions effectively. The most common method is to work with a collection of indented text encoding the tree structure, as shown in Figure 1b. In this work, we focus on the analysis of individual discourse trees (**Q1-3**) and present three different views. The support of global analysis on the entire corpus (**Q4-5**) has been reported in a previous version of this work (Zhao et al. 2012).

3.2.2 Visualization and Computational Linguistics

There is a growing body of research in the area of text visualization, with most efforts aimed at content analysis — revealing keywords in a document, topics in a corpus, and changes in streaming text data. In this work, we are interested in a specific subset of language-related visualizations: those works whose aim is to improve our understanding of linguistic phenomena or computational linguistic algorithms.

Visualization has been used to answer fundamental questions in linguistics — as evidenced by the various chapters of this volume. For example, the Diachronlex diagram is used to reveal changes in language constructs over time (Therón et al. 2011). Pilz et al. (2008) use multidimensional scaling to plot the similarities of spelling variants to understand the propagation of spelling changes through time and geography. Mayer et al. (2010) created a visualization of phonetic patterns across languages to investigate vowel harmony. Structured Parallel Coordinates can be used to understand common patterns in corpus linguistics (Culy et al. 2011). Other corpus linguistic visualizations aim to support visualizing variation (Siirtola et al. 2014) and feature engineering (Heimerl et al. 2012). There have also been a wealth of visualizations of text and documents which are designed to support digital humanities research, including linguistics. Jänicke et al. (2015) contributed a comprehensive survey.

More relevant to this work are visualizations designed to better understand, and even to improve, computational linguistic algorithms. The DerivTool is designed for computational linguists to interactively correct problems in a translation system by directly editing the translation model learned from training data (DeNeefe et al. 2005). The lattice visualization of Collins et al. (2007) and the Chinese Room visualization of Albrecht et al. (2009) both use visualization to reveal a collection of closely ranked translation hypotheses considered by an automated translation algorithm, and allow a user to select the most reasonable alternative. Finally, the Bubble Sets visualization was designed to support machine translation researchers, using a participatory approach similar to the one we adopted here (Collins et al. 2009). Bubble Sets are overlays on parse trees to improve their usefulness in the task of diagnosing translation errors in order to improve translation algorithms. Similarly, the three discourse tree visualizations that we study in this work — two of which we introduced in our earlier version of this work (Zhao et al. 2012) and the third we adapt from the Ego-Lines visualization (Zhao et al. 2016) — are designed to support the discovery of errors in discourse trees in order to inspire improvements to discourse parsing algorithms.

3.2.3 Visualization of Tree Structures

Tree diagrams have been used for several centuries (Lima 2014), inspiring a rich collection of designs ranging from logic diagrams (Baron 1969), H-Tree representations (Shiloach 1976) and icicle plots (Kruskal and Landwehr 1983) long before the Information Visualization and Graph Drawing communities emerged, to more recent nature-inspired styles (Neumann et al. 2006, Kleiberg et al. 2001) and advanced interactive visualizations (Blanch et al. 2015). Schulz (2011) provides a comprehensive visual bibliography of tree visualization.

Existing tree visualizations divide into *node-link* diagrams, *space-filling* representations and *matrix* representations. Each of these has its advantages and disadvantages depending on the underlying data and the task at hand. In general, node-link diagrams are more accessible to general audiences, but take up space. Space-filling approaches (e.g., sunburst, icicle plots, treemaps) are more space-efficient, but the hierarchical structure is more difficult to grasp. Finally, matrix representations are powerful for revealing structural patterns, but suffer from lack of readability for tasks involving following edge-paths.

Tree visualization is not limited to the representation of a single structure. Building on the above representations, a breadth of techniques have also been proposed for the visual comparison of multiple trees. These approaches can be classified under three main categories: side-by-side views (Bremm et al. 2011, Chevalier et al. 2007, Munzner et al. 2003), merged views (Tu and Shen 2007, van Ham 2003) and animation (Robertson et al. 2002). For an exhaustive review see the survey by Graham and Kennedy (2010).

Side-by-side views can be based on visual cues to convey the relationships. Explicit links can be drawn between the matched nodes in each view, and the transparency of the links tuned to indicate the similarity measure between the corresponding branches, as for example in the syntax trees (node-link diagrams) by Chevalier et al. (2007). However, such an explicit linking can lead to a cluttered view due to the numerous lines. Side-by-side views can leverage interaction through dynamic queries: for instance, TreeJuxtaposer (Munzner et al. 2003) allows the user to interactively visualize similar node-link subtree structures by highlighting a query pattern. A system particularly related to our work was developed by Bremm et al. (2011) for the comparison of phylogenic trees, where several visualization techniques are combined as coordinated views. Their work also includes a tabular view of the trees of interest and a similarity matrix view indicating similarity scores between the trees of the dataset, a concept that we also applied in DAViewer (Zhao et al. 2012).

An alternative approach is to use merged views where two trees are combined in a single visualization that encodes the differences. Similarity matrices fall into this category. The nodes of the trees to compare correspond to rows and columns, and the cells indicate the similarity between the nodes. Van Ham (2003) uses such an approach for software analysis. These techniques are a powerful and space-efficient way for comparing the different nodes with one another. This is, however, to the detriment of making the hierarchical structure apparent. Union Tree (Tu and Shen 2007), which integrates two trees into a single treemap visualization based on a structural match, and colour-codes the differences between the nodes are another example of merged views. Similarly, Candid Tree (Lee et al. 2007) visualizes structural differences between two trees by merging them into a single, color-coded, node-link representation. While such approaches make differences salient, they are limited to the comparison of two trees at a time.

Finally, a third approach is to use animation to convey changes between two different trees (Robertson et al. 2002, Bach et al. 2014). However, users may lose track of the overall difference since the positions of many nodes are varying during the animation (Graham and Kennedy 2010). In addition, while animation can help keep track of changes while smoothly transitioning between trees, only one of the trees is visible at any given time, making comparison difficult.

3.3 Visual Design Rationales

In order to design effective tree visualization techniques for discourse analysis, we carried out a design study by involving two domain experts in a user-centered process. One of them was an expert in both computational linguistics and visual design, and a co-author of this chapter; and the other was an external researcher, from a university computational linguistics group whose focus is discourse analysis. Based on our interviews with the domain experts, and in response to the questions **Q1-3** enumerated in Section 3.2.1, we identified the following key design rationales for visually representing discourse trees.

R1 Revealing important linguistics variables. Other than the tree structure itself, there exist several key domain-specific variables that should be explicitly encoded in the visualization, for example, node type (nucleus, satellite) and relation (e.g., Cause).

R2 Emphasizing specific tree structural information. To facilitate analysis, the presentation of leaf nodes in a discourse tree should be ordered the same as the associated text chunks (i.e., EDUs) appear in the document. Moreover, the visualization should facilitate the identification of text chunks (consisting of a set of sequential of EDUs) at any level of the tree as well as the relationships between them (Q1).

R3 Facilitating comparison of trees generated by different analyses. To gain actionable insights for designing new algorithms, linguists need to discover the pros and cons of different parsers, which demands easy comparison of multiple trees (Q3). For example, identifying whether the same (internal) node appears in different trees. Also, the similarity scores (or errors if compared to the gold standard) assigned to branches of the tree should be readily available, as they provide an important overview of the discourse structure and performance of the parsers (Q2).

While the above design rationales are grounded in the context of this specific NLP application, we note that the general ideas behind them are not exclusive to linguistic visualizations. Indeed, representing the tree structure and node details in a similar fashion to that commonly used by a general audience is likely to be valid in other domains, such as phylogenetic trees in biology (see e.g. Bremm et al. 2011). More importantly, visual comparison of multiple trees is an ubiquitous and recurrent theme in systems of analyzing tree structures. However, the general tree visualization tools that support these requirements would need to be adapted to effectively satisfy the specific domain constraints.

3.4 Visual Representations of Discourse Trees

In this work, we propose and investigate the potential of three visual representations of discourse trees (Figure 2), each of which corresponding to one of the main tree representation types, namely (a) node-link, (b) space-filling and (c) matrix based representations (Section 3.2.3). Our visualizations are specifically tuned for the scenario of discourse analysis based on the aforementioned design rationales. One aspect to note is that, unlike standard tree representations, such as Figure 1, all three of our tree representations display trees with leaves vertically aligned. This design mimics the flow of text chunks in an article (i.e., from top to bottom) and facilitates the comparison of multiple discourse trees generated from the same text (see Section 3.4.4).

3.4.1 Node-Link Based

The node-link representation (Figure 2a) is derived from the traditional dendrogram (Graham and Kennedy 2010), a branching node-link diagram particularly suited to reflect relationships, that resembles the classic representation as used by our target users (Figure 1a). In this visualization, the nodes are color-coded according to the assigned relation label from the 18 relations described by Hernault et al. (2010). To best encode them visually, the specific hues were selected from 18 of the 22 most distinguishable colors in Green-Armytage (2010) (R1). Also, the density of the links indicates the nuclearity of the children nodes with respect to their parent: black indicates a nucleus (the most prominent nodes), and gray indicates a satellite (R1). For example, in Figure 1, the highlighted node spanning from EDU 6 to 9 has the Explanation relation (encoded in green); its first child node is nuclear and the second one is satellite. To identify the EDU clusters at each tree level, one could follow the links to the leaf nodes to build the different groupings (R2).

3.4.2 Space-Filling Based

The space-filling representation (Figure 2b) is a variation of the icicle plot (Kruskal and Landwehr 1983). This visualization is a hybrid representation of dendrogram and icicle plot: we display nodes in the form of rectangles as in the traditional icicle plot, to make the embedding relation visually salient. However, our layout mimics the dendrogram in that we align all the leaves at the same rightmost level, and we expand each rectangle's width up to the level where the corresponding node is grouped in turn. In this way, when looking at the visualization in columns, one can clearly see the clustering of EDUs at each intermediary stage of the bottom-up grouping process (R2). For example, in Figure 2b, it is clear to see the range of EDUs covered by the highlighted node, as well as how it split at the lower level (e.g., equally by two children) and how it merged with its sibling (e.g., the darker green node). Likewise, we encode the relation with the same color scheme as the node-link representation and use black outlines of the rectangles to indicate nucleus EDUs and gray for satellite (R1).

3.4.3 Matrix Based

The matrix representation (Figure 2c) is inspired by the basic visual form introduced in Graham and Kennedy (2010) and the visualization

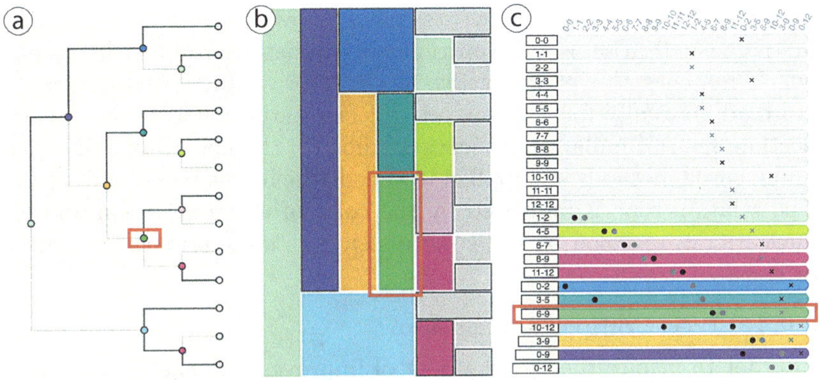

[0] The Singapore and Kuala Lumpur stock exchanges are bracing for a turbulent separation, [1] following Malaysian Finance Minister Daim Zainuddin's long-awaited announcement [2] that the exchanges will sever ties.<P> [3] On Friday, Datuk Daim added spice to an otherwise unremarkable address on Malaysia's proposed budget for 1990 [4] by ordering the Kuala Lumpur Stock Exchange "to take appropriate action immediately" [5] to cut its links with the Stock Exchange of Singapore.<P> **[6] The delisting of Malaysian-based companies from the Singapore exchange may not be a smooth process. [7] analysts say. [8] Though the split has long been expected, [9] the exchanges aren't fully prepared to go their separate ways.<P>** [10] The finance minister's order wasn't sparked by a single event [11] and doesn't indicate a souring in relations between the neighboring countries. [12] Rather, the two closely linked exchanges have been drifting apart for some years, with a nearly five-year-old moratorium on new dual listings, separate and different listing requirements, differing trading and settlement guidelines and diverging national-policy aims.

FIGURE 2 Different discourse tree representations that visualize the same data: (a) node-link based, (b) space-filling based, and (c) matrix based. The raw text data with EDUs numbered in bracelets is shown at the bottom. An example of the same node in different visual representations is highlighted in red boxes, and this node is also highlighted in the raw text.

for dynamic networks of Zhao et al. (2016). Each row or column in the matrix corresponds to a node (leaf or internal node) of the discourse tree, which is labeled with the starting and ending EDU indices of its sub-tree. For example, the node with index range 6-9 in Figure 2c corresponds to the highlighted nodes in Figure 2a, b, and the highlighted EDUs in the text.

Parent-child relationships between two nodes are indicated by a mark at the intersection of the corresponding rows and columns: a circle means the column node is the child of that of the row node, and a cross means the opposite relation. For example, in Figure 2c, on the highlighted row, node 6-9, the cross indicates its parent is node 3-9 from the column label; the two circles indicate its children are node 6-7 and node 8-9. To address R2, the nodes are sorted (top-to-bottom and left-to-right) according to their level in the tree, from the lowest level (leaf) to the highest level (root); the size of the rectangle around a node label also encodes its level (smaller nodes means lower level). The matrix visualization is row-centric as it emphasizes rows with ribbons, which matches the previous two visual representations where nodes are read vertically for a tree level and facilitates tree comparison (see Section 3.4.4). Similar approaches as those in the node-link and space-filling based methods are applied to encode the linguistic variables (R1). The relation type is indicated by the color of the row ribbon and the nuclearity is revealed by the color density of the link mark (i.e., circle or cross).

3.4.4 Tree Comparison Support

In order to inspire the development of improved parsing algorithms, it is essential for linguists to develop a good understanding of the specific flaws of the existing algorithms compared to the gold standard, or the strengths and weaknesses of different algorithms to imply under which conditions an algorithm should be used (R3). To support such comparative analysis, we align multiple discourse trees horizontally using the above three visual representations (Figures 3, 4 and 5).

For the node-link and the space-filling representations, we align the leaf nodes across multiple trees, each indicating the same EDU in the text document (Figure 3 and Figure 4). Thus, the user can observe the same EDUs (which should be in the same vertical position) across all the discourse trees to examine structural differences.

For the matrix representation, the internal nodes might vary across discourse trees produced by different algorithms, which result in different matrix sizes (i.e., the total number of nodes varies). In this representation, we connect the same nodes and their row ribbons across all matrices (Figure 5). If a node is missing in one matrix, it is indicated as a dashed line in the corresponding matrix. For example, in Figure 5, node 0-4 appears in all other trees except the second one. To prevent visual clutter caused by too many dashed lines, we only indicate a missing node for intermediary matrices where the same node exists both in a matrix placed on the left and on the right. For easier comparison, nodes in each matrix are sorted according to a tree that is specified by the user. Any tree can be selected for such node alignment.

Moreover, our experts are interested in identifying precisely which step(s) of the greedy bottom-up process fail or behave differently, and to what extent such errors have an impact on the steps that follow. To facilitate such analysis, we employ a similarity measure for comparing two tree structures proposed by Bremm et al. (2011), but other similarity measures could be considered. To visualize the similarity scores, we overlay a space-filling representation as the background of the node-link

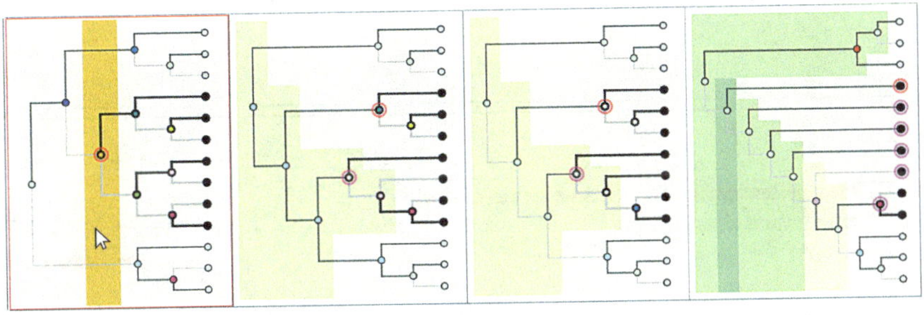

FIGURE 3 Comparison of multiple discourse trees for the same text, using the node-link representation. The first tree on the left is the reference tree for the similarity computation.

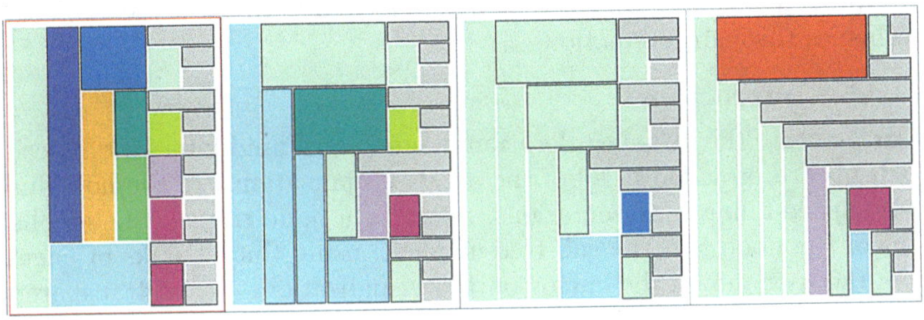

FIGURE 4 Comparison of multiple discourse trees for the same text, using the space-filling representation. The first tree on the left is the reference tree for the similarity computation.

representation, where the rectangle nodes are color-coded according to the similarity scores of the internal nodes using a yellow-to-green palette (Figure 3). This serves as a heatmap where errors (dissimilarity) are made more salient because of the darker color. For example, in Figure 3, the light background at the low levels of the second tree reveals that most of the tree is similar to the reference tree (i.e., the leftmost one); but the pink node at the third level from the leaves is in darker green (i.e., higher dissimilarity) and propagates the error to upper levels that are also shown in darker green. For the matrix representation, we color-code the nodes (row labels) with the similarity scores using the same color palette (Figure 5). As nodes can be sorted and aligned according to the reference tree, it is easy to see which nodes at which levels have more dissimilarity and whether they contain the same EDUs in the reference tree or not.

The space-filling representation is more challenging, as there is no easy way to encode the similarity scores at the same time as the linguis-

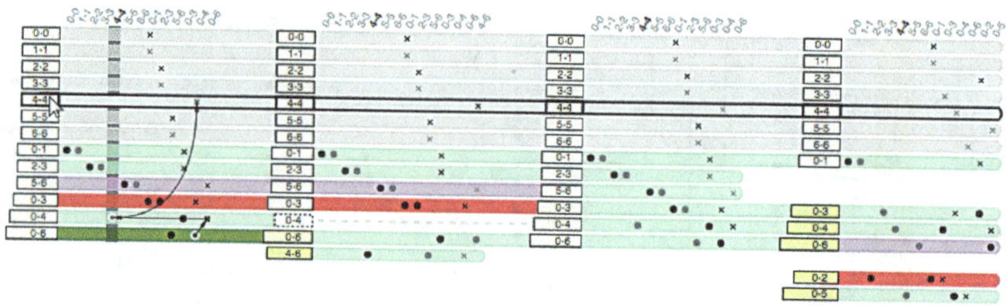

FIGURE 5 Comparison of multiple discourse trees of the same text, using the matrix representation. The first tree on the left is the reference tree for row ordering and similarity computation.

tic variables (i.e., nuclearity and relation). To address this shortcoming, we provide the user with the ability to switch between these two color schemes through interaction.

3.4.5 Interaction

To facilitate the visual exploration, a number of fluid interaction mechanisms are provided in all of the above visualizations. In the node-link and space-filling representations, selecting a node triggers the emphasis of the node and the sub-tree under it, using thicker links or edges. As the user moves the cursor on the visualization, a semi-transparent brown ribbon indicates the tree level where the cursor resides, as an aid to identify the nodes on the same tree level (Figure 3). The matrix representation uses a slightly different highlighting method to assist the user with interpreting the tree structure displayed in the matrix: hovering over a node in a row emphasizes this row and the corresponding column; a series of curved arrows traces reveal the path from the root to the hovered node, or from a user-selected source node to the hovered node. For example, in Figure 5, the curves indicate that the hovered node 4-4 is the child of node 0-4, which itself is the child of node 0-6 (the root). For all three visualizations, the text chunks associated with the nodes are accessible on pop-up tooltips and another text panel.

The support of visual comparison of multiple discourse trees is further empowered by rich interaction that allows for a flexible exploration of the trees. For example, selecting a sub-tree in the node-link and space-filling representations highlights the sub-trees that are composed by the same set of leaf nodes in other trees; hovering over a node or link mark in the matrix representation emphasizes the same entities in other matrices. This is particularly useful for a close analysis of the relations and the text associated with a problematic node, in order to identify the causes of a mislabeled relation (e.g., a keyword causing ambiguity). When comparing how a set of EDUs is clustered across several algorithms, the user can also explore parsing differences in detail, allowing her to infer hypotheses on the impact of parameter settings on the correct identification of specific relations.

3.5 Participatory Expert Review

While all three visual representations of discourse trees present the same data, they strongly differ in their design. Based on our design choices, we have the following intuitions regarding how each visualization will perform in analyzing discourse trees. We expect that the node-link representation is the easiest to interpret, as it is builds on the most common form of displaying trees in many application domains. We also believe that the space-filling representation could better support tasks based on identifying text chunk separations at multiple levels, because each rectangular bar clearly shows the portion of all of the EDUs it includes. Finally, we hypothesize that the matrix representation is best for comparison tasks across multiple discourse parsers' outputs. That is because it can interactively align all the nodes across different trees, unlike the other two visualizations that only align leaf nodes.

To better understand the strengths and weaknesses of the three visualizations, we conducted an in-depth interview with the external domain expert who specializes in discourse analysis of computational linguistics (see Section 3.3). During the interview, we first presented the three representations, explained the visual encoding and demonstrated how to interact with the visualizations. We then asked the expert to explore her own data with all three visualizations following a think-aloud protocol. We audio-recorded the session and took notes while the expert conducted observations.

In the remaining part of this section, we report the results of our participatory expert review. We first describe a usage scenario derived from our observation and interview with the expert. We then discuss the expert's specific feedback on the three visual representations as well as her general comments about analyzing discourse trees with visualization techniques.

3.5.1 Sample Usage Scenario

In this subsection, we describe a simple usage scenario that was developed based on our interview with the expert. Suppose that Rachel, who is a graduate student in computational linguistics, is developing different discourse parsers for her research, and is using the various views of our tool to compare the parser behavior.

First, Rachel wants to investigate errors produced by the HILDA parser (duVerle and Prendinger 2009), a popular algorithm in the do-

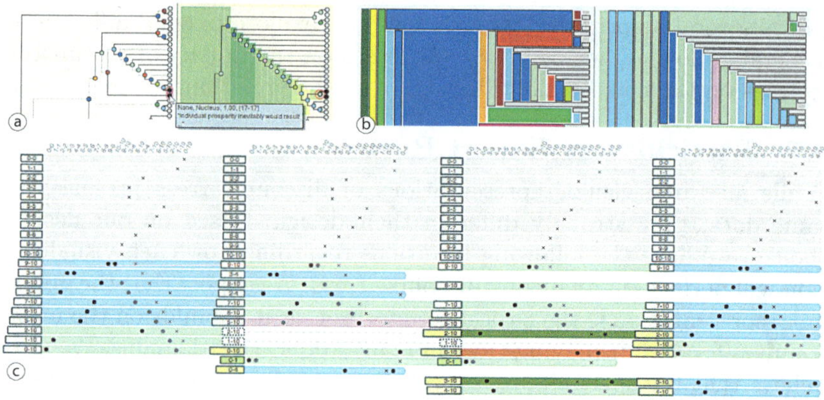

FIGURE 6 An analyst is exploring the results of different discourse parsers using the three representations.

main, in order to get inspiration about ways to improve on the previous work. She starts by picking a few cases where HILDA performs badly compared to the gold standard. For example, Figure 6a shows the gold standard (left) and the HILDA parser result (right) of one particular article. With the help of the heatmap background indicating the similarity, Rachel identifies where the error first occurs: HILDA groups EDUs 16 and 17 as early as the second level whereas the gold standard keeps the branches separated up to level 17. Thus, she finds that this first error, which propagates to the root node, is a major problem that strongly affects the overall parsing. By looking at the text, she finds that the EDU 17 says "individual prosperity inevitably would result" where the keyword "result" is a critical indicator of the Cause relation. Yet, the HILDA parser groups this node under an Elaboration relation (Figure 6a). A close examination of other results reveals that the above issue is common across the corpus.

By switching to the space-filling representation, Rachel observes the data from a different perspective (Figure 6b). It is clearer to see that, in the gold standard, the brown node labeled with the Cause relation (near the center of the left tree) has one large child node and the other child is a leaf node. By looking into the text, she confirms that EDUs 7-16 as a whole are the summary of previous content, that should be grouped together in a branch under the Cause relation, with EDU 17, as indicated by the gold standard. Moreover, it is more obvious with this representation to observe that the gold standard has large variety of relation types (e.g., more colors), whereas the HILDA parser tends to assign nodes with a few relations more often, such as Elaboration,

Background, and Joint. This is another weakness of HILDA which requires further attention on increasing the variety of relation labeling.

After identifying several issues in the HILDA parser, Rachel wants to investigate how her own parsers (referred to as algorithms A1 and A2) perform compared to the gold standard and HILDA. As shown in Figure 6c, she uses the matrix representation to compare four discourse trees of the same article, including the gold standard and the results of HILDA, A1, and A2 (from left to right). With a glance of the gray rows (leaf nodes), the patterns and distributions of circles and crosses are similar between the gold standard and HILDA, as well as between A1 and A2, indicating that HILDA generates better results at the lower level. However, by observing the colored rows (internal nodes), A2 seems to generate more accurate relation labels than both the other parsers, compared to the gold standard. Moreover, nodes 2-10 and 1-10 are missing in the HILDA results but exist in A2, the same as the gold standard. This further indicates A2 performs better in terms of constructing the structure at higher levels. Overall, A1 seems to generate the worst result with incorrect relation labels and hierarchies. Thus, Rachel decides to pursue algorithm A2 for future research.

3.5.2 Feedback on Different Visual Representations

In this particular interview, our expert was interested in investigating if and how tuning different parameters affects the outputs of her own parsers, as well as how they are compared to the gold standard (Carlson et al. 2001) and the classic HILDA parser (Hernault et al. 2010). The text inputs of these discourse parsers were articles from the *Wall Street Journal* and the gold standard contained discourse trees that are manually annotated by linguists based on the articles. Thus, for each visual representation, the expert loaded four discourse trees (gold standard, HILDA, and two of her own algorithms) that were generated from the same article for comparison.

Our expert outlined three main sub-tasks in comparing the results of multiple discourse parsers: 1) *where* the errors or discrepancies occur, 2) *how* they affect the discourse tree structures, and 3) *why* they happen. More particularly, for the first sub-task (where), the expert was interested in spotting where the first error occurred along the process of constructing the discourse tree. In her case, EDUs are merging from left to right (their order in the text) and bottom to top. For the second sub-task (how), she was curious about whether errors in the bottom levels would affect the tree structure in the top levels. For some applications, one may only care about the upper level relations between text chunks, for example, on the paragraph level, so errors happening in the sentence, phrase, or sub-phrase levels are not important as long as the upper level discourse tree structures are correct. In this case other criteria of the algorithms may be taken into consideration such as speed and memory usage. For the third sub-task (why), the expert wanted to drill down to the original text chunks and intermediate outputs of the parsers to study why the errors were produced.

Since the third sub-task (why) is outside the scope of visualizing tree structures and all tree visual representations are equipped with similar mechanisms for allowing users to browse the original text, in the following, we only discuss our expert feedback on the three different visual representations regarding sub-tasks 1 (where) and 2 (how).

Node-link representation. The expert mentioned that this representation (Figure 3) was the easiest to understand as it resembles the tree representation that she uses in her research, and the background that encodes the similarity scores helps quickly spot where the first error occurred (sub-task 1). However, she reported that the node-link representation is not optimal for sub-task 2: "*I have to trace the links down to the leaves to see which EDUs are included in the internal nodes so that I can figure out if the text partition at this level is correct.*" She further added that the similarity scores were not helpful in this task. Scores are computed recursively from the leaves and propagated up the tree — this supports tracing errors from the top down to the leaves, but it makes it difficult to distinguish errors occurring at a given level from errors propagated from the levels below.

Space-filling representation. The expert reported that this representation (Figure 4) could benefit sub-task 2 as the height of each rectangular node at a tree level clearly indicates the groupings of EDUs: "*This is more straightforward [than the node-link representation].*" She then further added: "*But the downside is the similarity scores are not shown here.*" To perform sub-task 1, the expert had to switch the color mapping to encode similarity, but in that case, she could not see the relation information anymore. However, compared to the node-link representation, she found that the linguistic variables were more salient than when visually encoded, because much more space is devoted to display the nodes compared to the two other representations. In general, she thought that this visualization had its strengths in revealing the partitions of the text at each tree level but could be enhanced by encoding more linguistic variables at the same time.

Matrix representation. At a first glance of the matrix representation (Figure 5), the expert thought it was difficult to understand and unlike anything she usually encounters in everyday work. Her first reaction was pretty revealing of her unfamiliarity with matrix-based representations: "*It doesn't look like a tree.*" After we explained the visual encoding and interaction, she experimented with the visualization for a few minutes and quickly commented that "*it is actually not that hard, and black curves [with arrows] are really helpful [to understand the tree structure].*" The expert then added: "*It is really easy to spot the first error because the nodes [i.e., rows] are ordered in the way that I like, [left to right, and top to bottom as in the tree], so I just need to browse the nodes from the top and find the darker green one.*" Another aspect of the matrix representation that the expert appreciated was that since it was straightforward to identify which internal nodes existed in which trees by following the lines, it was easier to discover differences between parsers than with other representations, where close examination or interaction is required. To some extent, this could facilitate sub-task 2 when the expert had a reference tree (e.g., the gold standard) to compare with: "*I can count the white gaps in the matrices to evaluate how good the upper level groupings are according to a reference.*"

Overall, these three visual representations have their own advantages and disadvantages, and could benefit to be used in complement to one another. The expert further reported that the node-link representation was suitable for high-level tasks such as obtaining the general impression of the tree structures, as it is similar to the traditional representation of trees; whereas the matrix representation was beneficial for low-level tasks to examine and compare the discourse trees in details, because it lays out the differences more clearly. She then said that the space-filling representation was somewhat in the middle, which was relatively easier to learn than the matrix representation but not optimal for certain types of tasks.

3.5.3 General Feedback

We also collected general feedback on using visualization techniques to aid the analyses of discourse trees produced by different parsers. Our expert pointed out that advanced visualization tools were not commonly used in her workflow, and through the interview sessions she reported to be highly satisfied with the visual design and interactions that she found to be "*handy and straightforward*" overall. She mentioned that visualization has significant benefits for analyzing the outputs of the parsers: "*It is great to have all the [discourse] trees available and see them visually. I can print [trees] in text files and look at them all day long, but never found it could be that clear and easy with the visual representations.*"

Visualization proved to be very efficient to our expert as it greatly increased her productivity: "*I used to draw trees by hand according to the output text files, so I could only compare 2 or 3 trees at the time and they are basically simple trees around 5 levels. Now I can compare many large trees efficiently. All trees are nicely aligned and the interactions allow me to focus on subtrees easily.*" The expert emphasized that her past experience of drawing trees of about 20 EDUs was "*awful*" (each tree taking her more than 10 minutes to draw) and highly error-prone due to the manual process. Then she mentioned: "*For the same data, now I can spot the [tree structure] differences in 2 seconds by observing visualizations of the [similarity] scores.*"

The visual representations of discourse trees were favored by the expert because they were efficient in showing the parsing process and comparing tree structures, though they were slightly different from the manually produced graphs. The expert said: "*I know I want the tree levels aligned from the bottom, but I can't draw such layout from the output file in one round since the tree nodes are indented in the depth-first order.*" Moreover, she commented that the separation of text and tree structure in the visual representations allowed her to focus on different aspects of the dataset, which is superior than the existing practice shown in Figure 1b. She also added that interactive aids such as tooltips and highlights of text provided the connections conveniently.

Our expert also provided some suggestions to further improve our proposed visual representations. For example, the node-link representation could be drawn beside the matrix representation to allow for better understanding and learning, or animation shown in NodeTrix can be applied to ease the learning of matrix representations (Henry et al. 2007). Moreover, to enable a deeper look into why and how the errors came from, some low-level algorithm information such as the intermediate probability distributions for each node merging operation could be displayed along with the visualizations. In summary, our expert was enthusiastic about further using the visualizations, and would like to continue using them in her research.

3.6 Discussion

We have introduced three dynamic visual representations designed for exploring and comparing discourse trees, each of which has its own benefits as reviewed by our external expert. Overall, the expert highly appreciated these visual and interactive approaches. This work is exploratory, and we identify several aspects that need to be enhanced for all three visual representations.

Scalability. One common issue across the different visual representations is to support effective visualization of larger discourse trees.

We support standard node collapsing and expanding operations in our designs, but once collapsed, much of the information (e.g., lower-level structures and similarities) is hidden from the user. It is an interesting venue to investigate in the future about how to address the scalability by aggregating the trees and at the same time keep the information loss minimal.

Richer set of linguistic variables. Another aspect is that there are many linguistic variables to encode in the three visualizations. In this chapter, we focus on a few key variables such as relation and nuclearity. Enriching the visual encoding, by e.g. using glyphs, complicates the visualization, and on the other hand, allowing users to interactively choose which to encode (e.g., relation or similarity for node color in the space-filling representation), although suitable, hides certain information. Thus, there is a trade-off, which is interesting to study further.

Trade-offs and different flavors of visual representations. As the expert pointed out, the space-filling representation (Figure 2b), when visually browsed vertically, reveals key features of hierarchical clustering as the traditional icicle plot does, which in our case reflects the greedy process of merging of text chunks from the original EDUs. Taking the benefits of dendrogram, nodes that remain unmerged across many levels, are shown saliently as rectangles with larger horizontal widths, making it easier to identify the nodes that reside on the levels covered by the width of a specific node, than when using a traditional dendrogram. In some studies of clustering algorithms such as classifiers in machine learning applications, this is useful for checking why a specific node is not combined with others in the algorithm as well as spotting the anomalies.

In addition, when a space-filling representation encoding the similarity score is displayed as the background of the node-link representation (Figure 2a), the analyst can more easily locate the structural differences, as large color-coded areas are easy to spot at a glance. Our external expert extensively relied on this background to quickly find the very first merging anomaly propagated to the top levels when comparing parsers. The matrix representation was initially viewed as "*out of the box*" by our expert, but in the end it turned to be effective for the key discourse tree comparison tasks identified by the expert, once she figured out the visual encoding. This implies that we sometimes need to break the convention to embrace new forms of visualizations with an open mind. Supporting easy learning of new visualizations is an important and challenging area of research (Ruchikachorn and Mueller 2015, Lee et al. 2016). Perhaps, as our expert suggested, combining familiar and unfamiliar visual representations in the same view (e.g., matrix plus node-link) is a promising direction to get users in the door of visual thinking with new visualizations.

Generalizability. All the proposed visualizations are general enough to be applied to any other hierarchical structure, whether it is for comparison purposes. For example, they are not constrained for representing only discourse trees in computational linguistics, it is possible to encode other kinds of hierarchical structures and linguistic information (on the tree nodes or links) in a similar design, to facilitate comparison across different structures. Moreover, in other application domains, the visualizations can be used for studying the difference of evolutionary relationships between organisms in phylogenetic trees. They can also be simply augmented with the visualization of an additional attribute associated to the nodes, e.g., displaying the space that files and folders take on the hard drive on the background of a file system browser.

3.7 Conclusion and Future Work

In this chapter, we have introduced three visual representations of tree structures, including node-link, space-filling, and matrix-based visualizations, further tailored for comparing discourse trees based on a set of design rationales obtained from expert users. We have also conducted an in-depth interview with experts to assess the effectiveness of the three types of visual representations. In general, the results indicate that visualizations indeed help users improve their efficiency in analyzing discourse trees generated by different algorithms, thus allowing them to better derive insights for developing new discourse parsers. We have further discussed the advantages and disadvantages of the three different visual representations in comparing multiple discourse trees.

In the future, we would like to explore opportunities to encode more linguistic variables by extending the current visual representations, and address the scalability issues by experimenting with techniques for visually aggregating tree structures. We also see potential benefits for combining the advantages of each visualization in a single interactive tool for comparing discourse trees. Finally, it would be interesting to test these visualization types with tree datasets from other domains, such as biology.

References

Albrecht, Joshua, Rebecca Hwa, and G. Elisabeta Marai. 2009. The Chinese Room: Visualization and interaction to understand and correct ambiguous machine translation. *Computer Graphics Forum* 28(3):1047–1054.

Bach, Benjamin, Emmanuel Pietriga, and Jean-Daniel Fekete. 2014. Graphdiaries: Animated transitions and temporal navigation for dynamic networks. *IEEE Transactions on Visualization and Computer Graphics* 20(5):740–754.

Baron, Margaret E. 1969. A note on the historical development of logic diagrams: Leibniz, Euler and Venn. *The Mathematical Gazette* 53(384):113–125.

Blanch, Renaud, Rémy Dautriche, and Gilles Bisson. 2015. Dendrogramix: A hybrid tree-matrix visualization technique to support interactive exploration of dendrograms. In S. Liu, G. Scheuermann, and S. Takahashi, eds., *Proceedings of the IEEE Pacific Visualization Symposium*, pages 31–38.

Bremm, Sebastian, Tatiana von Landesberger, Martin Heß, Tobias Schreck, Philipp Weil, and Kay Hamacherk. 2011. Interactive visual comparison of multiple trees. In *Proceedings of the IEEE Symposium on Visual Analytics Science and Technology*, pages 29–38.

Carlson, Lynn, Daniel Marcu, and Mary Ellen Okurowski. 2001. Building a discourse-tagged corpus in the framework of Rhetorical Structure Theory. In *Proceedings of the Second SIGdial Workshop on Discourse and Dialogue – Volume 16*, pages 1–10.

Chai, Joyce Y. and Rong Jin. 2004. Discourse structure for context question answering. In *Proceedings of the HLT-NAACL Workshop on Pragmatics in Question Answering*, pages 23–30.

Chevalier, Fanny, David Auber, and Alexandru Telea. 2007. Structural analysis and visualization of C++ code evolution using syntax trees. In *Ninth International Workshop on Principles of Software Evolution: In Conjunction with the 6th ESEC/FSE Joint Meeting*, pages 90–97.

Collins, Christopher, Sheelagh Carpendale, and Gerald Penn. 2007. Visualization of uncertainty in lattices to support decision-making. In K. Museth, T. Möller, and A. Ynnerman, eds., *Proceedings of the 9th Joint Eurographics / IEEE VGTC Conference on Visualization*, pages 51–58.

Collins, Christopher, Gerald Penn, and Sheelagh Carpendale. 2009. Bubble sets: Revealing set relations with isocontours over existing visualizations. *IEEE Transactions on Visualization and Computer Graphics* 15(6):1009–1016.

Culy, Chris, Verena Lyding, and Henrik Dittmann. 2011. Structured parallel coordinates: A visualization for analyzing structured language data. In *Proceedings of the International Conference on Corpus Linguistics*, pages 485–493.

DeNeefe, Steve, Kevin Knight, and Hayward H. Chan. 2005. Interactively exploring a machine translation model. In *Proceedings of the ACL 2005 on Interactive Poster and Demonstration Sessions*, pages 97–100.

duVerle, David A. and Helmut Prendinger. 2009. A novel discourse parser based on support vector machine classification. In *Proceedings of the 47th Annual Meeting of the ACL and the 4th International Joint Conference on Natural Language Processing of the AFNLP*, pages 665–673.

Feng, Vanessa Wei and Graeme Hirst. 2012. Text-level discourse parsing with rich linguistic features. In *Proceedings of the 50th Annual Meeting of the Association for Computational Linguistics*, pages 60–68.

Feng, Vanessa Wei, Ziheng Lin, and Graeme Hirst. 2014. The impact of deep hierarchical discourse structures in the evaluation of text coherence. In *Proceedings of the International Conference on Computational Linguistics 2014*, pages 940–949.

Ghosh, Sucheta, Richard Johansson, and Sara Tonelli. 2011. Shallow discourse parsing with conditional random fields. In *Proceedings of the 5th International Joint Conference on Natural Language Processing*, pages 1071–1079.

Graham, Martin and Jessie Kennedy. 2010. A survey of multiple tree visualisation. *Information Visualization* 9(4):235–252.

Green-Armytage, Paul. 2010. A colour alphabet and the limits of colour coding. *Colour: Design and Creativity* 5(10):1–23.

Heimerl, Florian, Charles Jochim, Steffen Koch, and Thomas Ertl. 2012. Featureforge: A novel tool for visually supported feature engineering and corpus revision. In *Proceedings of the International Conference on Computational Linguistics 2012: Posters*, pages 461–470.

Henry, Nathalie, Jean-Daniel Fekete, and Michael J. McGuffin. 2007. Nodetrix: A hybrid visualization of social networks. *IEEE Transactions on Visualization and Computer Graphics* 13(6):1302–1309.

Hernault, Hugo, Helmut Prendinger, David A. duVerle, and Mitsuru Ishizuka. 2010. Hilda: A discourse parser using support vector machine classification. *Dialogue and Discourse* 1(3):1–33.

Jänicke, Stefan, Greta Franzini, Muhammad Faisal Cheema, and Gerik Scheuermann. 2015. On close and distant reading in digital humanities: A survey and future challenges. In R. Borgo, F. Ganovelli, and I. Viola, eds., *Eurographics Conference on Visualization (EuroVis) – STARs*, pages 83–103.

Kleiberg, Ernst, Huub van de Wetering, and Jarke van Wijk. 2001. Botanical visualization of huge hierarchies. In K. Andrews, S. Roth, and P. C. Wong, eds., *Proceedings of the IEEE Symposium on Information Visualization*, pages 87–94.

Kruskal, Joseph B. and James M. Landwehr. 1983. Icicle plots: Better displays for hierarchical clustering. *The American Statistician* 37(2):162–168.

Lascarides, Alex and Nicholas Asher. 2007. Segmented discourse representation theory: Dynamic semantics with discourse structure. In H. Blunt and R. Muskens, eds., *Computing Meaning: Volume 3*, pages 87–124. Dordrecht: Springer.

Lee, Bongshin, George G. Robertson, Mary Czerwinski, and Cynthia Sims Parr. 2007. Candidtree: Visualizing structural uncertainty in similar hierarchies. *Information Visualization* 6(3):233–246.

Lee, Sukwon, Sung-Hee Kim, Ya-Hsin Hung, Heidi Lam, Youn-ah Kang, and Ji Soo Yi. 2016. How do people make sense of unfamiliar visualizations? A grounded model of novice's information visualization sensemaking. *IEEE Transactions on Visualization and Computer Graphics* 22(1):499–508.

Lima, Manuel. 2014. *The Book of Trees: Visualizing Branches of Knowledge*. New York: Princeton Architectural Press.

Mann, William C. and Sandra A. Thompson. 1988. Rhetorical structure theory: Toward a functional theory of text organization. *Text* 8(3):243–281.

Marcu, Daniel. 1999. Discourse trees are good indicators of importance in text. In I. Mani and M. Maybury, eds., *Advances in Automatic Text Summarization*, pages 123–136. Cambridge, MA: MIT Press.

Mayer, Thomas, Christian Rohrdantz, Miriam Butt, Frans Plank, and Daniel A. Keim. 2010. Visualizing vowel harmony. *Linguistic Issues in Language Technology* 4(2):1–33.

Munzner, Tamara, François Guimbretière, Serdar Tasiran, Li Zhang, and Yunhong Zhou. 2003. Treejuxtaposer: Scalable tree comparison using focus + context with guaranteed visibility. *ACM Transactions on Graphics* 22(3):453–462.

Neumann, Petra, Sheelagh Carpendale, and Anand Agarawala. 2006. PhylloTrees: Phyllotactic patterns for tree layout. In B. S. Santos, T. Ertl, and K. Joy, eds., *Proceedings of the Eurographics /IEEE VGTC Symposium on Visualization*, pages 59–66.

Pilz, Thomas, Wolfram Luther, and Ulrich Ammon. 2008. Retrieval of spelling variants in nonstandard texts – automated support and visualization. *SKY Journal of Linguistics* 21:155–200.

Prasad, Rashmi, Aravind K. Joshi, and Bonnie L. Webber. 2010. Exploiting scope for shallow discourse parsing. In *Proceedings of the Seventh International Conference on Language Resources and Evaluation*, pages 2076–2083.

Prendinger, Helmut, Paul Piwek, and Mitsuru Ishizuka. 2007. A novel method for automatically generating multi-modal dialogue from text. *International Journal of Semantic Computing* 1(3):319–334.

Robertson, George, Kim Cameron, Mary Czerwinski, and Daniel Robbins. 2002. Animated visualization of multiple intersecting hierarchies. *Information Visualization* 1(1):50–65.

Ruchikachorn, Puripant and Klaus Mueller. 2015. Learning visualizations by analogy: Promoting visual literacy through visualization morphing. *IEEE Transactions on Visualization and Computer Graphics* 21(9):1028–1044.

Schulz, Hans-Jörg. 2011. Treevis.net: A tree visualization reference. *IEEE Computer Graphics and Applications* 31(6):11–15.

Shiloach, Yossi. 1976. *Arrangements of Planar Graphs on the Planar Lattice*. Ph.D. thesis, Weizmann Institute of Science.

Siirtola, Harri, Tanja Säily, Terttu Nevalainen, and Kari-Jouko Räihä. 2014. Text variation explorer: Towards interactive visualization tools for corpus linguistics. *International Journal of Corpus Linguistics* 19(3):417–429.

Therón, Roberto, Laura Fontanillo, Andrés Esteban Marcos, and Carols Seguín Herrero. 2011. Visual analytics: A novel approach in corpus linguistics and the Nuevo Diccionario Histórico del Español. In M. Carrió Pastor and M. Candel Mora, eds., *Actas del III Congreso Internacional de Lingüística de Corpus*, pages 335–342.

Tu, Ying and Han-Wei Shen. 2007. Visualizing changes of hierarchical data using treemaps. *IEEE Transactions on Visualization and Computer Graphics* 13(6):1286–1293.

van Ham, Frank. 2003. Using multilevel call matrices in large software projects. In T. Munzner and S. North, eds., *Proceedings of the 9th Annual IEEE Conference on Information Visualization*, pages 227–232.

Zhao, Jian, Fanny Chevalier, Christopher Collins, and Ravin Balakrishnan. 2012. Facilitating discourse analysis with interactive visualization. *IEEE Transactions on Visualization and Computer Graphics* 18(12):2639–2648.

Zhao, Jian, Michael Glueck, Fanny Chevalier, Yanhong Wu, and Azam Khan. 2016. Egocentric analysis of dynamic networks with egolines. In *Proceedings of the SIGCHI Conference on Human Factors in Computing Systems*, pages 5003–5014.

4

Interactive Visualizations in INESS

PAUL MEURER, VICTORIA ROSÉN AND KOENRAAD DE SMEDT

4.1 Introduction

Both on paper and on computer screens, grammatical structures are often drawn as diagrams consisting of nodes connected by lines or by arrows. Such diagrams, exemplified by the simple constituent structure in Figure 1, make it easier to grasp grammatical information than linear notations, such as the equivalent labeled bracketing in (1).

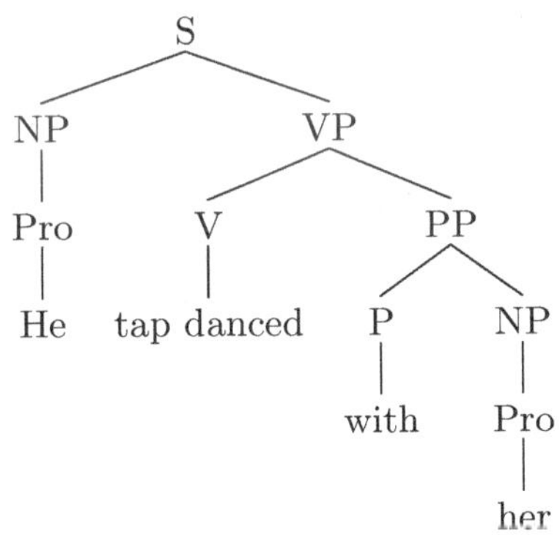

FIGURE 1 A simple example of a constituent tree structure for the sentence *He tap danced with her.*

Visual Analytics for Linguistics (LingVis).
edited by Miriam Butt, Annette Hautli-Janisz and Verena Lyding.
Copyright © 2020, CSLI Publications.

(1) [S [NP [Pro [He]]] [VP [V [tap danced]] [PP [P [with]] [NP [Pro [her]]]]]]

In contrast to fixed diagrams on paper, visualizations on computer systems offer opportunities for dynamic interaction, such that the computer assists the user in navigating and adapting the flow of information, depending on the user's choices and the task at hand. In this chapter, we focus on innovative visualizations in the context of the online construction and exploration of treebanks.

Treebanks are syntactically annotated corpora. They take their name from the inverse tree-shaped diagrams, such as the one in Figure 1, that all linguists are familiar with. Beyond trees, treebanks may however also contain more general graphs, such as directed acyclic and even cyclic graphs, which are represented in more complex kinds of diagrams, as will be shown below. The grammatical annotations in treebanks may provide important empirical information to linguists and language scholars, and may also be useful in developing language technology applications.

Treebanks are usually created by a combination of automatic parsing and manual processing. Good visualizations are helpful in manual intervention, which often involves text preparation as well as the inspection, disambiguation and correction of parse results. Inspection and disambiguation can be challenging due to the number of possible readings of sentences and the size and detail of the structures. Therefore, methods for showing structures at different levels of detail, and for pointing out differences between readings, are helpful. Color highlighting and collapsing or graying out information may be useful visual features in this respect.

Sometimes there is a need to edit displayed syntactic structures. When editing is performed through the manipulation of displayed items by drag and drop, color differences and highlighting of selectable items offer important visual clues.

In exploring treebanks, various ways of displaying search results may be helpful to users. We will show how highlighting helps users to identify those parts of syntactic structures that match queries. Furthermore, tables with aggregated, clickable search results provide good overviews and ease of navigation.

In what follows, we describe several concrete innovative features of effective visualizations in the INESS treebanking infrastructure. INESS is the *Infrastructure for the Exploration of Syntax and Semantics* and is part of the CLARINO Bergen Center.[1] It offers access to treebanks

[1]`http://clarino.uib.no/iness`

of different types, such as LFG (Lexical-Functional Grammar), HPSG (Head-driven Phrase Structure Grammar), dependency grammar, and phrase structure grammar (constituency). It also provides online LFG parsing and disambiguation for several languages.

Although various aspects of the infrastructure have been described in other publications (Rosén et al. 2009, 2012), neither its approach to visualization nor its recently updated visualization components have been sufficiently described. We therefore focus now on the visual presentation and inspection of complex syntactic analyses, including interactive visualizations that combine multiple levels of syntactic description and represent the relations between them.

Although appropriate visualizations are provided for all types of treebanks, we will in the present chapter pay most attention to LFG analyses. We also discuss visual aspects of the interface for displaying and manipulating structures in some other types of treebanks as well. We will not discuss text preprocessing and interaction with the lexicon (Rosén et al. 2016), nor several interactive "management" aspects of the treebanking interface, such as selecting treebanks and monitoring treebank versions.

Section 4.2 introduces the visualization of LFG structures in the infrastructure. Section 4.3 presents visual techniques for disambiguation. Section 4.4 discusses the visualization of dependency and constituency structures, and Section 4.5 shows how dependency structures are interactively edited. Section 4.6 presents some aspects of visualization in parallel treebanks. Section 4.7 explains different ways of presenting search results and navigating in these. In Section 4.8 we briefly present the implementation of the system, and in Section 4.9 we make comparisons with other systems. Section 4.10 is the conclusion.

4.2 Interactive Visualization of LFG Structures

Syntactic data, especially those resulting from deep parsing, are among the most complex types of linguistic data and rely heavily on user-friendly visualization. While many treebanks have only one level of syntactic analysis, LFG analyses have at least two separate but inter-related levels. One is the c-structure (constituent structure), which is a phrase structure tree representing projective constituency imposed on a string (i.e. respecting linear order and without crossing branches). The other is the f-structure (functional structure), which is a feature-value matrix (a labeled directed graph) representing functional relations and features. C- and f-structures are related to each other by projections as defined by the grammar: each c-structure node projects some (subsidiary) f-structure. For instance, an NP in the c-structure may project the value of the OBJ (object) in the f-structure. Such projection relations are important and should be appropriately visualized.

The Xerox Linguistic Environment (XLE) is a platform for developing LFG grammars (Maxwell and Kaplan 1993, King et al. 2004). XLE offers an efficient parser and generator for LFG grammars, and it interfaces with finite-state preprocessing modules for tokenization and morphological analysis. Whereas XLE offers a visual display based on X11 and Tcl/Tk, INESS uses only the XLE parser and has developed its own visualizations in a web browser interface, which is far easier to access than the outmoded X11 platform. The following two main modes of operation are available for LFG analyses in INESS:

1. XLE-Web is an online interface to XLE where users can parse sentences in a web browser, with a number of grammars for different languages including English, French, German, Polish, Norwegian and others.[2]
2. The LFG Parsebanker (Rosén et al. 2009) also interfaces to XLE and uses some of the same visualizations as XLE-Web but is embedded in an elaborate environment for the construction and exploration of LFG treebanks.

In particular, whereas XLE has implemented a basic juxtaposed rendering of the c- and f-structures (Maxwell and Kaplan 1993), we have implemented a more advanced visualization that extends these ideas. Here we present mainly the aspects of visualization that are novel in INESS; a more specific comparison to XLE is provided in Section 4.9.

Figure 2 shows the c- and f-structures for the sentence *The president offended two journalists.* This sentence was parsed in XLE-Web with the English ParGram LFG grammar,[3] developed in the Parallel Grammar project (Butt et al. 2002). For reasons of space we have chosen a simple sentence of only five words to demonstrate that the c- and f-structures are rich representations encoding many different types of linguistic information. For longer and more complex sentences the amount of information will of course increase accordingly; the sheer size of the representations suggests not only that a large screen will be practical, but also that good visualization techniques will be essential. For ease of viewing, a similar coloring scheme is used in both structures. In the c-structure, black is the basic color but terminal nodes (words)

[2] `http://clarino.uib.no/iness/xle-web`

[3] Parsing with this grammar results in structures where sentence-initial uppercase letters are represented by a preposed circumflex, reflecting preprocessing in terms of tokenization.

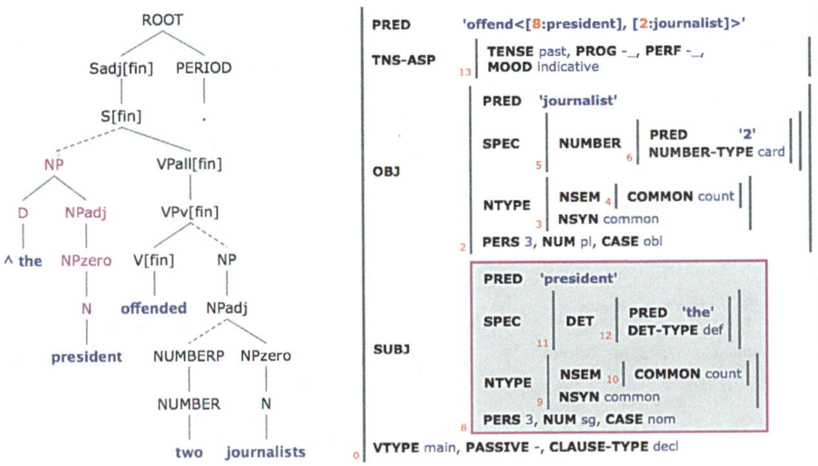

FIGURE 2 Parse result for the sentence *The president offended two journalists*, with mouse over visualizing the projection from an NP node in the c-structure (left) to the value of the SUBJ in the f-structure (right).

are in blue. In the f-structure, the feature names are in black and their atomic values in blue, while indices are displayed in orange.

The set of c-structure nodes that project to the same (subsidiary) f-structure constitute a functional domain. The functional domains partition the c-structure. These partitions are indicated by the use of solid and dotted lines in the branches of the tree. Nodes connected by solid lines project to the same functional domain, whereas dotted lines connect parts of the tree which project to different functional domains.

The projection relations between the two representations are of interest to researchers and should therefore be available for visual inspection. The approach which we have followed is the simultaneous highlighting of corresponding parts in both representations. This may be seen by mousing over nodes in the c-structure. In the example in Figure 2, mousing over the leftmost NP node highlights the corresponding subsidiary f-structure with a magenta border, thus showing that the NP *the president* is the subject (SUBJ) of the sentence. On mouse over, all nodes that belong to the same functional domain (i.e. all nodes that project the same f-structure) are highlighted in magenta; holding the mouse over any of the other nodes in this NP, i.e. D, NPadj, NPzero or N, produces the same result.

One can also use mouse over in the reverse direction, from the f-structure to the c-structure. In this case, mousing over the index num-

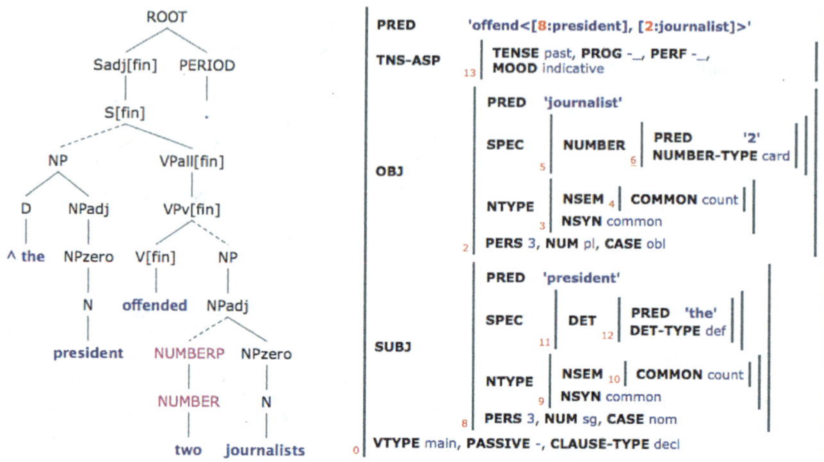

FIGURE 3 Mouse over on index 6 on the value of the NUMBER attribute in the f-structure results in highlighting NUMBERP in the c-structure.

ber of an f-structure results in all c-structure nodes projecting that f-structure being highlighted. Figure 3 shows the effect of mousing over the index 6; this results in highlighting of the subtree headed by NUMBERP in the c-structure which projects the value of the NUMBER attribute in the f-structure.

Whether going from c- to f-structure or vice versa, the correspondence between highlighted parts of the two representations is entirely dependent on and derived from the projections defined by the particular LFG grammar used for each treebank. If the grammar allows discontinuities, i.e. a projection of non-contiguous nodes to the same f-structure, then these will be visualized as such. This is illustrated in Figure 4 for the Norwegian sentence (2), parsed with the NorGram grammar (Dyvik 2000, Dyvik et al. 2016); the subtree for *vi* and the one for the floating quantifier *alle* are both highlighted since they project to the same f-structure, which is both topic and subject of the sentence.

(2) Vi kom alle.
we came all
'We all came.'

In order to make the inspection of large structures manageable, it is possible to collapse or expand certain parts of the c-structure, depending on what the user is interested in viewing. Clicking on a preterminal node expands it to display the sublexical structure of the terminal node,

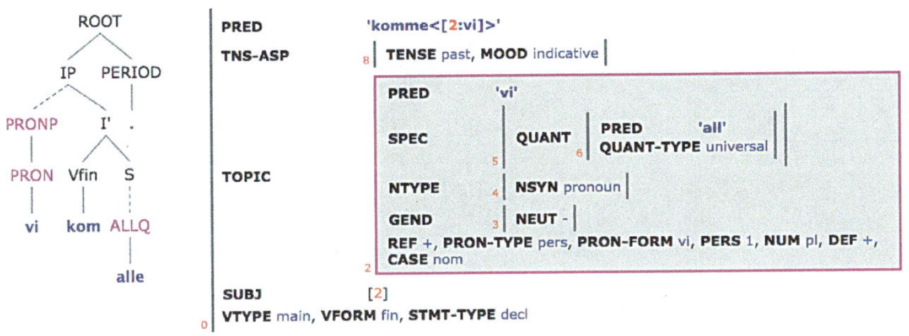

FIGURE 4 Visualization of the projection from discontinuities in example (2).

thus making visible the features encoded by the morphological analyzer. Clicking again collapses the sublexical tree. Clicking on any c-structure node that is not a terminal or preterminal collapses the dominated subtree into a triangle over the entire substring. If the substring is too long, the middle of the substring may be elided. Clicking once again on the same node replaces the substring by ellipsis dots surrounded by square brackets. A third click will return the full subtree.

These visualizations can be useful for viewing very large c-structures, since parts of the c-structure that are not relevant to what the user wants to examine may be abbreviated, while other parts the user does wish to view may be expanded. Figure 5 illustrates these features in the c-structure of the sentence *All of the Republican senators on the bus waved to the smiling president.* The leftmost NP is collapsed, the rightmost NP is further collapsed to ellipsis dots, and the preterminal node V[fin] is expanded to display its morphological features.

F-structures can also be made more compact; the options "Show PREDs only" and "Suppress CHECK" were originally implemented in XLE (Maxwell and Kaplan 1993). The option "Show PREDs only" suppresses attributes which do not contain a path to a PRED (predicate) value; the "PREDs only" view of the f-structure in Figure 3 is shown in Figure 6. Here only the functional backbone of the f-structure is shown. In this view, the f-structure resembles a dependency structure. In addition, "Suppress CHECK" is an option which suppresses auxiliary attributes which are internally used in the grammar for wellformedness checks; this option is on by default.

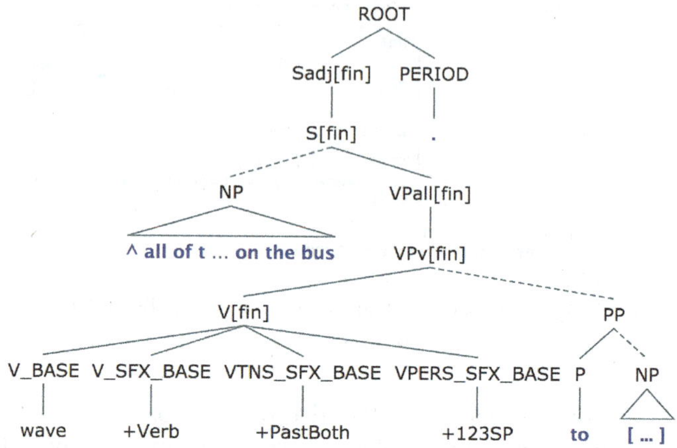

FIGURE 5 Expansion into sublexical nodes and collapsing of c-structure nodes, illustrated for the analysis of the sentence *All of the Republican senators on the bus waved to the smiling president.*

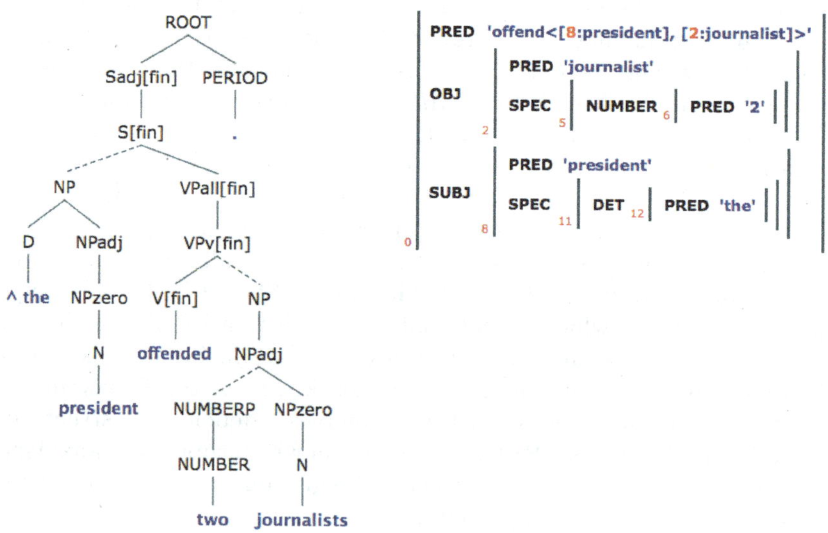

FIGURE 6 Compact "PREDs only" view of f-structure.

4.3 Visualizing the Effects of Discriminants on Packed Structures

Because of lexical and syntactic ambiguity, parsing often produces multiple analyses. When there are many possible analyses, it is difficult or practically impossible to find the intended one by sequentially inspecting all the visual structures. There are several solutions to this problem.

One way of visualizing multiple analyses compactly is to use a *packed* representation in which all analyses are viewed together in one graph, with choice indices on nodes, indicating which analyses the subtree pertains to. Whereas the XLE interface offers such a representation for f-structures, called an *f-structure chart* (King et al. 2004), INESS offers packed representations for c-structures as well as f-structures. Figure 7 shows the packed representations of the sentence *The journalists saw the tweets*, with choice indices shown in green. In this figure the choice index *a1* is used in both the c- and the f-structure to indicate the analysis of the verb as the present tense of *saw*, while the choice index *a2* indicates the solution where the verb is the past tense of the verb *see*. The subtrees headed by the choice indices *a1* and *a2* in the c-structure look identical, but clicking on the preterminal nodes will expand the terminal nodes to show their different stems and morphological features.

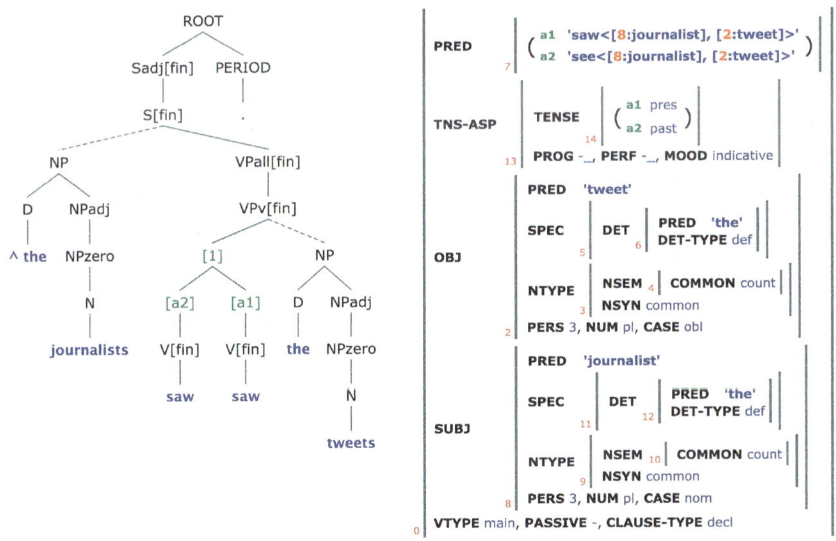

FIGURE 7 Packed c- and f-structures for *The journalists saw the tweets.*

NorGramBank, a large LFG treebank for Norwegian, was created by automatically parsing a corpus followed by manual disambiguation (Dyvik et al. 2016). When there are multiple ambiguities in a sentence, the packed structures may become so large or complex that they are difficult to read, and they are thus not by themselves sufficient for disambiguation. We have therefore implemented a system of discriminants (Carter 1997, Oepen et al. 2004), which are simple properties of analyses. Discriminants make it possible to choose between arbitrarily many solutions by consecutively selecting properties of the desired analysis rather than selecting one of many analyses. INESS computes discriminants and presents them to annotators of treebanks or users of XLE-Web, who can choose or reject discriminants in order to disambiguate a sentence. Usually, a small number of discriminants is sufficient to select one of potentially many possible analyses. In INESS, discriminants for LFG are computed and grouped by kind (Rosén et al. 2007), as illustrated in Figure 8 for the sentence *The detective saw the bag with his binoculars.* Since packed representations for a large number of analyses tend to be too complicated to be useful for visual inspection, the packed structures are only displayed together with the discriminants when there are 20 or fewer solutions. This default number can be changed by the user to a higher or lower number. In the present example there are only two solutions, as indicated in the figure by "Selected solutions: 2 of 2".

Choosing a discriminant results in the removal of all analyses not compatible with that discriminant from the parse forest. It is often useful to preview the effect on the packed representation of selecting a certain discriminant, especially because there are often interdependencies between discriminants. Figure 8 illustrates the effect of mousing over the discriminant *the || bag with his binoculars.*[4] The parts of the c-structure that are not compatible with this discriminant are grayed out. If the user clicks on this discriminant, the grayed-out part of the tree will no longer be displayed, and the discriminants that no longer distinguish between analyses will not be shown. In this case, disambiguation will then be complete since this sentence only has two readings.

4.4 Visualization of Dependency and Constituency Treebanks

Other treebank formalisms besides LFG are also catered for in INESS. We will briefly discuss some features for the visualization of dependency

[4]The double bar in the string is a shorthand for the bracketing *[the][bag with his binoculars]*.

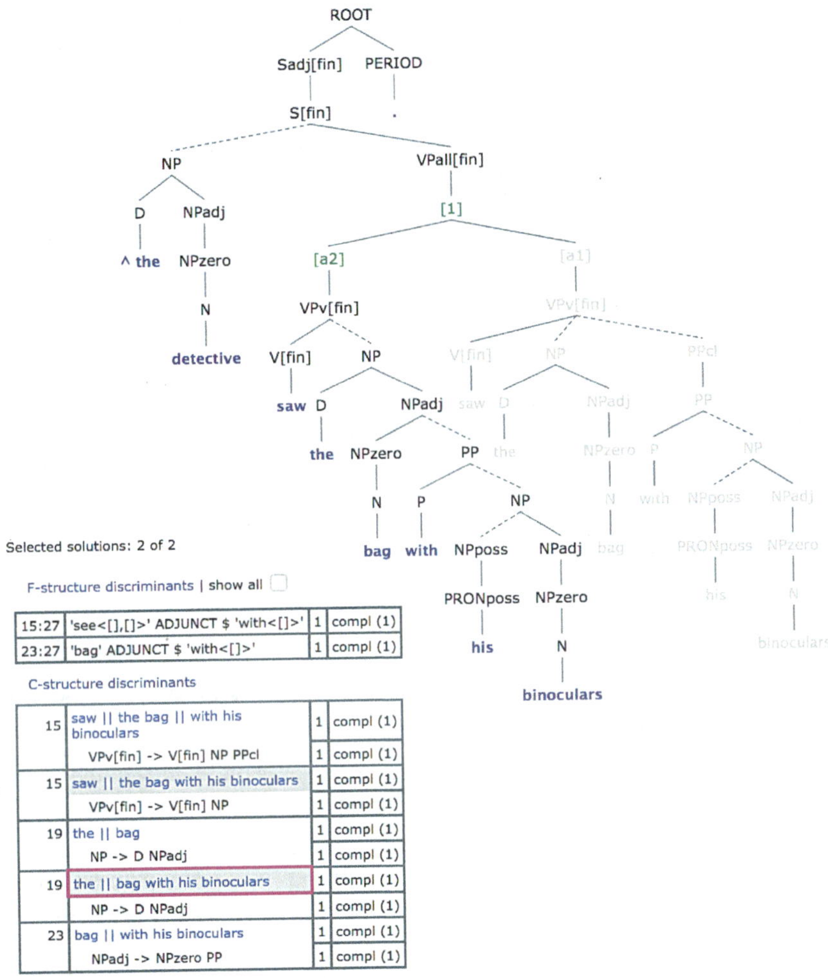

FIGURE 8 Previewing the effect of mousing over a discriminant for the sentence *The detective saw the bag with his binoculars*. The moused over discriminant is marked by a red border. The part of the packed c-structure which is not compatible with this discriminant is grayed out.

and constituency treebanks.

Sentences in dependency treebanks are traditionally represented with the nodes in linear order and with dependency relations shown as labeled edges in the shape of arrows above the sentence, as illustrated on the left in Figure 9 for example (3) from the PROIEL Classical Armenian treebank. Because the multitude of arrows can be difficult to read, the mouse over action over a word highlights all edges to and from that word. Red arrows are incoming edges and blue arrows are outgoing ones, as illustrated in Figure 9 in which the mouse focus is on the word *ēr*.

(3) ná ēr i skzbanē aṙ Astowác
it.NOM.SG was.IMPF.3SG in beginning.ABL.SG with God.ACC.SG
'He was in the beginning with God.'

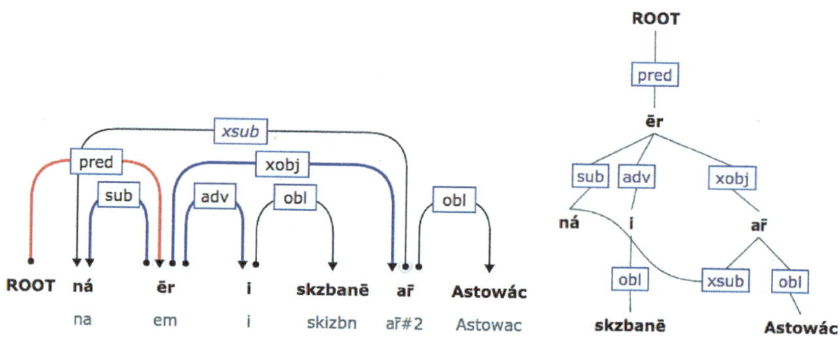

FIGURE 9 Dependency structure in linear (at left) and tree (at right) visualizations for example (3), with mouse over on *ēr* in the linear representation.

Dependency structures can also be represented as (unordered) trees with an implicit vertical direction of the edges, making arrows unnecessary. Incoming edges are always at the top of the node and outgoing edges at the bottom. This is illustrated on the right in Figure 9. Furthermore, multiple incoming edges are easy to spot, since secondary edges are drawn as curved lines, e.g. the secondary edge to *ná* in the figure.

Constituency structures are sometimes straightforward trees, but they can have secondary edges and can be drawn in different formats, depending on the user's choice. The TIGER style formatting, with angled edges, is particularly well suited for the display of non-projective trees, that is, trees with crossing edges. The alternative is the more generally used tree style with slanted edges, which tends to be more compact. Both styles are illustrated in Figure 10.

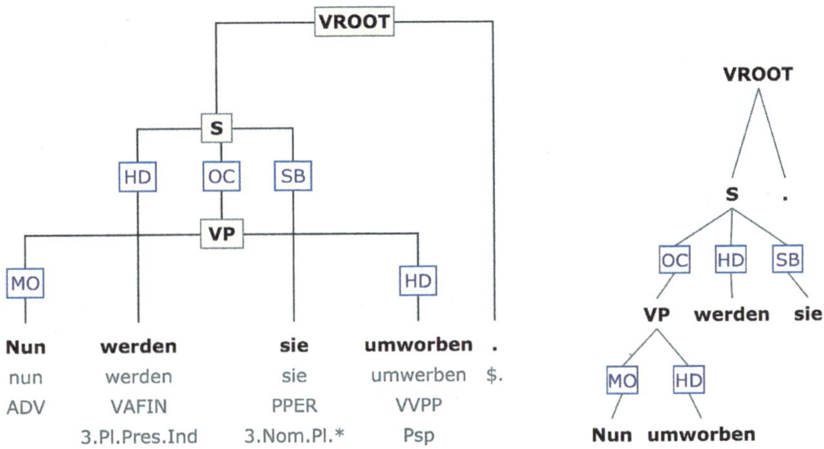

FIGURE 10 Constituency structure visualizations in TIGER style (at left) and alternative tree style (at right) for example (4) from the German TIGER treebank.

(4) Nun werden sie umworben.
Now become they wooed
'Now they are being wooed.'

4.5 Editing of Dependency Structures

In linear view, dependency structures can be edited. This function is implemented for the Universal Dependency (UD) treebanks (Nivre et al. 2016). All editing can easily be undone and redone. Changes are not stored in the database until the user saves them. The illustrations in the following discussion will be based on fragments of some structures taken from the English UD v2.0 treebank.

Figure 11 shows dependency relations for the name *Muqtada al-Sadr* as annotated in the treebank. Suppose that one wants to change the *punct* relation so that *al* is the new head. By clicking and dragging the start circle originating at the head node of a dependency relation edge and dropping it on a different node, a new head can be assigned to the relation. Figure 12 shows the situation when the start circle of the *punct* edge is moved. This causes highlighting of the edited edge in red, as well as highlighting of all valid new heads with red borders. The circle is about to be dropped on the node for *al*, which gets a red

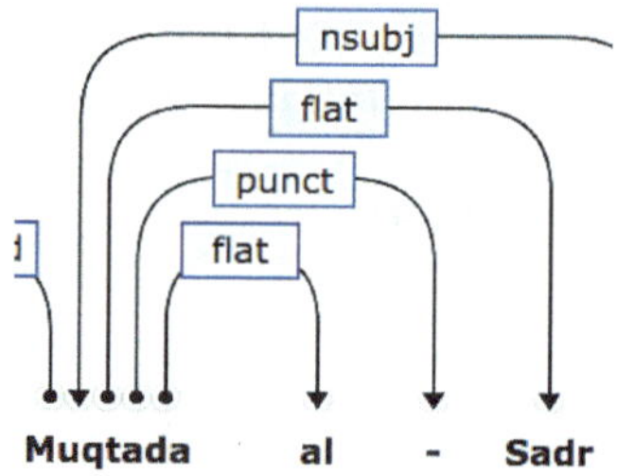

FIGURE 11 Example dependency relations for the name *Muqtada al-Sadr* from the English UD v2.0 treebank.

fill color. Only destinations which do not result in circular structures are valid.

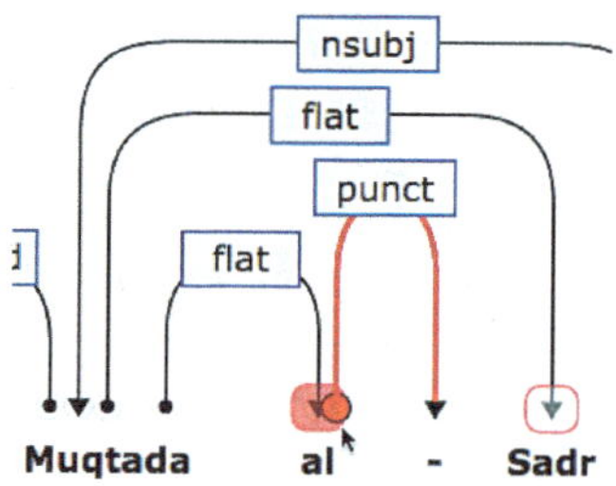

FIGURE 12 Selecting a head node highlights possible new heads.

Suppose that one instead would like to change the dependency relation *punct* to *flat*, in order to treat the whole name as a 'flat' multiword expression. Edge labels can easily be changed by clicking on the label and choosing a new one from a context pop-up menu, as shown in Figure 13.

Occasionally it is necessary to change the tokenization of the underlying sentence, which amounts to merging two adjacent nodes, or splitting a node in two. One might for instance wish to merge the three tokens *al,* - and *Sadr* into a single token. Adjacent nodes can be merged by dropping one node onto the other, as illustrated in Figure 14. In the first step (top left) the node with the hyphen is dragged to the left onto the *al* node. The relation of the node on which another is dropped is kept (top right). The next step shows a similar procedure in which the node *Sadr* is dropped onto *al-* (bottom left), resulting in the single token with spaces *al - Sadr* (bottom right).

In this and other cases, it may be necessary to edit the attributes

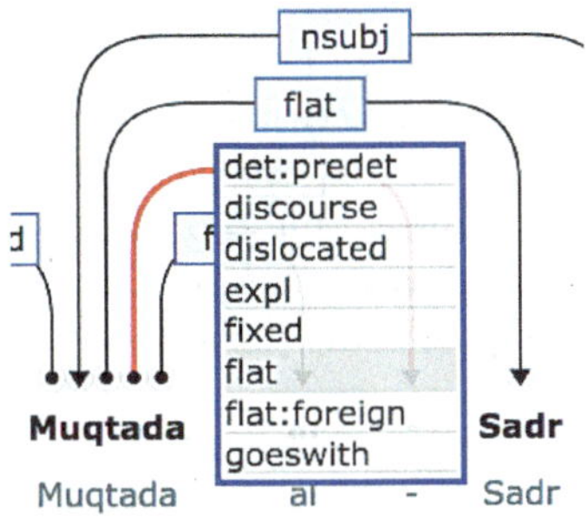

FIGURE 13 Choosing a new label for a dependency from a context pop-up menu.

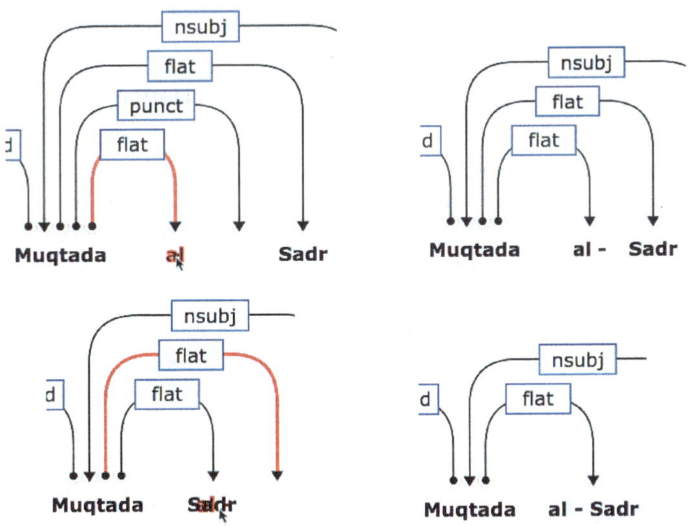

FIGURE 14 Consecutive steps in merging nodes by dropping one onto the other.

of a node. The word form itself, the lemma, the part of speech, or the grammatical features may need to be changed. This can be done by clicking on a node, which makes a context menu appear where the attributes can easily be edited. In Figure 15, for instance, the word form has been edited so that the spaces have been removed. The presented choices for grammatical features are context sensitive: if the part of speech is PROPN, for instance, only morphological features that apply to proper nouns can be chosen; the possible values are restricted to those values that actually appear in the treebank.

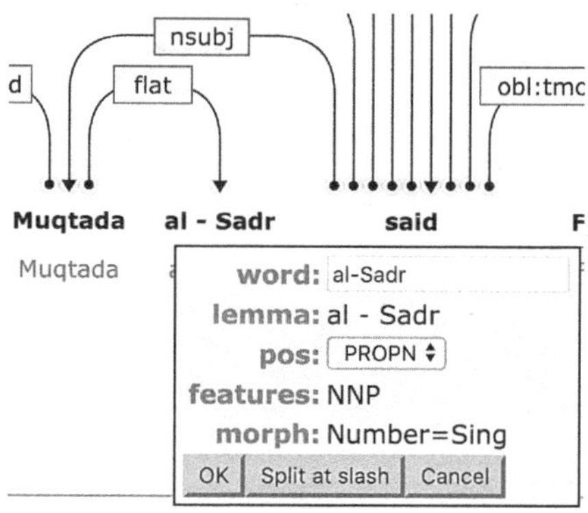

FIGURE 15 Menu for changing node attributes.

To split a node in two, the user inserts a slash or a backslash in the word form at the place where it should be split. Thus, a new daughter node of the original node is inserted in the structure to the left if a backslash was chosen, and to the right if a slash was chosen. The attributes of both nodes will need to be adjusted afterwards.

Secondary edges can be created by clicking and dragging the arrowhead that marks the end of an edge. This is illustrated in Figure 16, where one might want to add a secondary edge for the object control relation. When the arrowhead over *Hamas* is clicked, the start circle of the new secondary edge appears and can be dragged and dropped on a node which will become the head of the relation. In the figure, the start circle is being dragged towards the node for the word *end*. During its creation, the secondary edge is green, in order to mark a difference with the editing of existing edges, which are red. After creation of a new secondary edge, it must be assigned a label by clicking on the preliminary label and choosing a new one from the context menu (cf. Figure 13).

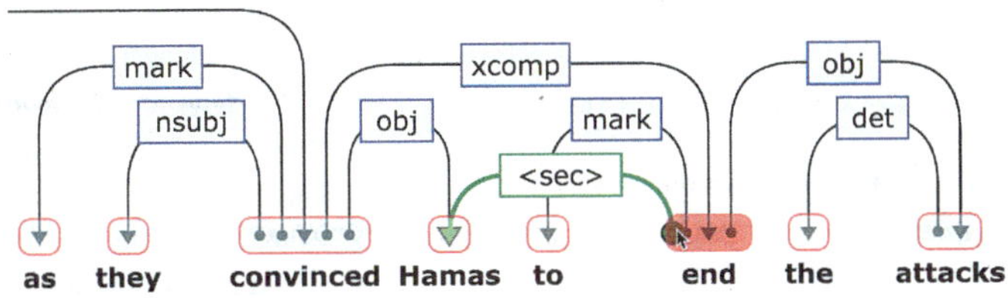

FIGURE 16 Creation of a secondary edge by selecting the end node of a dependency relation and dropping the start circle on the node which is to become head.

4.6 Parallel Treebanks

Parallel treebanks are sets of treebanks which are aligned so as to indicate certain correspondences between them; usually these are translational correspondences between sentences. Such treebanks may be useful in comparative language studies, in translation studies, or for the development of machine translation systems. We will not discuss all possibilities and intricacies of parallel treebanks, but only focus on core features of their visualization in INESS, which offers tools for building and exploring treebanks aligned on the sentence level and optionally also on the sub-sentence level. INESS currently supports alignment, exploration and visualization of one pair of treebanks at a time. Source and target treebanks do not need to be of the same type.

When browsing a parallel treebank, the structures of aligned sentences are displayed next to each other, as illustrated in Figure 17. This figure also shows structural alignments below the sentence level, which are presently implemented for LFG treebanks only. Alignments between sub-f-structures of parallel sentences are constructed by dragging the index of a source f-structure onto the index of a target f-structure. These alignments are displayed by small arrows linking the source and target f-structure indices; the red number on the left of the arrow is the regular index of the f-structure, while the green number on the right is the index of the target f-structure. When the aligned f-structures are compatible according to criteria described in detail in Dyvik et al. (2009), a linking of c-structure nodes is automatically induced. The links between source and target c-structure nodes are shown by curved, colored lines to make them easily distinguishable from the straight lines in the two c-structures.[5]

[5]In the example, Georgian is transliterated for readability, but INESS can also display strings in the Georgian script.

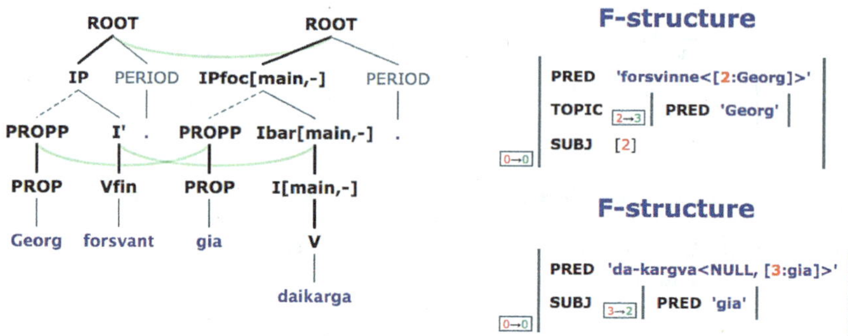

FIGURE 17 Structural alignment between a Norwegian and a Georgian LFG analysis for example (5).

(5) a. Georg forsvant.
Georg disappeared
'Georg disappeared.'

b. gia daikarga.
Georg disappeared
'Georg disappeared.'

4.7 Visualization of Search Results

INESS has a powerful search mechanism, INESS Search (Meurer 2012), which allows users to formulate queries that specify structural properties of sentences. Without going into detail about the query language itself, we will discuss how the search results are visually presented. As an example, consider searching for sentences where *tractor* is the object of a predicate in the ParGram English treebank, part of a multilingual test suite for the comparative exploration of syntactic structures in LFG (Sulger et al. 2013). Example query (6) matches sentences with a predicate (PRED) (marked with the variable *#p*), which has an object (OBJ) (marked with the variable *#obj*), which has as its PRED 'tractor'.

(6) *#_f* >PRED *#p* & *#_f* >(OBJ PRED) *#obj*:'tractor'

Overviews of search results from INESS Search can be displayed in different ways. Figure 18 shows one way: a list of sentence IDs is displayed; clicking on an ID displays its c- and f-structures. At the top, under the search expression, a list of pointers to matching sentences is given, and the first matching sentence is displayed with its c- and f-structures. Because it is helpful to also clearly visualize which parts of the structure match the query, the values of the variables are highlighted with red borders in the f-structure, while the variables themselves are also included as red indices. In this example, nothing is highlighted in the c-structure, because the search expression only matches parts of the f-structure.

Another way of displaying search results is tabular mode, where results are given as a table in which the values of variables are aggregated and sorted according to node variables (and possibly features) in the query. The table has one column for every variable, and each row of the table represents a distinct combination of values for the selected variables. This is illustrated in Figure 19. Variables containing an underscore ($\#\_f$ in the example) may be necessary in the query but are not shown in the table of results.

Clicking on a row displays a table of all matching sentences where those feature values are assumed. This is illustrated in Figure 20, where the sixth row, showing that there are nine sentences in which $\#obj$ has the value *tractor* and $\#p$ has the value *buy*, has been clicked. This action opens a display window with a black border listing those nine sentences.

It is possible to see the matching nodes and structures in the tabular view at a glance, without having to go to a different web page and navigate back to the tabular view afterwards. Mousing over a sentence, as highlighted in orange in Figure 20, pops up a window with a preview of only the essential parts of the c- and/or f-structure, depending on what has been searched for.[6] In our example, this is the "PREDs only" f-structure displayed on the right in Figure 20. It includes all matching nodes, while parts of the structure not containing a matching node are collapsed, but can be expanded if desired. Each matching node is highlighted with a red border and is indexed with its corresponding variable in the search expression.

INESS Search also works on other treebank types, such as dependency or constituency treebanks, and highlighting of search results works equally well for syntactic structures of those types. By way of illustration, Figure 21 shows the tabular results of searching for divergent annotations for dependencies with the *fixed* label in all UD v2.0 treebanks. In particular, the expression in (7) matches sentences in which $\#x$ precedes $\#y$ while there is a *fixed* dependency relation from $\#y$ to $\#x$.

(7) $\#y$ >fixed $\#x$ & $\#x$.* $\#y$ :: lang

The resulting table in Figure 21 shows columns for these variables,

[6] This shows the one analysis that is indexed. When a parse has been manually disambiguated down to one analysis, that analysis is indexed; if manual disambiguation has not been done, the stochastically highest ranked analysis is indexed.

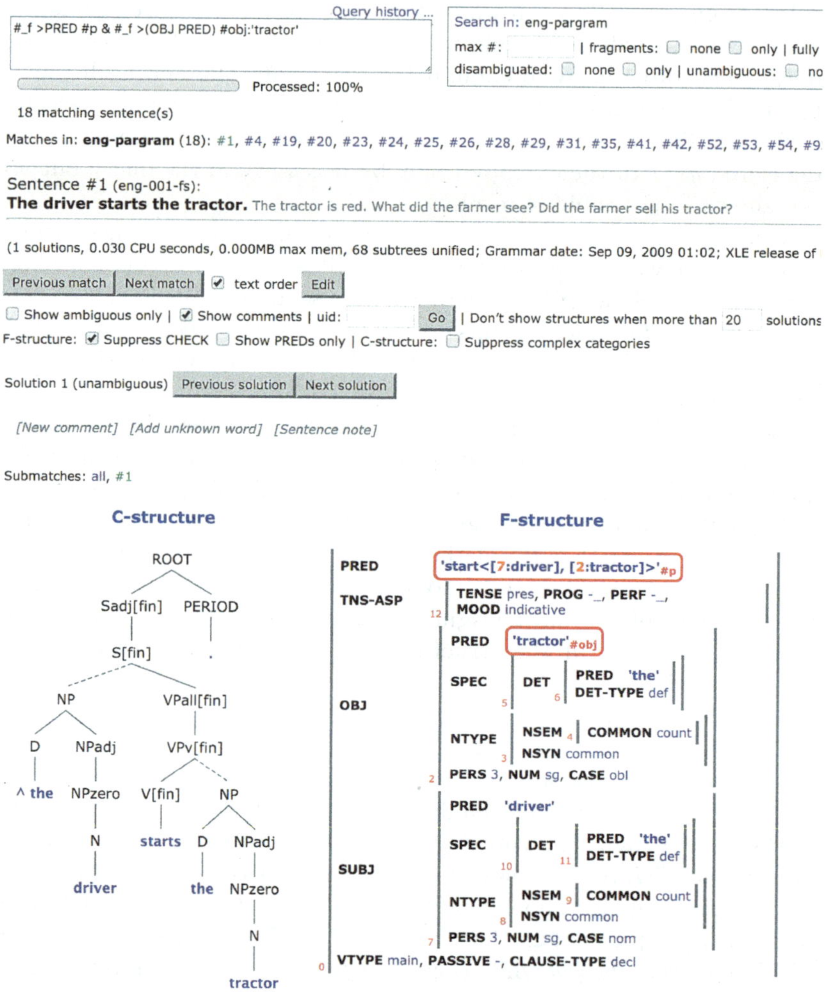

FIGURE 18 Highlighting of matching nodes in search results.

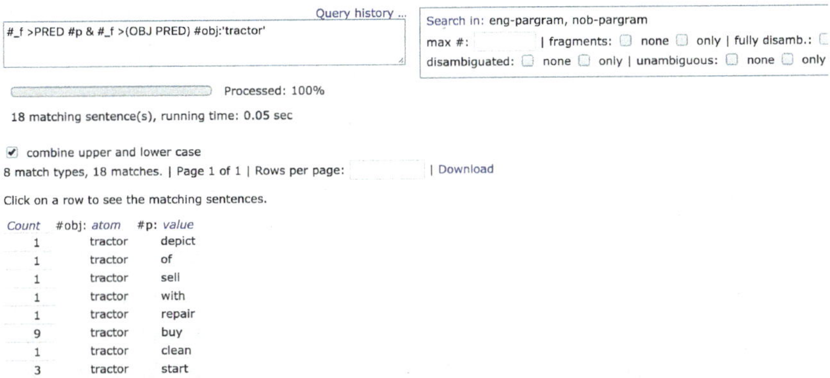

FIGURE 19 Table view of search results, with a list of matching values for each variable.

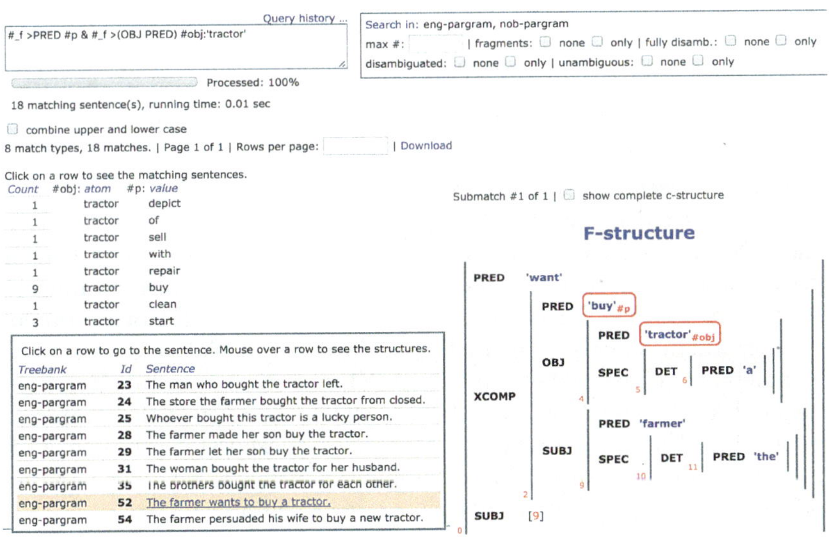

FIGURE 20 Table view of search results, with a list of matching sentences when clicking a row, and compact f-structure display on mouse over, with highlighting of matching nodes.

as well as a column for the metavariable *lang* (the language of the treebank). Clicking on a row in the table (the row starting with 9 in the figure) brings up a list of matching sentences, which can be further inspected. Figure 22 shows matching elements of one of the matching sentences in linear and tree visualizations; in this case the Portuguese expression *uma vez que* 'since, because' is matched.

4.8 Implementation

The treebanking system is fully online and can be used in any modern web browser. Both the visualization code and the remainder of the treebanking framework are written in Common Lisp. Web pages are generated as XML documents that are converted into CSS-styled HTML on the server using XSLT transformations. XML is an abstract representation which indicates hierarchical structure without committing to visualization, so that there is a clean separation between the content structure and the different possible visualization modes. For the interactive features, Javascript is used. The tree and linear dependency visualizations are implemented in SVG (Scalable Vector Graphics), whereas f-structures are coded as tables in plain HTML. The SVG code is currently generated directly from Common Lisp.

4.9 Comparison with Related Systems

Although INESS is inspired by the graphic environment in XLE, the design of the two systems is different. INESS caters to treebank constructors as well as to end users wishing to consult treebanks. XLE is mainly targeted at an audience of grammar developers, not treebank users. XLE visualizations therefore show details which are relevant for grammar development but not relevant for linguists only wishing to see parsing results. For instance, XLE allows the detailed inspection of valid syntactic structures as well as structures that violate coherence or completeness constraints. In addition, XLE shows, for instance, certain negated and completeness constraints which are relevant for grammar debugging. Users have reported that large packed structures in XLE present usability problems in disambiguation tasks, for which INESS offers discriminant-based solutions, as described above.

An example of a packed f-structure representation in XLE is shown in Figure 23. This sentence, *They can fish*, has three analyses. One analysis has *can* as a modal auxiliary that takes an XCOMP. The other two analyses involve *can* as a main verb taking an OBJ; in addition, *fish* can either be a singular noun or the plural of a count noun. Even with only three analyses, this visualization is difficult to read. The INESS

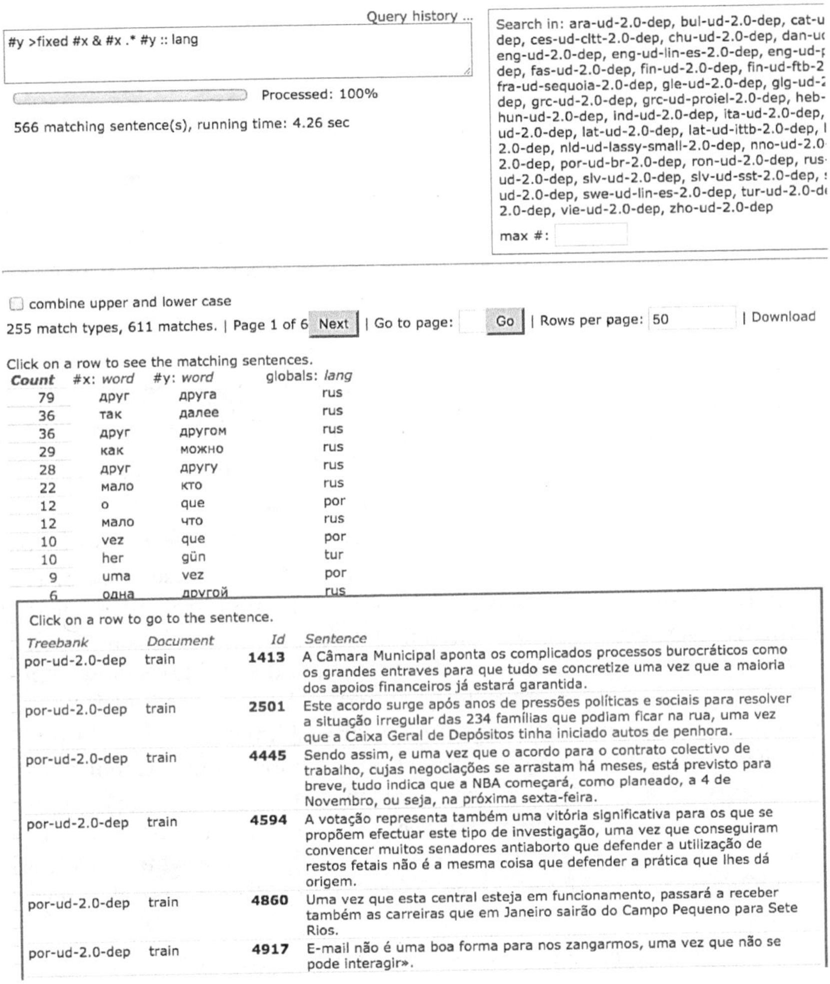

FIGURE 21 Table view of search results. Clicking on the row with *uma vez* displays matching sentences. Clicking on a sentence will display its structure, as illustrated in Figure 22.

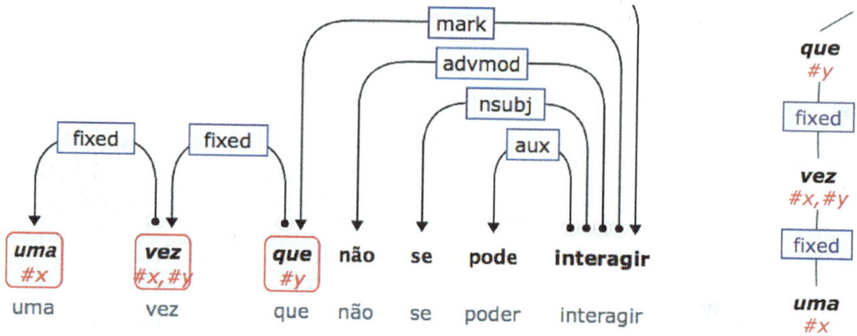

FIGURE 22 Linear view (left) and tree view (right) of a fragment of the dependency structure of a matching sentence, with highlighting of matching nodes; *uma vez que* is a fixed expression meaning 'since, because'.

packed f-structure for the same sentence in Figure 24 is easier to read. This is partly because some less relevant information and superfluous brackets are left out. It is also partly due to the use of colors and boldface and the less obtrusive placement of the indices, which together offer a clearer visual separation of structural elements.

TüNDRA (Martens 2013) is an extensive application for browsing, searching and visualizing the contents of treebanks. Like INESS, it is entirely offered through a web browser and users are authenticated through federated single sign-on. TüNDRA supports both constituency and dependency treebanks, as well as mixed and hybrid treebank types, but has only limited support for directed graphs as required for LFG, and it does not support discriminant disambiguation. In addition to TIGER-style (square angled) branches and more conventional phrase structures, it also offers colored labeled bracketing. For dependency structures, there is a choice between a visualization with arcs or as a tree (TrED style). TüNDRA has a query language which is similar to TIGERSearch and has appropriate highlighting in red for search results.

ANNIS3 (Krause and Zeldes 2016) offers search and visualization of multi-level corpora, including treebanks. It is available both as a standalone application and online through a browser. Its visualization modes are rich and varied, depending on the information to be rendered. Visualizations of syntactic structures include dependency arcs, hierarchical or ordered dependencies, and TIGER-style trees with right-angled branches. Visualizations of token and span annotations include KWIC with interlinear glossing, grids with layered spans for information structure, colors and underscoring for coreference, and Rhetorical

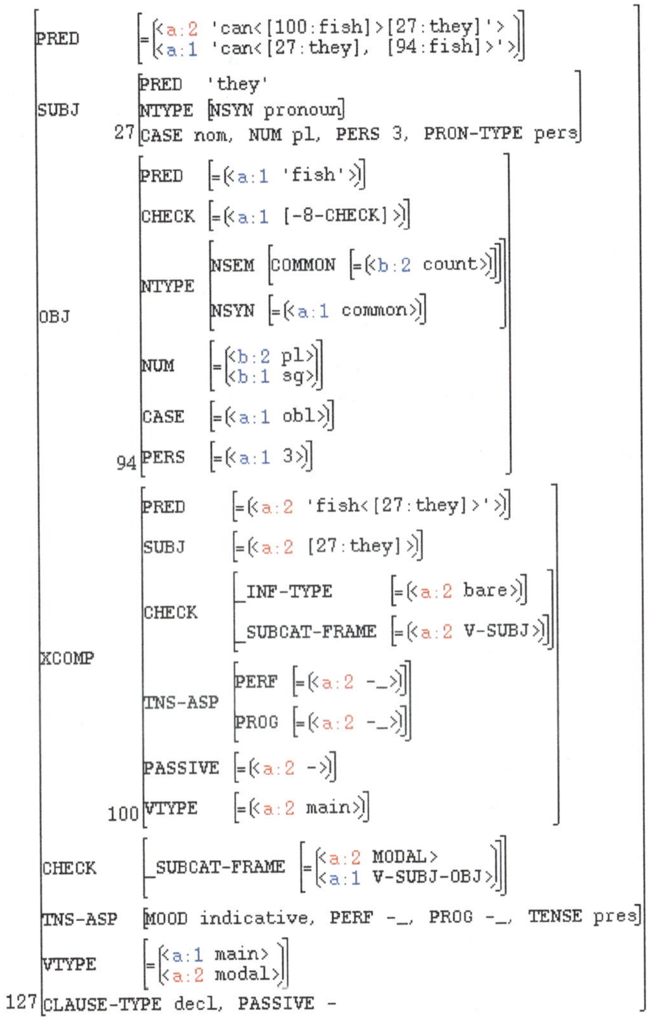

FIGURE 23 Packed f-structure for *They can fish* in XLE.

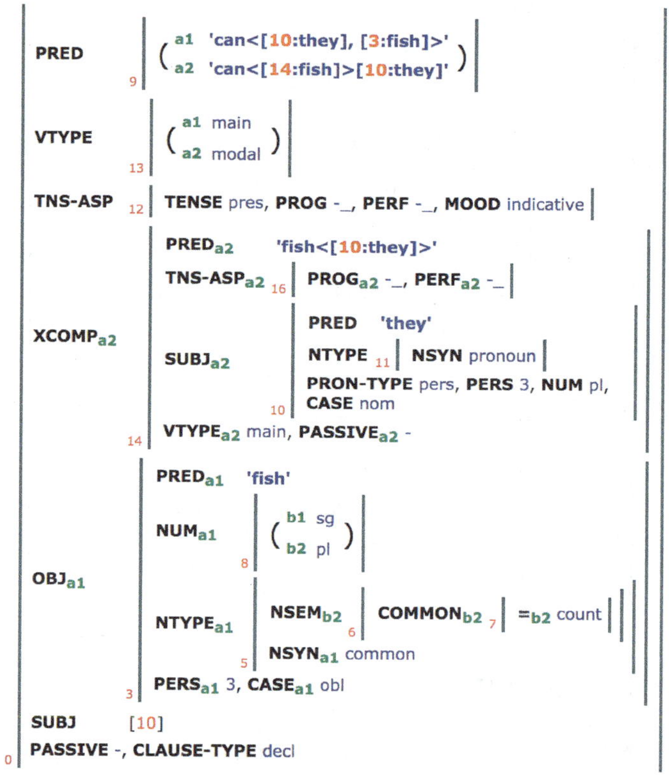

FIGURE 24 Packed f-structure for *They can fish* in INESS.

Structure Theory (RST) representations. LFG representations and discriminants are not supported. ANNIS3 can render parallel structures for corpora aligned at sentence level. Like TüNDRA and INESS, ANNIS3 uses a modified form of the TIGERSearch query language to search treebanks. Importing large volumes of data can be slow because ANNIS3 uses a conventional relational database as backend, with heavy use of auxiliary index tables to speed up query execution; INESS on the other hand uses an efficient custom index format.[7]

The PML Tree Query system (also referred to as PML TQ) has a graphical web client (Pajas and Štěpánek 2009) which has also been linked to KWIC concordance lines in Kontext (Klyueva and Straňák 2016). It displays syntactic dependency structures compatible with the Prague Markup Language (PML) and allows exploration of many dependency treebanks. LFG structures and discriminants are not supported. PML Tree Query has several highlighting modes, such as colored frames around nodes, and differentiated color coding of nodes in case several nodes referred to in a query are displayed in one structure. PML TQ also allows the user to put together a query interactively by choosing color-coded components from menus. The color coding assists users in constructing complex queries.

GrETEL (Augustinus et al. 2012, 2013) provides a web-based query interface for some Dutch language treebanks. It partly circumvents the problems that many users face in constructing search expressions. It has an interface in which users can build a query based on an example sentence or phrase which is interactively parsed. From the user's options about the extent to which the words in the example are fixed or may vary, an Xpath query is constructed; this query can optionally be modified. GrETEL presently only supports constituency treebanks which may have edge labels. Trees are visualized with layered nodes displaying edge label, part of speech, lemma and word.

None of the above-mentioned systems have support for LFG representations in a way that is comparable to the features of INESS. Also, none of these systems offer interactive editing of UD graphs.

[7] For an informal account on problematic aspects of the ANNIS3 index implementation, see `http://www.laudatio-repository.org/laudatio/wp-admin/tmp/2014/10/ANNIS_fuer_EntwicklerKrause2014.pdf`.

4.10 Concluding Remarks

We have discussed some approaches to the visualization of grammatical structures. In particular, we have discussed interactive graphical interfaces for treebanking in the context of the INESS treebanking infrastructure. Although most interfaces for treebanking handle constituency treebanks, and therefore can visualize c-structures, only INESS can visualize f-structures and the links between c-structures and f-structures. INESS is also the only system that handles search and discriminant-based disambiguation of LFG structures and offers appropriate interfaces for these tasks.

Since grammatical structures are quite complex, in particular in LFG, smart techniques must be used to overcome the problem of the sheer size of the structures in relation to computer screens, even quite big ones. One of our guiding principles has been that visualizations of syntactic structures should be able to present different levels of detail, dependent on user needs in different tasks (e.g. annotation, search, or preview). This includes ways to collapse or expand information, dependent on user choices, while "hidden" information remains accessible upon request through clicking or mouse over movements. Color is used to separate different kinds of information; clutter is avoided by using lighter colors and smaller font sizes for necessary but less visually important information (such as indices in f-structures). These principles are reflected in the implementation of INESS, which annotators and users have experienced to be more user-friendly than the original XLE interface.

Syntactic structures in other treebank formalisms, such as dependency, constituency and HPSG structures, can also be handled and searched in INESS. Their visualization benefits from some user definable options. For UD graphs, several editing operations are available. INESS is currently the only online treebanking system in which these interactive editing possibilities are offered.

The INESS framework as described here is fully functional and available for use. ParGram and many other projects use it for constructing, managing, disseminating and exploring treebanks. Many treebanks and operations are accessible without authentication, while some treebanks and some editing functions require authentication and authorization due to licensing and security considerations. Federated single sign-on authentication is available, as promoted by CLARIN.[8]

INESS remains under active development and more visualization features are planned as feedback from users is collected. A potentially

[8] `http://clarin.eu`

useful addition would be the ability to shrink large structures with zooming so that the user can mouse over with an intuitive virtual magnifying glass in order to zoom into parts. Another addition might be the option to lock highlighting which is now only shown during mouse over. Also, it may be useful to have interactions (e.g. highlighting) between words in a linear version of the sentence and their corresponding nodes in syntactic structures. Finally, the construction of queries would benefit from some interactive support, e.g. through feedback on the query as it is being written, by means of color coding or otherwise.

4.11 Acknowledgements

The work reported on in this chapter was funded by the Research Council of Norway under the INESS and CLARINO infrastructure projects and by the University of Bergen. The authors thank two anonymous reviewers for their comments.

References

Augustinus, Liesbeth, Vincent Vandeghinste, Ineke Schuurman, and Frank Van Eynde. 2013. Example-based treebank querying with GrETEL – now also for spoken Dutch. In *Proceedings of the 19th Nordic Conference of Computational Linguistics*, pages 423–428.

Augustinus, Liesbeth, Vincent Vandeghinste, and Frank Van Eynde. 2012. Example-based treebank querying. In N. Calzolari, K. Choukri, T. Declerck, M. U. Doğan, B. Maegaard, J. Mariani, J. Odijk, and S. Piperidis, eds., *Proceedings of the Eighth International Conference on Language Resources and Evaluation*, pages 3161–3167.

Butt, Miriam, Helge Dyvik, Tracy Holloway King, Hiroshi Masuichi, and Christian Rohrer. 2002. The Parallel Grammar project. In J. Carroll, N. Oostdijk, and R. Sutcliffe, eds., *Proceedings of the Workshop on Grammar Engineering and Evaluation at the 19th International Conference on Computational Linguistics (COLING)*, pages 1–7. Taipei, Taiwan: Association for Computational Linguistics.

Carter, David. 1997. The TreeBanker: A tool for supervised training of parsed corpora. In *Proceedings of the 14th National Conference on Artificial Intelligence*, pages 598–603.

Dyvik, Helge. 2000. Nødvendige noder i norsk: Grunntrekk i en leksikalsk-funksjonell beskrivelse av norsk syntaks [Necessary nodes in Norwegian: Basic properties of a lexical-functional description of Norwegian syntax]. In Ø. Andersen, K. Fløttum, and T. Kinn, eds., *Menneske, språk og felleskap*, pages 25–45. Oslo: Novus forlag.

Dyvik, Helge, Paul Meurer, Victoria Rosén, and Koenraad De Smedt. 2009. Linguistically motivated parallel parsebanks. In M. Passarotti, A. Przepiórkowski, S. Raynaud, and F. Van Eynde, eds., *Proceedings of the Eighth International Workshop on Treebanks and Linguistic Theories*, pages 71–82.

Dyvik, Helge, Paul Meurer, Victoria Rosén, Koenraad De Smedt, Petter Haugereid, Gyri Smørdal Losnegaard, Gunn Inger Lyse, and Martha Thunes. 2016. NorGramBank: A 'deep' treebank for Norwegian. In N. Calzolari, K. Choukri, T. Declerck, M. Grobelnik, B. Maegaard, J. Mariani, A. Moreno, J. Odijk, and S. Piperidis, eds., *Proceedings of the Tenth International Conference on Language Resources and Evaluation*, pages 3555–3562.

King, Tracy Holloway, Stefanie Dipper, Anette Frank, Jonas Kuhn, and John T. Maxwell III. 2004. Ambiguity management in grammar writing. *Research on Language and Computation* 2(2):259–280.

Klyueva, Natalia and Pavel Straňák. 2016. Improving corpus search via parsing. In N. Calzolari, K. Choukri, T. Declerck, S. Goggi, M. Grobelnik, B. Maegaard, J. Mariani, H. Mazo, A. Moreno, J. Odijk, and S. Piperidis, eds., *Proceedings of the Tenth International Conference on Language Resources and Evaluation*, pages 2862–2866.

Krause, Thomas and Amir Zeldes. 2016. Annis3: A new architecture for generic corpus query and visualization. *Digital Scholarship in the Humanities* 31(1):118–139.

Martens, Scott. 2013. TüNDRA: A web application for treebank search and visualization. In S. Kübler, P. Osenova, and M. Volk, eds., *Proceedings of the Twelfth Workshop on Treebanks and Linguistic Theories*, pages 133–144.

Maxwell, John and Ronald M. Kaplan. 1993. The interface between phrasal and functional constraints. *Computational Linguistics* 19(4):571–589.

Meurer, Paul. 2012. INESS-Search: A search system for LFG (and other) treebanks. In M. Butt and T. H. King, eds., *Proceedings of the LFG '12 Conference*, pages 404–421. Stanford, CA: CSLI Publications.

Nivre, Joakim, Marie-Catherine de Marneffe, Filip Ginter, Yoav Goldberg, Jan Hajič, Christopher D. Manning, Ryan McDonald, Slav Petrov, Sampo Pyysalo, Natalia Silveira, Reut Tsarfaty, and Daniel Zeman. 2016. Universal Dependencies v1: A multilingual treebank collection. In N. Calzolari, K. Choukri, T. Declerck, S. Goggi, M. Grobelnik, B. Maegaard, J. Mariani, H. Mazo, A. Moreno, J. Odijk, and S. Piperidis, eds., *Proceedings of the Tenth International Conference on Language Resources and Evaluation*, pages 1659–1666.

Oepen, Stephan, Dan Flickinger, Kristina Toutanova, and Christopher D. Manning. 2004. LinGO Redwoods: A rich and dynamic treebank for HPSG. *Research on Language and Computation* 2(4):575–596.

Pajas, Petr and Jan Štěpánek. 2009. System for Querying Syntactically Annotated Corpora. In *Proceedings of the ACL-IJCNLP 2009 Software Demonstrations*, pages 33–36.

Rosén, Victoria, Koenraad De Smedt, Paul Meurer, and Helge Dyvik. 2012. An open infrastructure for advanced treebanking. In J. Hajič, K. De Smedt, M. Tadić, and A. Branco, eds., *META-RESEARCH Workshop on Advanced Treebanking at LREC2012*, pages 22–29.

Rosén, Victoria, Paul Meurer, and Koenraad De Smedt. 2007. Designing and implementing discriminants for LFG grammars. In M. Butt and T. H. King, eds., *Proceedings of the LFG '07 Conference*, pages 397–417. Stanford, CA: CSLI Publications.

Rosén, Victoria, Paul Meurer, and Koenraad De Smedt. 2009. LFG Parsebanker: A toolkit for building and searching a treebank as a parsed corpus. In F. Van Eynde, A. Frank, G. van Noord, and K. De Smedt, eds., *Proceedings of the Seventh International Workshop on Treebanks and Linguistic Theories*, pages 127–133.

Rosén, Victoria, Martha Thunes, Petter Haugereid, Gyri Smørdal Losnegaard, Helge Dyvik, Paul Meurer, Gunn Inger Lyse, and Koenraad De Smedt. 2016. The enrichment of lexical resources through incremental parsebanking. *Language Resources and Evaluation* 50(2):291–319.

Sulger, Sebastian, Miriam Butt, Tracy Holloway King, Paul Meurer, Tibor Laczkó, György Rákosi, Cheikh Bamba Dione, Helge Dyvik, Victoria Rosén, Koenraad De Smedt, Agnieszka Patejuk, Özlem Çetinoglu, I Wayan Arka, and Meladel Mistica. 2013. ParGramBank: The ParGram parallel treebank. In *Proceedings of the 51st Annual Meeting of the Association for Computational Linguistics*, vol. 1, pages 550–560.

5

Visual Analytics in Diachronic Linguistic Investigations

ANNETTE HAUTLI-JANISZ, CHRISTIAN ROHRDANTZ, CHRISTIN SCHÄTZLE, ANDREAS STOFFEL, MIRIAM BUTT AND DANIEL A. KEIM

5.1 Introduction

Beginning with seminal work by Collins et al. (2007) and Collins (2010), the visualization methods developed within computer science have been introduced to work on a small but growing range of linguistic problems. These range, for example, from visualizing syntactic categories (Honkela et al. 1995), the comparison of linguistic features across languages, e.g. vowel harmony (Mayer et al. 2010), syntactic trees (Culy et al. 2012), typological features (Mayer et al. 2014), pitch contours (Sacha et al. 2015, Asano et al. 2016), to discourse analysis (Gold et al. 2015a,b). The existing work has demonstrated that combining insights from Visual Analytics (Thomas and Cook 2005, Keim et al. 2010) with theoretical and computational linguistics offers the potential for groundbreaking new approaches with respect to understanding the complex, multifactorial and high-dimensional data that typically underlies linguistic work. We see Visual Analytics for Linguistics (LingVis) as an emerging field with high potential and demonstrate this with respect to two phenomena within historical linguistics.

The main goal of historical linguistics is to understand how different types of linguistic structure at different levels (e.g. phonology, morphology, syntax and semantics) have changed over time and how these

Visual Analytics for Linguistics (LingVis).
edited by Miriam Butt, Annette Hautli-Janisz and Verena Lyding.
Copyright © 2020, CSLI Publications.

different parts of the grammar interact with each other in order to effect a diachronic change in the first place. So far, quantitative approaches have mainly focused on statistical analysis as a means to make sense of the available data and the patterns contained in it. This can be appropriate because it provides insights into whether a particular factor is significant or not — verifying a priori hypotheses of the individual investigator.

However, the amount of data available is often limited, questioning the applicability of purely statistical methods. It is also a priori unclear if a researcher can anticipate all relevant and significant interactions between different dimensions of the data, particularly because linguistic data tends to feature complex interactions between phenomena/dimensions. The central issue remains, namely the ability to detect significant factors without previous knowledge of the data or the structures found in it. This type of research is crucial because the relevance of a particular factor for language change is often fiercely debated or may even have been previously unknown.

The aim of Visual Analytics is to enable interactive and exploratory access to a given data set and to automatically identify and saliently present interesting or significant correlations. In terms of historical linguistics, this facilitates the identification of relevant diachronic factors. Moreover, the user can detect anomalies in the data, and — more importantly — is supported in hypothesis generation, furthering the understanding of a given phenomenon.

In turn, from the point of Visual Analytics, diachronic linguistic research is interesting because the data is typically challenging and the research questions may be quite complex, so that methods commonly used in Visual Analytics to date need to be advanced to cope with the requirements of the linguistic investigator. This means that both sides benefit from a collaboration: Linguistics can arrive at a deeper understanding of language and Visual Analytics is faced with novel interesting challenges.

In this chapter, we discuss two approaches to using Visual Analytics in diachronic linguistic research with a particular focus on developing a generalized design space for diachronic visualizations. This design space, we claim, is valid for diachronic visualizations in general and can be used as a guideline for further research in the area, specifically with respect to how the type of data and the research questions related to it determine the design of the visual analysis system. As examples, we situate two exploratory and interactive visual analysis systems with respect to the design decisions inherent in this framework. The first visualization uses English newspaper data to track the semantic change of English verbs by looking at the contexts these verbs appear in. The second example tracks syntactic change in Icelandic by investigating determining factors for two well-known phenomena in the history of Icelandic: V1 (verb first) word order and dative subjects.

The chapter proceeds as follows: Section 5.2 presents the design space underlying the visualizations discussed in this chapter, with the case studies of semantic change in English (Section 5.3) and syntactic change in Icelandic (Section 5.4) being related to it in detail. Section 5.5 summarizes the findings and concludes the chapter.

The use cases presented in this chapter were designed for specific types of investigations within historical linguistics. Such problem specific visualizations have been designed only in rare cases. Apart from the two applications discussed in this chapter, further examples are an investigation of changes in the use of modal verbs within academic discourse (Lyding et al. 2012), and an analysis of the appearance and cross-linguistic spread of new suffixes throughout mass media (Rohrdantz et al. 2012, Rohrdantz 2014). Another novel visualization approach proposed by Therón and Fontanillo (2015) are diachronlex diagrams, which provide an overview of the evolution of meanings based on historical dictionaries. Standard type visualizations for historical linguistic work have included, for example, Lin et al. (2012), who use standard line charts for the comparison of the frequency developments of the verb forms 'burnt' vs. 'burned' in the Google Books Ngram Corpus (Michel et al. 2011, Lin et al. 2012).

5.2 Design Space for Diachronic Visualizations

Designing visualizations for research is both a structured and creative process. This process involves coming up with optimal solutions of mapping data values to visual representations, i.e. mapping different data dimensions, such as numerical, ordinal, or categorical dimensions, to different , such as color, position, shape, size, and orientation (Bertin 1983).

The number of visual variables is limited and not every visual variable is well suited for every kind of data dimension. For example, color is often used for representing categorical data dimensions and position is often used for plotting numerical data dimensions. There is an interplay in the choice of visual variables, as they depend on one another: A good choice in one visualization might be a bad choice in another one.

A good design fosters the emergence of visual patterns that are likely to point to relevant hidden patterns within the raw data. The designer has to anticipate the kinds of patterns that might be of interest, in order to choose a design which makes them emerge visibly. In general, the design process should be a back and forth between the disciplines: Domain experts have knowledge and hypotheses about the data and visualization experts have knowledge and experience about the usefulness of different visual components for different analysis tasks and settings.

In the following, we elaborate on the parameter and design space for using visualizations in diachronic linguistic research. Most design decisions that have to be made relate to the characteristics of the time dimension and to the nature of the other data dimensions to be explored. Moreover, a central factor is whether potential correlations among different dimensions are of interest.

5.2.1 Visualization of the Time Dimension

In diachronic research, the time dimension plays an essential role as many tasks revolve around the question: "What does (not) change over time?" For the visual design of the time dimension, different data characteristics must be considered:

- Time resolution: In diachronic research, each data object can be considered a time-stamped observation of language or language use, e.g. a document or sentence. It is usually not the case that days or even hours or minutes play a role. Still, the time resolution given in the data or implied by the research task is important for the visualization design. Do we consider years, decades, or centuries?
- Distribution of observations over time: It is quite often the case that many more data objects are available for the recent past than for the longer-standing past. When plotting such data along a linearly scaled timeline, some epochs might be sparsely populated, while others will suffer from overplotting. Instead of using a timeline, it might be a good choice to analyze data points in time sequences or aggregate them according to time frames of fixed or variable sizes.
- Amount of observations: The amount of data objects also has a decisive influence on the design. When there are only a few data objects, each individual object might be given an individual visual representation within the resulting visualization. In contrast, when dealing with tens of thousands of data objects or more, aggregation might be the better choice, i.e. aggregating different data objects by time in order to arrive at a meaningful visualization.

5.2.2 Data Dimensions under Investigation

The purpose of diachronic linguistic research is to establish the kinds of linguistic patterns that have changed over time and to derive hypotheses as to why those have changed. The visualization has to represent these patterns in data dimensions that complement the time dimension. These dimensions can be either edited manually or computed from the raw data, see Table 1 for an overview.

TABLE 1 Overview of the different data dimensions and their characteristics.

	Manually edited data dimensions		**Computed data dimensions**	
	Manually created (A)	**Manually revised (B)**	**Predefined (C)**	**Open (D)**
Complexity of annotations	+++	++	+	+
Accuracy of annotations	+++	+++	++	+
Interpretability of results	+++	+++	++	+
Amount of data processed	+	++	+++	+++

There are two different kinds of manually edited data dimensions:

- (A) Manually created data dimensions: These dimensions result from annotations of the data done manually by a domain expert. These annotations can cover quite complex facts or relations and in most cases will be very accurate. However, the amount of data might be limited.
- (B) Manually revised data dimensions: These dimensions result from annotations of the data created with automated means followed by a manual supervision. This allows experts to achieve good annotation quality for a larger data set.

There are two different kinds of computed data dimensions:

- (C) Predefined computed data dimensions. These dimensions are computed automatically from the raw data and are used as is, as the quality is known or expected to be good enough. The advantage is that very large datasets can be made use of, enabling much more detailed insight. Such dimensions indicate, for example, if (or how frequently) a certain phenomenon (word form, syntactic pattern, etc.) occurs. The challenge is to exclude the possibility of systematic biases due to processing errors.
- (D) Open computed data dimensions. This also refers to data dimensions that have been computed on the basis of the raw data. In these cases, however, it is typically not clear beforehand how to interpret the resulting dimension. One example are clustering algorithms which group data objects according to their similarity. The task is then twofold: (1) understand what the clustering into groups

is actually sensitive to; (2) understand how these clustered groups develop over time. Open computed data dimensions may lead to novel insights that have not been anticipated.

5.2.3 Correlation of Dimensions

Observing change in one data dimension can either confirm an anticipated hypothesis, lead to an insightful interpretation or generate a new hypothesis. Often several different dimensions of the data are correlated and in some cases, the researcher will not have anticipated which dimensions these are. The Visual Analytic approach allows for two kinds of investigations. First, an easy interactive way of experimenting with the correlations of different dimensions, some of which may prove to be revealing. These dimensions may correlate with the primary dimension under investigation, either semantically or statistically, thus leading to further, new hypotheses on the nature of the historical change. Second, potentials for model improvements may be revealed and improvements can be implemented through feedback loops. This will in turn lead to better automated analyses and, consequently, a better data foundation for research, for example through explicit or implicit parameter tuning of algorithms, or even the selection of alternative algorithms.

5.2.4 Summary

This section laid out the design space and variables that are necessary for an implementation of successful visualizations for investigations into diachronic data. In the following sections we discuss this with respect to two concrete diachronic visualizations, namely an application for detecting semantic change in English newspaper texts (Section 5.3) and a visualization on syntactic change in Icelandic (Section 5.4). These visualizations represent very different diachronic problems and work with different diachronic material. Both visualizations are discussed in light of the design space presented above. In particular, we discuss how the type of data and the question underlying the linguistic investigation led to the design decisions pursued in each of the approaches.

5.3 Semantic Change

The first Visual Analytics approach sets out to automatically identify and saliently present changes in word meaning by visually modeling and representing word contexts over time. The challenge is to analyze semantic change in more detail than in previous work, ideally finding starting points of change and tracking the development over time, paired with a quantitative comparison of prevailing senses. The aim is to (1) verify existing hypotheses of lexical items that have undergone semantic change, (2) to learn more about the triggers of the change, and (3) to generate new hypotheses based on the patterns emerging from the data. Whereas previous approaches (Sagi et al. 2009, Cook and Stevenson 2010) concentrated on measuring general changes in the meaning of a word (e.g., narrowing or pejoration), our work, first presented in Rohrdantz et al. (2011), deals with cases where words acquire a new sense by extending their contexts to other domains.

For the scope of this investigation we restrict ourselves to cases of semantic change in English even though the methodology is generally language-independent. Our choice is on the one hand motivated by the extensive knowledge available on semantic change in English. On the other hand, our choice was driven by the availability of large corpora for English. In particular, we used the New York Times Annotated Corpus[1] (Sandhaus 2008). Given the variety and the amount of text available, we are able to track changes from 1987 until 2007 in 1.8 million newspaper articles.

In order to explore our approach in a fruitful manner, we concentrate on words which have acquired a new dimension of use due to the introduction of computing and the internet, e.g., 'to browse', 'to surf', 'bookmark'. In particular, the Netscape Navigator was introduced in 1994 and our data show that this does indeed correlate with a change in use of these words.

Processing From a computational viewpoint, the modeling of word senses is based on the assumption that the meaning of a word is reflected by its immediate context (Firth 1957). The idea of computationally determining and inferring the sense of a word on the basis of its context has been the subject of intensive research (e.g., Schütze 1998 and Yarowsky 1995). In general, the representation of a keyword consists of a numerical vector where each of the dimensions corresponds to a context word candidate. The entry in a dimension is zero if the candidate word does not appear in the context window of the key word. If, in turn, a candidate word does appear in the context window, the corresponding dimension gets a positive numerical entry, e.g. the frequency or the tf-idf value (Spärck Jones 1972). The data processing involves the following steps: (a) context extraction, and (b) sense modeling. Extracting the keywords under investigation, we extract a context of 25 words before and after the keyword (as suggested by Schütze 1998). Each context is complemented with a time stamp from the corpus.

For modeling the senses, we use Latent Dirichlet Allocation (LDA;

[1] https://catalog.ldc.upenn.edu/LDC2008T19.

Blei et al. 2003).[2] LDA is able to find groups of words that belong together, in the sense that the words within a group tend to co-occur within documents. When applying LDA to large document collections, the resulting groups can be interpreted as describing different topics contained within the document collection. Consequently, when applying LDA to word contexts, the resulting groups of words can be interpreted as describing different contextual senses of the word under investigation. LDA does not typically assign one word context unambiguously to a certain contextual sense, but assigns different probabilities to a word context as belonging to different contextual senses. By having a large number of word contexts, it is possible to determine degrees of overlap among different contextual senses, which can and do differ over time. In addition to each context having a probability for belonging to a certain contextual sense, each word in that context is assigned to one contextual sense, see Figure 1 for an example. This means that a certain word context could be assigned to sense X with a high probability, while some of its individual words could be assigned to a different sense Y. The aim of the visualization is to model the gradually overlapping senses as time progresses so that the stochastic analysis becomes more transparent to the linguist investigating variation and change.

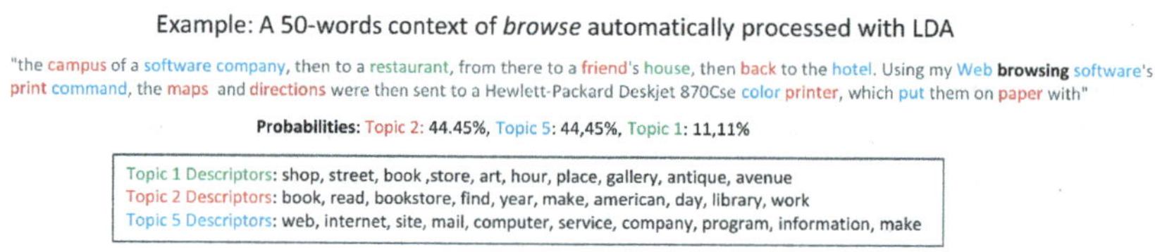

FIGURE 1 Example for automatically generated LDA topics/contextual senses for a word context. Each word in this context of 'browsing' was automatically assigned to different color-coded contextual senses. Consequently, the whole context can be assigned to different contextual senses with different probabilities. Characteristic terms describing one sense are listed in the box.

Visualization The visualization offers two views on the data: In the scatterplot, see Figure 2, each context is represented as one dot. This allows us to investigate the underlying text passages of the individual data points — a prerequisite for generating valid hypotheses. With the axes corresponding to contextual senses of a word (LDA dimensions), the further to the right a dot is situated, the more the corresponding

[2]The toolkit MALLET (McCallum 2002) was used for LDA (`http://mallet.cs.umass.edu/`).

word occurrence relates to the sense described by the horizontal axis. Accordingly, the further to the top a dot is situated, the more the corresponding word occurrence relates to the vertical axis sense. When the probability of a context belonging to a certain contextual sense is less than 40%, it is scaled down to 0% for visualization, because it cannot be assigned to that contextual sense unambiguously. Before plotting the points, a random jitter is added, which prevents the overplotting of contexts with the same or similar vector entries. The jitter can be reduced or eliminated interactively using a slider. Contexts that equally belong to both selected senses, i.e. a context which for both senses have probabilities above 40%, are displayed along the diagonal of the plot. In Figure 2, this is not the case as the two selected contextual senses are very different. Those contexts having between 0-40% probability for both selected senses are lumped into the area in the lower left.

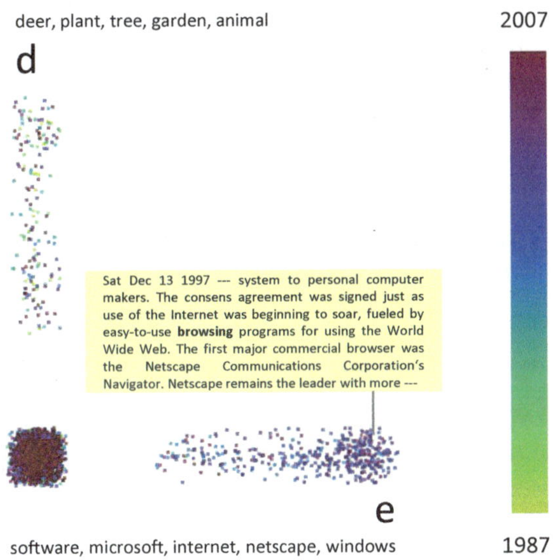

FIGURE 2 Overview of two contextual senses of 'browse'. It becomes evident that while sense *d* had been around in the whole time interval (all colors present), the usage of sense *e* came up heavily towards the last third of the time range (blueish towards purple coloring).

Time is encoded via the visual variable "color", which marks a dot as belonging to a particular year. The chosen colormap covers a wide range of colors, going from yellow over green and blue to purple, and thus enables a more fine-grained distinction of different time points than a simple unipolar or bipolar color map. The data is characterized by a comparatively high time resolution, i.e. the design of the time slider has to be fine-grained enough to go beyond the year (or decade/century) level necessary for other diachronic data. This time slider is also relevant to deal with the amount of observations, because, despite having a fairly large amount of contexts across the investigated time span (3062 contexts for 'to browse' from 1987 to 2007), the requirement was to be able to investigate each context individually, while still maintaining the possibility to aggregate. To manage the balancing act, we created two separate views on the data: the individual plotting for the detailed investigation (Figure 2) and the aggregated view for a general observation (Figure 3). With respect to the distribution of observations over time, we were dealing with a data set that had fairly equal distribution of keyword occurrences over time.

With respect to the data dimensions under investigation, we focus on the LDA sense dimensions. These are open dimensions, computed from the raw data, which have to be interpreted. They are not necessarily self-explanatory and the linguistic expert has to consult the contexts underlying the data in order to fully understand the "meaning" of a contextual sense. The text passages underlying the individual data points can be displayed by mouse-over interaction.

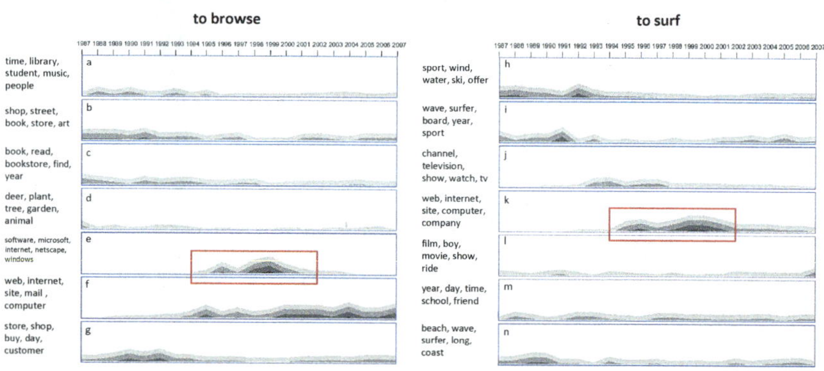

FIGURE 3 Temporal development of different contextual senses concerning the verbs 'to browse' (left) and 'to surf' (right). Reprinted from Rohrdantz et al. (2011), © 2011 Association for Computational Linguistics.

While plotting every word occurrence individually offers the opportunity to detect and inspect outliers and pinpoint single word contexts for text content exploration, aggregated views on the data are able to provide further insights into more general developments. Figure 3 shows the percentage of word occurrences belonging to the different contextual senses over time. For the verbs 'to browse' and 'to surf' seven contextual senses have been learned with LDA. Each sense corresponds to one line and is described by the top five terms identified by LDA. The higher the gray area at a certain x-axis point, the more of the contexts of the corresponding year belong to the specific sense. Each shade of gray represents 10% of the overall data, i.e., three shades of gray mean that between 20% and 30% of the contexts can be attributed to that sense.

This method of presenting the data focuses less on the detection of outliers and more on general trends, for instance that certain contextual senses appear at particular points in time, e.g., the senses *e*, *f*, *j* and *k*. This provides a strong indication that the outlined senses correspond to new ways of word usage.

Case study For the case study, we investigate the verbs 'to browse' and 'to surf' based on the temporal sense development in Figure 3. Interestingly, sense *e* for 'to browse' and sense *k* for 'to surf' pattern quite similarly across time. Consulting their contexts reveals that both patterns appear shortly after the introduction of web browsers, peaking during the so-called first browser war when by mid-1995 the Internet Explorer 1.0 was released by Microsoft as a competition to the widely spread Netscape Navigator, introduced in 1994. For the verb 'to browse', another broader sense (sense *f*) of the verb, namely browsing the internet and digital media collections, shows a continuous increase over time, dominating in 2007. As can be seen with senses *e* and *f*, there may be some semantic correlation in that sense *e*, which reflects the heavy presence of the first browser war in mass media in the mid-1990s, influences the longer-standing change reflected by sense *f*.

Overall, the visualization shows that open computed data dimensions, the LDA senses, and patterns over time can be interpreted in a meaningful way, revealing influencing factors on language change. In a preliminary evaluation comparing the computed contextual senses with senses coming from dictionaries, Rohrdantz et al. (2011) show that this type of visualization is able to track semantic change, given the size of the corpora and the investigated items. In some cases, the visualization produced even more precise senses than those from the dictionary. This shows that the method is not only appropriate from a visualization point of view, but also from a linguistic point of view.

5.4 Syntactic Change

Our study of Icelandic is an example of syntactic change. Icelandic is interesting as it is known as the most conservative Germanic language, with comparatively little change attested over the centuries. However, change has occurred and we have to date investigated two phenomena: verb placement and dative subjects. These turn out to be interrelated as Icelandic has moved towards a more fixed word order over time, while still retaining a rich case marking system.

5.4.1 Data, Annotations and Processing

Icelandic is also of interest from a computational perspective as the Icelandic Parsed Historical Corpus (IcePaHC; Wallenberg et al. 2011) has recently become available. IcePaHC consists of 61 texts from different genres with over one million words dating from the 12th to the 21st century, covering all attested time stages for Icelandic. The documents are not evenly distributed across the different genres; however each sentence in IcePaHC provides information about the age (year dates), the name and the genre of the document it appears in as well as its position therein (sentence number).

We chose IcePaHC as the basis for our investigations as it is syntactically annotated according to the Penn Treebank scheme (Marcus et al. 1993) and includes a sophisticated annotation of sentence types (e.g., matrix declaratives, questions, etc.), constituents, word order, grammatical relations, tense, voice, and case. The original annotations were generated semiautomatically with manual checking and revision (Rögnvaldsson et al. 2012).

We automatically extracted the features we were particularly interested in from the deep linguistic annotations of IcePaHC via Perl scripts and thus generated data sets which contain several linguistic dimensions, for example, word order, verb type, subject type, subject case, and voice. We calculated these for each sentence, which in turn provides information on the genre and the age of the utterance. With respect to our investigation of dative subjects, we added a further layer of annotation to the corpus that specified the verb class of the verbs in the clause. To determine verb class information, we used a combination of Levin's verb classification for English (Levin 1993) and the verb classes which Barðdal et al. (2012) postulate for dative subject predicates in Icelandic.

The resulting data set is thus one that consists of a structured data matrix with multiple, interacting dimensions. The challenge was then to design a visualization that could do justice to the high-dimensional, complex data while allowing the user to generate and explore hypotheses both by investigating generalizations over the data and by having interactive access to individual data points.

5.4.2 Visualization

The amount of relevant details within the data as well as their partly interrelated structure do not match well with any standard visualization approach. Consequently, we designed a novel visualization tailored to the data and research task at hand, which provides an overview of the phenomenon across the entire corpus as well as allowing for insights at different levels of detail. We hereby follow Shneiderman's (1996) Visual Information Seeking Mantra "Overview first, zoom and filter, then details-on-demand".

Each text in IcePaHC is visualized as a glyph representing its different data dimensions. Glyph representations of documents are known from the field of Information Retrieval and the TileBars technique (Hearst 1995, reprinted in this volume). These provide a compact and informative iconic representation of a document's contents with respect to certain query terms. With respect to the time dimension (Section 5.2.1), each of the 61 texts (or glyphs) is plotted onto a fixed position on the y-axis according to its time stamp (year dates), see Figure 4. The y-axis, in this case, is not a linearly scaled timeline, but presents the texts sequentially in the order of their age, thus avoiding both gaps and overplotting. The distribution of documents is generally equal across the centuries. Moreover, the exact year date of a given text can be accessed via mouse-over. Additionally, each glyph is equipped with a tick mark on a timeline plotted to its right side indicating the position of the text on the complete diachrony. The x-axis was used to position the documents according to their genre, as displayed in Figure 4.

The text glyphs are mainly composed of three parts, see e.g. Figure 5 (top left). The black horizontal bar on top of the glyph indicates the length of the text in comparison to the longest text in the corpus (which would cover the whole width of the glyph). The light gray stripes drawn into the horizontal bar correspond to the occurrences of the phenomenon in question (i.e. V1 or datives subjects) in the narrative flow of the text. The horizontal line on the right side of the glyph is the timeline which indicates the time span covered by the corpus with a tick mark providing information about the specific age of a text.

A matrix containing colored items forms the central component of the glyph and represents the interactions of the data dimensions. We used different visual variables, i.e. "shape", "color", and "position", in

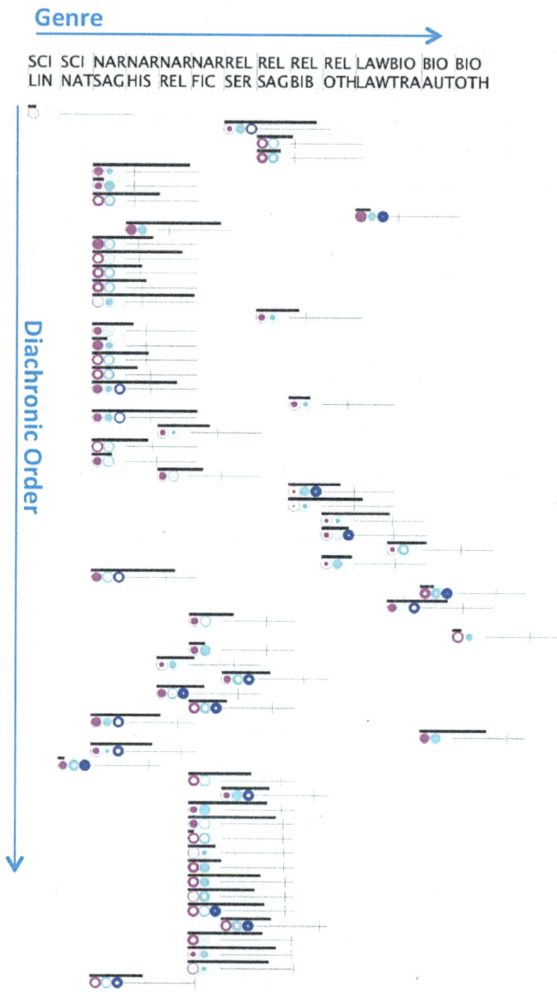

FIGURE 4 All texts from IcePaHC are positioned among each other on the vertical axis (diachronic order) and, in the genre-shifted layout mode, aligned on the horizontal axis with respect to their genre. Genre labels are shown on top and can be read as columns (scientific texts SCI, narratives NAR, religious texts REL, law texts LAW, and biographies BIO).

order to redundantly encode sentence features with respect to the predefined data dimensions occurring together with the phenomenon under investigation. Those were aggregated on the document level so that the design enables the researcher to spot interesting patterns in the whole corpus at a glance. The data dimensions under investigation, apart from the temporal component and different genres, are those identified as relevant by the researcher and are typically based on previous information gleaned from the existing theoretical literature. These data dimensions were extracted from the processed corpus (cf. Section 5.4.1).

Dimensions depicted on the rows of the matrix are encoded via different shapes, while dimensions mapped onto columns are represented via different colors for better visibility, see e.g. Figure 5 (bottom left). An empty matrix cell means that the corresponding feature interaction does not occur in the text. In order to be able to cope with a large number of text features and data dimensions, e.g. the high number of lexical semantic verb classes,[3] we provide the possibility of visualizing features as systematically aggregated glyph representations which provide an overview (see top left of Figure 5). The aggregated feature representations can be extended for more details (horizontal expansion, see top right of Figure 5) or to show interactions with other features (e.g. voice; vertical expansion, see bottom of Figure 5) on demand (keystroke or mouse click on a text).

The colored cells encode whether a given feature combination appears more or less often than expected in the analyzed text. The deviation of the observed from the expected value is quantified via the scale depicted in Figure 6. Both the observed and the expected occurrences are calculated based on the text length and the average occurrences of the feature interaction in the whole corpus.

During the initial testing of the visualization we noticed that the genre-shifted layout of the text glyphs made it difficult to track specific features over time. In order to facilitate the comparison of documents across genres and along the history of Icelandic respectively, the user can switch between an overview where the documents are placed among each other horizontally for an easier temporal comparison, see Figure 7, and a genre-shifted alignment to track genre-specific differences, see Figure 4. On demand, the tick mark can be extended to

[3]The following categories were used in the investigation: psych, existence, motion, sending, concealment, social interaction, permission, measure, put, communication, change of possession, change of state and aspectual verbs, verbs with predicative complements and verbs involving the body. These categories can be aggregated into the higher class categorization experiencer predicates, happenstance predicates and verbs of modality in the visualization.

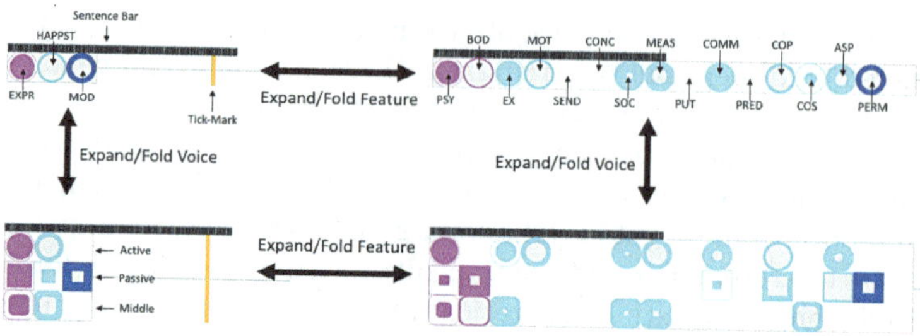

FIGURE 5 Each text representation consists of a sentence bar on top, a colored matrix, and a tick mark which indicates a selected feature value when hovered, or the age of the text as default. Top left: aggregated verb classes, top right: detailed verb classes, bottom left: interaction of aggregated verb classes with voice, bottom right: interaction of detailed verb classes with voice.

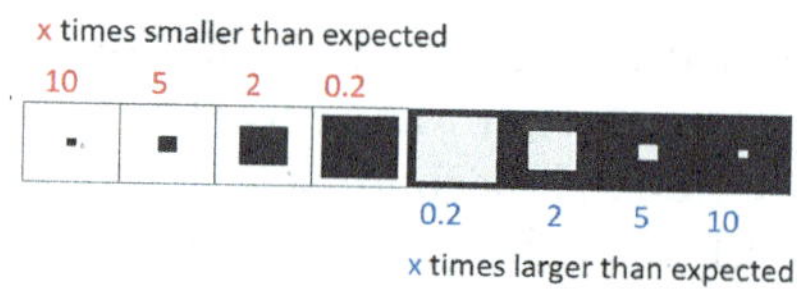

FIGURE 6 The colored glyphs are visualized according to the occurrence of a given feature interaction. The glyph is filled from inside if the interaction is smaller than expected, and filled from outside if it is larger than expected.

show the diachronic as well as genre-dependent occurrence of a hovered feature interaction and allows the user to track the distribution of data dimensions throughout the whole diachrony. In this case, the tick marks of all texts are repositioned to indicate the relative frequency of the hovered feature value.

Several interaction techniques were implemented into our visualization offering the possibilities to drill down into the data if desired: First, we added zooming and panning interactions in order to navigate within the visualization's viewport. Furthermore, our visualization is equipped with details on demand through tooltip operations providing the analyst with information about meta data. The interface also gives access to the underlying data connecting a statistical analysis with the actual sentences involved in the calculations, see e.g. Figure 8 for sentences with experiencer predicates and dative subjects involved in the calculations of the hovered feature interaction.

Finally, we noticed that the variety of interactions we implemented (tooltip, tick marks, expand/fold, etc.) disturbed each other. Thus, we

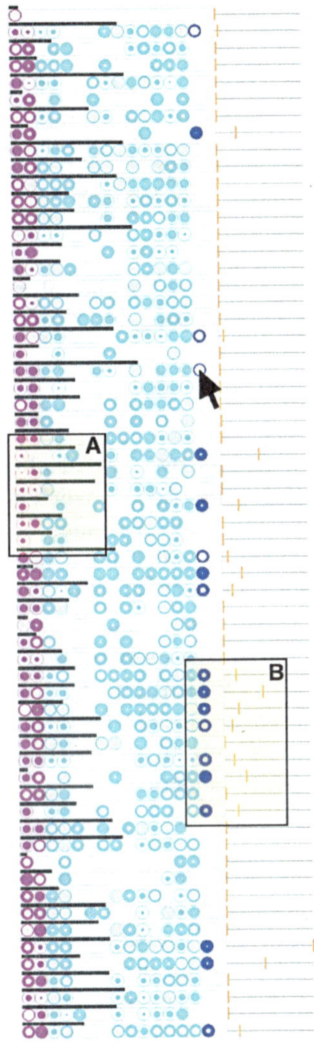

FIGURE 7 Visualization showing all texts with the detailed feature classes selected in temporal comparison layout. Tick marks show the occurrence of a selected/hovered feature enabling the diachronic comparison of this feature. Additionally, this representation allows to spot deviating visual patterns at a glance, e.g. the patterns A and B.

allow the user to disable or enable the tooltips to switch between detail and comparison mode in order to facilitate the comparison of features from a diachronic perspective.

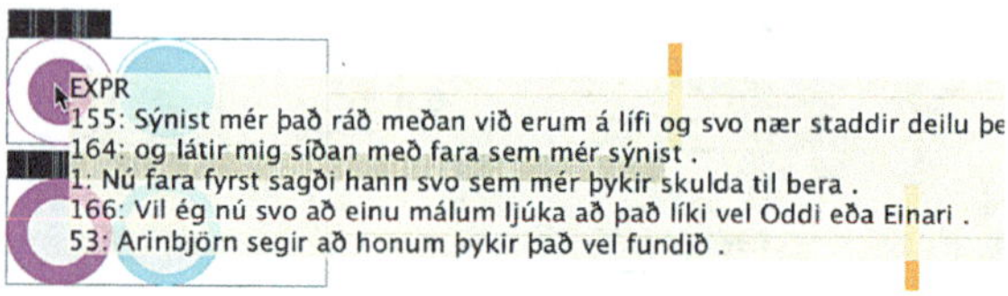

FIGURE 8 Sentences which are involved in the calculation of a given feature interaction can be accessed via mousing over the interaction in the glyph.

5.4.3 Case Studies

In this section, we briefly discuss two case studies being conducted on the basis of the visualization presented above. The case studies concern V1 word order and dative subjects.[4] Although V1 declaratives and dative subjects are attested throughout the history of Icelandic (Sigurðsson 1990, Barðdal and Eythórsson 2009, Butt et al. 2014, Schätzle and Sacha 2016, Schätzle et al. 2015), the exact factors that license V1 word order and dative subjects synchronically as well as diachronically have been fiercely debated. The visualization not only helped to shed light on previous established theories about the respective phenomena, but also led to the generation of new hypotheses and uncovered complex interrelations between data dimensions.

V1 in Icelandic

V1 word order is generally used to signal yes/no questions or imperatives in Germanic. Icelandic however, which is an SVO-language with a V2-constraint (Thráinsson 2007), also regularly allows for V1 in matrix declarative sentences. These V1 structures mainly occur in narrative texts and have been characterized as "narrative inversions" (Sigurðsson 1990). Moreover, V1 declaratives can be attested throughout the recorded history of Icelandic (e.g., see Sigurðsson 1990, Butt et al. 2014). Example (8) shows a V1 declarative sentence from IcePaHC which employs the verb *vera* 'be' in the initial position of the matrix clause and has an empty expletive subject.

[4]Abbreviations used in glossing examples are: DAT/dative, GEN/genitive, NOM/nominative, PAST/past tense, PL/plural, SG/singular, 3/third person.

(8) Var fátt manna heima.
be.PAST.3SG few.NOM.SG man.GEN.PL at-home
'There were few men at home.'
(IcePaHC: *Finnbogi saga ramma*, 1350)

Nevertheless, exactly what licenses V1 declaratives synchronically as well as diachronically has been the subject of controversy. Previous studies on V1 in Icelandic (e.g., by Franco 2008, Sigurðsson 1990) have proposed syntactic factors such as topicality (null pronouns, expletives, definiteness) and the co-occurence with particular verb types (i.e. unaccusatives) to be relevant. Other studies on V1 however (e.g. Hinterhölzl and Petrova 2010, Petrova 2011 for German) focus on information structural theories by which V1 occurs in presentational clauses and existential constructions which lack a topic-comment structure placing the entire clause into the scope of the assertion (focus).

Our investigations on V1 in Icelandic are ongoing, building on initial work and visualizations as presented in Butt et al. (2014) and Schätzle and Sacha (2016), and we are currently also exploring the diachronic correlation among the development of a fixed clause-initial subject position, verb placement, and subject case in Icelandic.

With respect to V1, we visualized the interaction of different subject types (i.e. pronominal subjects, definite or indefinite subjects, empty subjects, and expletives) and verbal type (main verbs, modals, 'do', 'have', 'be', and 'become') in order to investigate the syntactic approaches as brought forward by Franco (2008) and Sigurðsson (1990). We generally found that proposals put forward to explain the occurrence of V1 declaratives in Icelandic so far can not be confirmed by the actual patterns observed in the visualization. However, we can confirm some of the findings of the previous literature, e.g. that V1 is mainly found in narrative texts (cf. Sigurðsson 1990), i.e. the Sagas in IcePaHC, which can be identified at a glance through the genre alignment of the visualization.

A marked decrease of V1 structures as of 1900 is also immediately shown in the overview mode of the visualization. This decrease could hypothetically be explained via Franco's (2008) assumption that some of the old V1 structures were effectively rendered into V2 constructions in Modern Icelandic via the establishment of an overt expletive in initial position. However, we found that expletives overall only occurred sparsely in V1 declaratives and the innovation of an overt expletive itself should hence not be powerful enough to provoke such a large drop in V1.

Additionally, we found that the appearance of V1 is not primarily bound to the occurrence of empty subjects overall because these generally do not appear more often than expected in the visualization. Moreover, V1 declaratives occur with all verb types along the corpus and in particular with modals and main verbs. Thus, our data does not support the syntactic accounts from the previous literature which mainly take V1 declaratives to be underlying V2 constructions meaning that they should primarily appear together with unaccusative verbs.

The visualization also led to the identification of data properties we were not aware of and made one specific set of data stand out in the visualization, i.e. the texts of around 1550 which show a comparative absence of V1. This absence is due to a genre effect because the documents within this range are religious and legal texts which can be identified at a glance via the visualization.

Further insights on the decrease of V1 as of 1900 are provided by our ongoing research. We recently found that subjecthood becomes increasingly associated with the clause-initial position along the history of Icelandic, in particular during the time post-1900. This fixing of a structural position of subjecthood places the verb in second position, in turn lowering the occurences of V1 constructions. Moreover, presentational constructions with the overt expletive *það* in the initial position are increasingly used after 1900 and replace V1 constructions which lack a topic-comment structure. This in turn argues for an information-structural approach to V1 in Icelandic (cf. Hinterhölzl and Petrova 2010, Petrova 2011).

Dative Subjects

Dative subjects are known to exist in a variety of modern Indo-European languages. However, how they came into existence in these languages has been the point of controversial debates among historical linguistic researchers. These debates mainly concentrate on two competing narratives. On the one hand, the Object-to-Subject Hypothesis assumes that dative subjects are a historical innovation in Indo-European and have been innovated through the reanalysis of former objects (cf. Haspelmath 2001). This hypothesis draws evidence from Indo-Aryan: While Old Indo-Aryan shows no proof for the existence of dative subjects (Hock 1990), Modern Indo-Aryan generally exhibits dative subjects from at least the 12th century on (Deo 2003, Butt and Deo 2013). The so-called Oblique Subject or Semantic Alignment Hypothesis on the other hand takes dative subjects to be inherited from Proto Indo-European and is supported by the pervasiveness and stability of dative subjects along the history of Icelandic (Barðdal and Eythórsson 2009, Barðdal et al. 2012). Example (9) shows a dative subject together with the experiencer verb *líka* 'like' and stems from one of the first attested Icelandic manuscripts (taken from IcePaHC).

(9) Vel líkuðu goðrøði góð røði
well like.PAST.3PL Goðrøður.DAT.SG good.NOM.PL oar.NOM.PL
'Goðrøði (the good oarsman) liked good oars well'
(IcePaHC: *Fyrsta málfræðiritgerðin*, 1150)

However, the Icelandic case system is currently undergoing a change in progress called "Dative Substitution" or "Dative Sickness" (see, e.g. Smith 1996) by which accusative experiencers are replaced with datives in a systematic manner. Furthermore, dative subjects may generally appear with all three Icelandic voices, active, passive, and middle, but are heavily constrained by lexical semantic factors with respect to middle formation (dative only on benefactives/goals).

Lexical semantic factors and in particular the increasing systematic relation between dative case and experiencer/goal arguments have been found to be conditioning factors for the innovation of dative subjects in Modern Indo-Aryan (e.g. by Deo 2003). Given that the written record of Icelandic only goes back to the 12th century which is about when dative subjects first emerged in Indo-Aryan and the lexical semantic constraints on case marking in Icelandic, the semantic coherence and stability of the dative subject construction throughout the history of Icelandic is highly doubtful.

Thus, with respect to dative subjects, we visualized the interaction of lexical semantic verb class and voice in dative subject constructions to shed more light on the diachrony of dative subjects in Icelandic. The visualization shows immediately that dative subjects already exist in the earliest Icelandic texts and are common throughout the history of Icelandic as dative subjects are present in each glyph, see Figure 4. In the visualization, dative subjects are mainly associated with experiencer predicates (magenta), but also appear together with happenstance predicates (light blue). Verbs of modality (which are in essence permission verbs; dark blue) however rarely occur with dative subjects in the first half of the corpus, but start to appear more often in the latter part of the corpus, see pattern B in Figure 7 in which the PERM feature (permission verbs) is hovered.

Moreover, disabling the horizontal genre alignment uncovered that experiencer verbs are increasingly used from the end of the 19th century on. Furthermore, by expanding the glyphs for voice, we found that this increase correlates with an increasing use of experiencer predicates with middle morphology. With respect to voice, the visualization showed that while experiencer and happenstance predicates may occur with all three voices throughout the corpus, modality verbs most often occurred in passives and more rarely in middle constructions, but never in an active construction.

Again, we were able to identify a genre effect in the corpus which caused a striking absence of experiencer predicates (magenta) in texts within the range of pattern A in Figure 7. This genre effect could be easily identified via the possibility to switch between horizontal alignments and again recognized the texts from this segment as mainly religious and legal in nature.

In sum, these findings suggest that the distribution of dative subjects has been changing over the past millennium in Icelandic. Furthermore, lexical semantic factors, that is the increasing systematic association of dative case with experiencer arguments and middle voice in turn, speak against dative subjects as a stable, common Proto Indo-European inheritance (e.g. contra Barðdal and Eythórsson 2009, Barðdal et al. 2012). The visualization provided us with an exploratory access to the complex relationship between verb class, voice and dative subjects, and moreover uncovered complex salient patterns in the data, such as the interrelatedness of middle voice and experiencer semantics, furthering the understanding of dative subjects in Icelandic.

5.5 Conclusion

In this chapter, we demonstrated the potential of integrating Visual Analytics into data-driven diachronic linguistic investigations by way of two sample visualizations. Each visualization system differs in how the data is presented. These differences are motivated by the type of data underlying the approach and the type of linguistic research that is being pursued. But both visualization systems have been designed so that new hypotheses can be generated via an interactive and exploratory access to the data. The user can effectively track changes without necessarily presetting time epochs and also track changes which take place within short periods of time. This allows to pinpoint change in time, breaking the analysis down into arbitrary finer-grained time intervals that are independent of given epochs, e.g. Old or Modern Icelandic in the syntactic change visualization.

In both cases the multidimensional raw data and the further derived dimensions or statistics, which have been calculated on the basis of the raw data, are mapped onto a combination of different visual variables, with a focus on shape, color, and spatial position. The interactivity in both cases is essential, enabling researchers to make deeper sense of the visual representations and the underlying data. This is crucial for the visualization on syntactic change, where the number of features and dimensions is much higher than in the visualization of semantic change, and with it the number of potential correlations. Without the option to swap between different aggregations and levels of detail, the results of the case study could not have been obtained.

Moreover, the visualizations serve as means to detect noise and outliers in the data, a particularly pressing issue if the data contain abstract linguistic information such as syntactic hierarchies and dependencies. Even widely used diachronic corpora may contain quite a number of unexpected errors that might lead to erroneous results. Pechenick et al. (2015) show this nicely, discussing pitfalls of the Google Books NGram Corpus using visualization. This also holds for potential flaws caused by biased data distributions, data sparsity, or representativity biases. One example for the latter are the genre effects in the study on syntactic change in Icelandic: Without the use of visualization these would probably have remained undiscovered.

Overall, the chapter shows that the design space in diachronic linguistics can be realized very differently across visualization applications. The process of "translating" the linguistic research questions and the prerequisites of the data into a visualization application is more time-consuming than might be assumed prima facie. However, it is a crucial process that needs to be gone through in order to make the visualization usable by an analyst, actually leading to new insights. In the process, case studies are indispensable: They help to refine and optimize the visualization, best illustrated with the move from the default glyph layout to the genre-shifted layout in the Icelandic visualization that prevented a misinterpretation of the data.

In conclusion, the proper and well-motivated use of Visual Analytics in quantitative historical linguistics helps researchers to gain insights and to discover unexpected correlations in the data than with traditional statistical analysis. In this chapter we hope to have motivated the opportunities LingVis holds for future linguistic research, in particular historical linguistic work.

Acknowledgements

We thank the Deutsche Forschungsgemeinschaft (DFG, German Research Foundation) for funding within project BU 1806/7-1 "Visual Analysis of Language Change and Use Patterns" and project D02 "Evaluation Metrics for Visual Analytics in Linguistics" of the TRR 161 – Project-ID 251654672.

References

Asano, Yuki, Michele Gubian, and Dominik Sacha. 2016. Cutting down on manual pitch contour annotation using data modeling. In *Proceedings of Speech Prosody 2016*, pages 282–286.

Barðdal, Jóhanna and Thórhallur Eythórsson. 2009. The origin of the oblique subject construction: An Indo-European comparison. In V. Bubenik, J. Hewson, and S. Rose, eds., *Grammatical Change in Indo-European Languages*, pages 179–193. Amsterdam: John Benjamins.

Barðdal, Jóhanna, Thomas Smitherman, Valgerður Bjarnadóttir, Serena Danesi, Gard B. Jenset, and Barbara McGillivray. 2012. Reconstructing constructional semantics: The dative subject construction in Old Norse-Icelandic, Latin, Ancient Greek, Old Russian and Old Lithuanian. *Studies in Language* 36(3):511–547.

Bertin, Jacques. 1983. *Semiology of Graphics.* Translated by William J. Berg. Madison, WI: The University of Wisconsin Press.

Blei, David M., Andrew Y. Ng, and Michael I. Jordan. 2003. Latent dirichlet allocation. *Journal of Machine Learning Research* 3:993–1022.

Butt, Miriam, Tina Bögel, Kristina Kotcheva, Christin Schätzle, Christian Rohrdantz, Dominik Sacha, Nicole Dehe, and Daniel Keim. 2014. V1 in Icelandic: A multifactorical visualization of historical data. In *Proceedings of the LREC 2014 Workshop VisLR: Visualization as Added Value in the Development, Use and Evaluation of Language Resources*, pages 33–40.

Butt, Miriam and Ashwini Deo. 2013. A historical perspective on dative subjects in Indo-Aryan. Paper presented at the LFG'13 Conference.

Collins, Christopher. 2010. *Interactive Visualizations of Natural Language.* Ph.D. thesis, University of Toronto.

Collins, Christopher, Sheelagh Carpendale, and Gerald Penn. 2007. Visualization of uncertainty in lattices to support decision-making. In K. Museth, T. Möller, and A. Ynnerman, eds., *Proceedings of the 9th Joint Eurographics / IEEE VGTC Conference on Visualization*, pages 51–58.

Cook, Paul and Suzanne Stevenson. 2010. Automatically Identifying Changes in the Semantic Orientation of Words. In *Proceedings of the Seventh International Conference on Language Resources and Evaluation*, pages 28–34.

Culy, Chris, Corina Dima, and Emanuel Dima. 2012. Through the looking glass: Two approaches to visualizing linguistic syntax trees. In *Proceedings of the 16th International Conference on Information Visualisation*, pages 214–219.

Deo, Ashwini. 2003. Valency change and case marking: Marathi dative experiencers. Handout from the Pioneer Workshop on Case, Valency and Transitivity.

Firth, John R. 1957. *Papers in Linguistics 1934–1951.* London: Oxford University Press.

Franco, Irene. 2008. V1, V2 and criterial movement in Icelandic. *Studies in Linguistics* 2:141–165.

Gold, Valentin, Mennatallah El-Assady, Tina Bögel, Christian Rohrdantz, Miriam Butt, Katharina Holzinger, and Daniel Keim. 2015a. Visual linguistic analysis of political discussions: Measuring deliberative quality. *Digital Scholarship in the Humanities* 32(1):141–158.

Gold, Valentin, Christian Rohrdantz, and Mennatallah El-Assady. 2015b. Exploratory text analysis using lexical episode plots. In E. Bertini, J. Kennedy, and E. Puppo, eds., *Eurographics Conference on Visualization: Short Papers*, pages 85–90.

Haspelmath, Martin. 2001. Non-canonical marking of core arguments in European languages. In A. Y. Aikhenvald, R. Dixon, and M. Onishi, eds., *Non-Canonical Marking of Subjects and Objects*, pages 53–83. Amsterdam: John Benjamins.

Hearst, Marti A. 1995. TileBars: Visualization of term distribution information in full text information access. In *Proceedings of the SIGCHI Conference on Human Factors in Computing Systems*, pages 59–66. New York: ACM Press/Addison-Wesley Publishing Co. [Reprinted in this volume].

Hinterhölzl, Roland and Svetlana Petrova. 2010. From V1 to V2 in West Germanic. *Lingua* 120.2:315–328.

Hock, Hans Henrich. 1990. Oblique subjects in Sanskrit. In M. Verma and K. Mohanan, eds., *Experiencer Subjects in South Asian Languages*, pages 119–139. Stanford, CA: CSLI Publications.

Honkela, Timo, Ville Pulkki, and Teuvo Kohonen. 1995. Contextual relations of words in Grimm tales, analyzed by self-organizing map. In *Proceedings of International Conference on Artificial Neural Networks*, pages 3–7.

Keim, Daniel A., Jörn Kohlhammer, Geoffrey Ellis, and Florian Mansmann, eds. 2010. *Mastering The Information Age: Solving Problems with Visual Analytics*. Goslar: Eurographics Association.

Levin, Beth. 1993. *English Verb Classes and Alternations: A Preliminary Investigation*. Chicago, IL: Chicago University Press.

Lin, Yuri, Jean-Baptiste Michel, Erez Lieberman Aiden, Jon Orwant, Will Brockman, and Slav Petrov. 2012. Syntactic annotations for the Google Books Ngram corpus. In *Proceedings of the 50th Annual Meeting of the Association for Computational Linguistics: System Demonstrations*, pages 169–174.

Lyding, Verena, Stefania Degaetano-Ortlieb, Ekaterina Lapshinova-Koltunski, Henrik Dittmann, and Christopher Culy. 2012. Visualising linguistic evolution in academic discourse. In *Proceedings of the EACL 2012 Joint Workshop of LINGVIS & UNCLH*, pages 44–48.

Marcus, Mitchell P., Mary Ann Marcinkiewicz, and Beatrice Santorini. 1993. Building a large annotated corpus of English: the Penn Treebank. *Computational Linguistics* 19(2):313–330.

Mayer, Thomas, Christian Rohrdantz, Miriam Butt, Frans Plank, and Daniel A. Keim. 2010. Visualizing vowel harmony. *Linguistic Issues in Language Technology* 4(2):1–33.

Mayer, Thomas, Bernhard Wälchli, Michael Hund, and Christian Rohrdantz. 2014. From the extraction of continuous features in parallel texts to visual analytics of heterogeneous areal-typological datasets. In B. Nolan and C. Periñán-Pascual, eds., *Language Processing and Grammars. The Role of Functionally Oriented Computational Models*, pages 13–38. Amsterdam: John Benjamins.

McCallum, Andrew Kachites. 2002. MALLET: A Machine Learning for Language Toolkit. `http://mallet.cs.umass.edu`.

Michel, Jean-Baptiste, Yuan Kui Shen, Aviva Presser Aiden, Adrian Veres, Matthew K. Gray, Joseph P. Pickett, Dale Hoiberg, Dan Clancy, Peter Norvig, Jon Orwant, Steven Pinker, Martin A. Nowak, and Erez Lieberman Aiden. 2011. Quantitative analysis of culture using millions of digitized books. *Science* 331(6014):176–182.

Pechenick, Eitan Adam, Christopher M. Danforth, and Peter Sheridan Dodds. 2015. Characterizing the google books corpus: Strong limits to inferences of socio-cultural and linguistic evolution. *PLOS ONE* 10(10):1–24.

Petrova, Svetlana. 2011. Modeling word order variation in discourse: On the pragmatic properties of VS order in Old High German. *Oslo Studies in Language* 3(3):209–228.

Rögnvaldsson, Eiríkur, Anton Karl Ingason, Einar Freyr Sigurðsson, and Joel Wallenberg. 2012. The Icelandic Parsed Historical Corpus (IcePaHC). In *Proceedings of the Eighth International Conference on Language Resources and Evaluation*, pages 1978–1984.

Rohrdantz, Christian. 2014. *Visual Analytics of Change in Natural Language.* Ph.D. dissertation, University of Konstanz.

Rohrdantz, Christian, Annette Hautli, Thomas Mayer, Miriam Butt, Frans Plank, and Daniel A. Keim. 2011. Towards tracking semantic change by visual analytics. In *Proceedings of the 49th Annual Meeting of the Association for Computational Linguistics: Short Papers*, pages 305–310.

Rohrdantz, Christian, Andreas Niekler, Annette Hautli, Miriam Butt, and Daniel A. Keim. 2012. Lexical Semantics and Distribution of Suffixes – A Visual Analysis. In *Proceedings of the EACL 2012 Joint Workshop of LINGVIS & UNCLH*, pages 7–15.

Sacha, Dominik, Yuki Asano, Christian Rohrdantz, Felix Hamborg, Daniel A. Keim, Bettina Braun, and Miriam Butt. 2015. Self organizing maps for the visual analysis of pitch contours. In *Proceedings of the 20th Nordic Conference of Computational Linguistics*, pages 181–190.

Sagi, Eyal, Stefan Kaufmann, and Brady Clark. 2009. Semantic Density Analysis: Comparing Word Meaning across Time and Phonetic Space. In *Proceedings of the EACL 2009 Workshop on GEMS: GEometical Models of Natural Language Semantics*, pages 104–111. Athens, Greece.

Sandhaus, Evan. 2008. *The New York Times Annotated Corpus* LDC2008T19. DVD. Philadelphia, PA: Linguistic Data Consortium.

Schätzle, Christin, Miriam Butt, and Kristina Kotcheva. 2015. The diachrony of dative subjects and the middle in Icelandic: A corpus study. In M. Butt and T. H. King, eds., *Proceedings of the LFG'15 Conference*, pages 357–377. Stanford, CA: CSLI Publications.

Schätzle, Christin and Dominik Sacha. 2016. Visualizing language change: Dative subjects in Icelandic. In A. Hautli-Janisz and V. Lyding, eds., *Proceedings of the LREC 2016 Workshop VisLR II: Visualization as Added Value in the Development, Use and Evaluation of Language Resources*, pages 8–15.

Schütze, Hinrich. 1998. Automatic word sense discrimination. *Computational Linguistics* 24(1):97–123.

Shneiderman, Ben. 1996. The eyes have it: A task by data type taxonomy for information visualizations. In *Proceedings of the IEEE Symposium on Visual Languages*, pages 336–343.

Sigurðsson, Halldór Ármann. 1990. V1 declaratives and verb raising in Icelandic. In J. Maling and A. Zaenen, eds., *Syntax and Semantics 24: Modern Icelandic Syntax*, pages 41–69. New York: Academic Press.

Smith, Henry. 1996. *Restrictiveness in Case Theory*. Cambridge: Cambridge University Press.

Spärck Jones, Karen. 1972. A statistical interpretation of term specificity and its application in retrieval. *Journal of Documentation* pages 11–21.

Therón, Roberto and Laura Fontanillo. 2015. Diachronic-information visualization in historical dictionaries. *Information Visualization* 14(2):111–136.

Thomas, James J. and Kristin A. Cook. 2005. *Illuminating the Path: The Research and Development Agenda for Visual Analytics*. National Visualization and Analytics Center.

Thráinsson, Höskuldur. 2007. *The Syntax of Icelandic*. Cambridge: Cambridge University Press.

Wallenberg, Joel C., Anton Karl Ingason, Einar Freyr Sigurðsson, and Eiríkur Rögnvaldsson. 2011. Icelandic Parced Historical Corpus (IcePaHC). Version 0.9.

Yarowsky, David. 1995. Unsupervised word sense disambiguation rivaling supervised methods. In *Proceedings of the 33rd Annual Meeting on Association for Computational Linguistics*, pages 189–196.

6

Discourse Maps — Feature Encoding for the Analysis of Verbatim Conversation Transcripts

MENNATALLAH EL-ASSADY AND ANNETTE HAUTLI-JANISZ

6.1 Introduction

This chapter reports on work that extracts information about linguistic features from political deliberations in order to make the deliberative quality of political dialog measurable.[1] With *Discourse Maps*, a dynamic visualization that is tailored to both the requirements of the data and the theoretical framework on measuring deliberative quality as articulated within political science Gold et al. (2016), we showcase how Visual Analytics can combine theory-driven (top-down) analysis with a data-driven (bottom-up) view on the data. Unlike the Zhao et al. (this volume) paper, we do not work solely on the basis of discourse relations, but extact a plethora of relevant linguistic features and visualize these according to their type and contribution to the deliberative

[1]The work reported on here arose from within an intense collaboration between Miriam Butt, Valentin Gold, Katharina Holzinger and Daniel A. Keim. The initial work was funded via the Bundesministerium für Bildung und Forschung (BMBF) under grant no. 01461246 (eHumanities VisArgue project). The writing of this paper was made possible via funding by the Deutsche Forschungsgemeinschaft (DFG, German Research Foundation) within project P9 of the FOR 2111 "Questions at the Interfaces" — Project-ID 276395906 and the VolkswagenStiftung under grant 92182 (ADD-up).

Visual Analytics for Linguistics (LingVis).
edited by Miriam Butt, Annette Hautli-Janisz and Verena Lyding.
Copyright © 2020, CSLI Publications.

nature of the dialog.

Our system has the potential to provide political scientists, linguists, stakeholders in the debate or the general public with a visualized representation of the discourse, which can be employed for the comparison of discourse patterns between speakers, speaker parties, and different sequences.

The data underlying our work are verbatim transcripts of natural language discourse in the political sphere, a type of data that has gained momentum with the increasing availability of such resources. A particular interest lies in debates, i.e., argumentative discourse that is characterized by the interaction of multiple interlocutors who try to win a discussion on a controversial topic or convince the other participants. Verbatim transcripts of such discourses capture the rapid exchange of opinions, arguments, and information between interlocutors and thus, establish a rich data source for analysis. At the same time, this type of data presents challenges to the automatic processing of language: fragmented constructions, interruptions, filled pauses ('uhm', 'mh'), speech repairs, dialect, and transcription errors require a robust machinery that yields reliable results.

In order to ground our approach in theoretical work in political science, we work with the theoretical framework articulated by our political science partners, who analyze political deliberation by means of four high-level dimensions Gold and Holzinger (2015), namely, **(1)** 'Argumentation & Justification', **(2)** 'Accommodation', **(3)** 'Participation', and **(4)** 'Atmosphere & Respect'. Using tailored *micro-linguistic discourse features* we operationalize these dimensions and make them measurable. In total, we have currently computed, together with our domain experts, a set of 53 relevant discourse features for verbatim text in two languages (English, German).

Our contribution in this area is the following: We present a robust, hybrid system that pairs shallow text mining with linguistically motivated discourse analysis in noisy data, generating a rich set of micro-linguistic features that constitutes communication in the domain. Secondly, we introduce a novel visual design that rigidly maps all relevant aspects of communication (according to the deliberation framework) onto a glyph-based representation within the Discourse Maps, making all levels of a debate (starting with a single turn, all the way to an aggregation of all turns of a speaker/ within a topic), instantly comparable with respect to the analyzed features.

This paper proceeds as follows: We first lay out the necessary background, namely relevant work in discourse processing and visualization (Section 6.2). We then present the computational linguistic analysis with both shallow text mining and the deeper, more linguistically motivated annotation (Section 6.3). The annotation scheme and its encoding in Discourse Maps is discussed in Section 6.4, followed by the discussion of the data structure modeling and the visualization design in Section 6.5. We then present a use case, where Discourse Maps are used to shed light on a real debate scenario, namely the so-called S21 arbitration, a public arbitration process in the German city of Stuttgart in 2010 (Section 6.6). Section 6.7 provides a two-level evaluation of Discourse Maps. Section 6.8 concludes the paper.

6.2 Background

Our work is rooted in the areas of discourse processing and Visual Analytics. This section highlights the relevant related-work and literature in both areas, building the background for the design and implementation of our Discourse Maps approach.

Discourse Processing Natural Language Processing (NLP) of discourse data is as varied as the type of data underlying it: An important area deals with the automatic annotation of discourse relations, i.e., relations between segments in the text. Those are annotated in different granularity and style in frameworks such as Rhetorical Structure Theory (Mann and Thompson 1988) or Segmented Discourse Representation Theory (Asher and Lascarides 2003). In English, the majority of work is based on landmark corpora such as the Penn Discourse Treebank (PDTB; Prasad et al. 2008). In German, the parsing of discourse relations has only lately received increasing attention (Versley and Gastel 2013, Stede and Neumann 2014, Bögel et al. 2014).

Another strand of research is concerned with dialogue act annotation, to which end several annotation schemes have been proposed (e.g., Bunt et al., 2010; inter alia). Those have also been applied across a range of German corpora (Jekat et al. 1995, Zarisheva and Scheffler 2015). Another area deals with the classification of speaker stance, for instance regarding personality (Mairesse et al. 2007), agreement and disagreement (Sridhar et al. 2015) or politeness (Danescu-Niculescu-Mizil et al. 2013).

With Discourse Maps, we provide the first discourse analysis pipeline which extracts a multitude of discourse features from naturally occurring dialogue data in parallel. This is done with hybrid technology: shallow text mining extracts surface-structure patterns in the discourse such as sentence complexity, interruptions and filler words (Section 6.3.1). This is complemented by a linguistically informed rule-based approach for disambiguating and annotating linguistic information such as discourse relations, speech acts, emotion, modality and rhetorical framing (Section 6.3.2).

In order to work with a fine-grained structure of the discourse, we divide the text in smaller units of analysis, namely the *discourse unit*. While there is no consensus in the literature on what exactly these discourse units have to contain, it is generally assumed that each describes a single event (Polanyi et al. 2004). Following Marcu (2000), we term these units *elementary discourse units* (EDUs). For Discourse Maps, we aggregate the information of all EDUs on the level of the speaker turn (for more details on the aggregation see Section 6.5).

Visual Analytics Text is an inherently multimodal data source, comprised of many information channels for analysis. In particular, conversations and debates encompass a broad spectrum of information due to the diversity of their dynamics and the ambiguity of their language. Visual Analytics techniques can reveal such dynamics and enable an extensive analysis of the different aspects of discourse. One of the first examples to model the social interactions in chat systems was Chat Circles (Donath and Viégas 2002). Other approaches are GroupMeter (Leshed et al. 2009), Conversation Clusters (Bergstrom and Karahalios 2009), Trains of Thought (Shahaf et al. 2012), and MultiConVis (Hoque and Carenini 2016). The VisArgue framework (El-Assady et al. 2017a) introduced specialized visualization techniques for a faceted analysis of conversational text, most notably, the Lexical Episode Plots (Gold et al. 2015), ConToVi for mapping a conversation to a Topic Space View (El-Assady et al. 2016), NEREx for exploring named entity relationships (El-Assady et al. 2017b), the Argumentation Feature Alignment Visualization (Jentner et al. 2017), and ThreadReconstructor for untangling reply chains (El-Assady et al. 2018a). However, most of these approaches are not designed to give a full overview of discourse features and do not allow for the *fingerprinting* of turns, speakers, or topics in a discourse. To achieve this, Discourse Maps utilizes the design principles and guidelines for glyph-based visualizations, as outlined by Borgo et al. (2013).

A more recent survey on glyph-based visualizations has been recently provided by Fuchs et al. (2017). They systematically reviewed the results of experimental studies on data glyphs, suggesting that the background of a glyph might not influence its readability and that aligning the glyph design to the mental models of the users enhances the understanding of its underlying data. They also express caution about encoding too many data points into a single glyph as it negatively affects search. Hence, in this work, we explore the trade-off between a stable mental model and the information density of the visualization, resulting with an interactive (turning data points on and off) representation that uses a strict visual mapping of domain knowledge.

Another area of related work are dense-pixel displays. A prominent example is the work by Keim and Oelke (2007) on literature fingerprinting. In this work, pixel-based small-multiples are used for encoding measures extracted from text data. In contrast to the guidance provided for sophisticated glyph design, dense-pixel displays do not limit the number of data points encoded in one visual object. Our proposed visualization uses small, simple glyphs as pixels that are arranges using techniques comparable to the ones well known in dense-pixel displays.

6.3 Computational Linguistic Analysis

Discourse Maps are based on a hybrid set of features that are extracted via shallow text mining techniques (Section 6.3.1) or via a more in-depth, linguistically motivated annotation system (Section 6.3.2). In the following, we discuss both methods based on an sample feature set.

6.3.1 Shallow Text Mining

With shallow text mining the aim is to capture properties of the discourse that do not necessarily depend on context or a deep analysis of linguistic structure. One such property is the *average sentence complexity*, which ives us an approximation as to how complex the sentence structure of a particular speaker (or speaker position) is. To that end we count the number of EDUs in each sentence of a speaker turn and divide it by the number of sentences.

Another relevant measure is whether particular turns are *interruptions*. Given the postulate of deliberative communication to be respectful, this feature allows us to detect phases in the debate which are heated and do not adhere to deliberative standards. To determine this, we count the number of content-bearing words in a speaker turn (e.g., nouns) and check whether it exceeds a user-defined threshold, marking the turn as an interruption if it does not. In addition to some turns not significantly contributing to the conversation, we also count the *number of filler words* of each turn. With this step we do justice to the type of data we are dealing with: spontaneous, natural language speech is noisy and many turns (or parts of them) merely signal backchanneling (that the speaker is paying attention and possibly agreeing or disagreeing). These are defined using dictionaries (e.g., 'um', 'hm', 'ah') and regular expressions to capture variation in the transcriptions (e.g., 'uuum', 'hmm'). Furthermore, we also consider statistical measures and features based on the content of the text, as determined by topic modeling algorithms developed by us (El-Assady et al. 2018b). In the following, these features are described in more detail.

Statistical Measures In political science, the use of statistical measures is ubiquitous. Such measures inform models for empirical studies and are taken as essential for understanding dynamics in conversations (Gold and Holzinger 2015). In our work we implemented three measures that capture commonly studied phenomena in discourse analysis. The first two rely on a moving window approach to assess the context of a speaker turn. Hence, based on a user-defined window size (defined by the tuple (p, f) for the number of previous and the number of following turns, respectively), we regard for the neighborhood of each turn one measure, as for example, for the speaker of the turn his/her *expected probability to speak* or the *moving Gini* that determines the turn-taking distribution based on the Gini Coefficient (Ceriani and Verme 2012). The third statistical measure we included determines the eloquence of speakers, measuring the diversity of their vocabulary based on the *Maas index*, as outlined by McCarthy and Jarvis (2007).

Topic Modeling Content analysis is one of the major tasks when dealing with discourse data. Topic modeling algorithms automatically segment the turns of a discourse into thematically coherent groups. We, thus, rely on their output to aggregate the turns into a set of topics, but also derive measures based on this segmentation. These measures determine how a particular turn is situated, given the topic distribution of the whole corpus. To define the features we extract using the topic modeling results, we select turns to consider for the similarity calculation to a turn utr_i at hand, based on three distinct factors:

speaker {self, all}: *turns that are from the same speaker as* utr_i ***vs.*** *all turns.*

topics {self, all}: *turns that deal with the same topics as* utr_i ***vs.*** *all turns.*

position {previous, following}: *turns that have come before* utr_i ***vs.*** *turns that have come after* utr_i.

Hence, we compute a set of turns to consider based on these factors, as exemplified in the following scheme; for the similarity to all previous turns of the speaker of the selected turn utr_i, we denote: $sim_{top_{all}, spe_{self}, pos_{prev}}(utr_i)$. Note, that the similarity calculation between two turns is modular and can be defined by users — by default the cosine similarity is selected.

This method enables the segmentation of the corpus in various forms, and, in turn, allows us to define useful features based on ratios of calculated segments. In total, we define five novel features.

(1) *Topic shift* describes whether the topic of the turn advances the conversation, or whether the turn is continuing with an already established topic. It is defined as: $Topic\ Shift_{utr_i} = \frac{sim_{top_{all},spe_{all},pos_{prev}}(utr_i)}{sim_{top_{all},spe_{all},pos_{follow}}(utr_i)}$.

(2) *Self previous recurrence* describes the relative amount of content recurrence a selected turn has to previous turns from the same speaker, considering all previous turns; i.e., how much this turn is a repetition of what this person has already said. It is defined as: $Self\ Previous\ Recurrence_{utr_i} = \frac{sim_{top_{all},spe_{self},pos_{prev}}(utr_i)}{sim_{top_{all},spe_{all},pos_{prev}}(utr_i)}$.

(3) *Self following recurrence* is the counterpart to the self previous recurrence. It describes the relative amount of content recurrence a selected turn has to the following turns from the same speaker, considering all previous turns. This can be seen as a measure of how much influence this particular speaker turn will have on the remainder of the conversation. It is defined as:
$Self\ Following\ Recurrence_{utr_i} = \frac{sim_{top_{all},spe_{self},pos_{follow}}(utr_i)}{sim_{top_{all},spe_{all},pos_{follow}}(utr_i)}$.

(4) *Self recurrence shift* is a measure of the relation between the self previous recurrence and the self following recurrence. Hence this is a measure of whether the recurrence of the turn is a progressive one or not, i.e., whether this particular turn is more relevant to the preceding part (for example, as a summary) or whether it will become more relevant to the following part of the conversation (for example, through setting new agenda topics). It is defined as: $Self\ Recurrence\ Shift_{utr_i} = \frac{Self\ Previous\ Recurrence_{utr_i}}{Self\ Following\ Recurrence_{utr_i}}$.

(5) *Topic persistence* describes whether the speaker of a particular turn is persistent with regard to the topic of that turn or not. This measure is defined as $Topic\ Persistence_{utr_i} = \frac{so(utr_i)/sa(utr_i)}{ao(utr_i)/aa(utr_i)}$, through the following four similarities:

$$\begin{aligned}
so(utr_i) &= sim_{top_{self},spe_{self},pos_{prev+follow}}(utr_i);\\
sa(utr_i) &= sim_{top_{all},spe_{self},pos_{prev+follow}}(utr_i);\\
ao(utr_i) &= sim_{top_{self},spe_{all},pos_{prev+follow}}(utr_i);\\
aa(utr_i) &= sim_{top_{all},spe_{all},pos_{prev+follow}}(utr_i).
\end{aligned}$$

In total, these measures indicate how a turn is contributing to the general content of a discourse and in which capacity a given speaker is involved. This and other shallow-linguistic features build the basis to a better understanding of the role of particular speaker turns in conversations and have proven to be insightful indicators of characteristic dynamics in political debates (Gold et al. 2016).

6.3.2 Linguistic Annotation

In contrast to the shallow text mining, the linguistic annotation pipeline extracts discourse features based on a comparatively deep linguistic analysis. The annotation system is specifically designed to deal with noisy transcribed natural speech which contains ungrammatical/fragmented constructions, backchanneling ('hm', 'ah') and interruptions. It is based on a linguistically informed, hand-crafted set of rules that deals with the disambiguation of explicit linguistic markers and the identification of their spans and relations in the text (for more details on the general structure of these rules see Bögel et al. 2014).

The system analyzes several layers of information. With respect to *discourse relations*, we annotate spans as to whether they represent: reasons, conclusions, contrasts, concessions, conditions or consequences (Bögel et al. 2014). For German, we rely on the connectors in the Potsdam Commentary Corpus (Stede and Neumann 2014), for English we use the PDTB-style parser by Lin et al. (2014). In order to identify relevant *speech acts*, we annotate speech act verbs signaling agreement, disagreement, arguing, bargaining and information giving/seeking/refusing. In order to gage *emotion*, we use EmoLex, a crowdsourced emotion lexicon (Mohammad and Turney 2010) available for a number of languages, plus our own curated lexicon of politeness markers. With respect to *event modality*, we take into account all modal verbs and adverbs signaling obligation, permission, volition, reluctance or alternative. Concerning *epistemic modality* and speaker stance we use modal expressions conveying certainty, probability, possibility and impossibility. Finally, we add a category called *rhetorical framing* (Hautli-Janisz and Butt 2016), which accounts for the illocutionary contribution of German discourse particles. Here we look at different ways of invoking Common Ground, hedging and signaling accommodation in argumentation, for example.

Preprocessing We first divide up all turns into EDUs. For German, we approximate the assumption made by Polanyi et al. (2004) by inserting a boundary at every punctuation mark and every clausal connector (conjunctions, complementizers). For English we rely on clause-level splitting of the Stanford PCFG parser (Klein and Manning 2003) and create EDUs at the SBAR, SBARQ, SINV and SQ clause levels. The annotation is performed on the level of these EDUs, therefore relations that span multiple units are marked individually at each unit.

We were not able to use an off-the-shelf parser for German. For instance, an initial experiment using the German Stanford Dependency parser (Rafferty and Manning 2008) showed that 60% of parses are incorrect due to interruptions, speech repairs and multiple embeddings. We therefore hand-crafted our own rules on the basis of morphological and POS information from DMOR (Schiller 1994). For English, we used the POS tags from the Stanford parser.

Disambiguation Many of the crucial linguistic markers are ambiguous. We developed hand-crafted rules that take into account the surrounding context to achieve disambiguation. Important features include position in the EDU (for instance for lexemes which can be discourse connectors at the beginning of an EDU but not at the end, and vice versa) or the POS of other lexical items in the context. Overall, the German system features 20 disambiguation rules, the English one has 12.

Relation Identification After disambiguation is complete, a second set of rules annotates the spans and the relations that the lexical items trigger. In this module, we again take into account the context of the lexical item. An important factor is negation, which in some cases reverses the contribution of the lexical item, e.g., in the case of 'possible' to 'not possible'.

With respect to discourse connectors, for instance the German causal markers *da, denn, darum* and *daher* 'because/thus', we only analyze relations within a single speaker turn, i.e., relations that are expressed in a sequence of clauses which a speaker utters without interference from another speaker. As a consequence, the annotation system does not take into account relations that are split up between turns of one speaker or turns of different speakers. For causal relations (reason and conclusion spans), the system performs with an F-score of 0.95 (Bögel et al. 2014).

Taken together, shallow text mining and linguistic processing yields a set of 53 features that encode various properties of the debate. All of them serve as operationalizing features for analyzing communicative strategies in deliberative communication. For Discourse Maps, we combine all features into an annotation scheme with dimensions that are well motivated from the viewpoint of political science. This annotation scheme serves as the mental model for Discourse Maps and is discussed in the following.

6.4 Annotation Scheme

The framework used to analyze deliberative communication comes from political science and comprises four larger dimensions, namely Argumentation & Justification, Accommodation, Atmosphere & Respect and Participation (Gold and Holzinger 2015). This model serves as the backbone for the annotation scheme and is populated with the features from the shallow text mining and the linguistic annotation pipeline. It also defines the design structure of the Discourse Maps visualization in that the map is divided into four quadrants — illustrated by the template in Figure 1. The annotation scheme and its relation to Discourse Maps is discussed in more detail in the following.

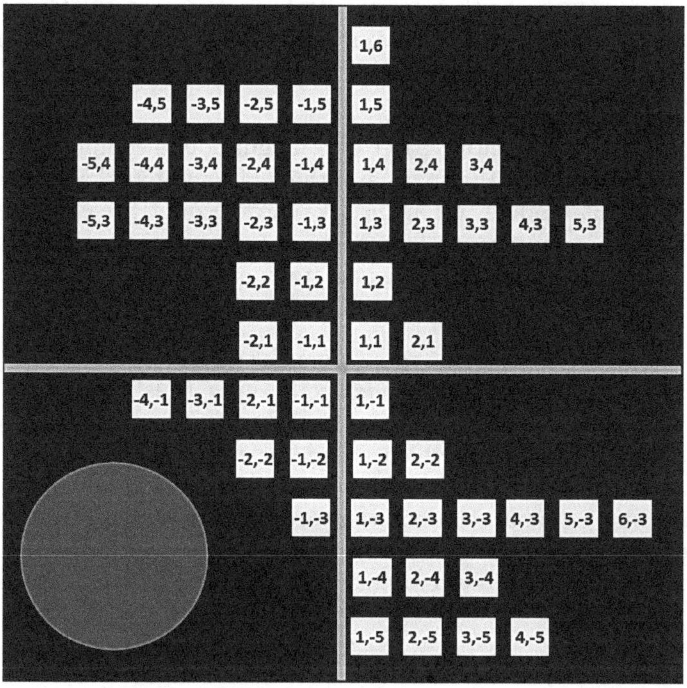

FIGURE 1 Index map, with each index position indicating the position of a glyph in the Discourse Map. Overall, the map shows the four quadrants, depicting the four deliberation dimensions. In addition, all quadrants combine 19 subdimensions, that, in turn, span 53 measures. The circular shape on the bottom left is scaled to the length of the underlying turns, indicating the relative size of the underlying text.

6.4.1 Atmosphere & Respect

The first subdimension, Atmosphere & Respect, is encoded in the upper right (Northeast; NE) quadrant of the Discourse Map. This dimension encompasses features that represent central standards in deliberative communication, namely respect, conscientiousness and civility (Gerhards 1997, Fishkin and Luskin 2005:inter alia). For a good deliberative process, Landwehr and Holzinger (2010) also require a conversational back-and-forth in the debate instead of a passive listening to monologues by the interlocutors.

TABLE 1 Dimension "Atmosphere & Respect"

Subdimension	Feature/Measure	Index	Type
Emotion	**Emotion Count**	1, 1	NUM CONT
	Emotion Relation	2, 1	NUM BIPOL
Interruptions	**Interruption**	1, 2	BINARY
Responsiveness	**Topic Shift**	1, 3	NUM BIPOL
	Self Previous Recurrence	2, 3	NUM CONT
	Self Following Recurrence	3, 3	NUM CONT
	Self Recurrence Shift	4, 3	NUM BIPOL
	Topic Persistence	5, 3	NUM BIPOL
Conventional Politeness	**Politeness**	1, 4	NUM CONT
	Impatience	2, 4	BINARY
	Unobtrusiveness	3, 4	BINARY
Face Issues	**Resignation Acceptance**	1, 5	NUM CONT
Sentiments	**Sentiment**	1, 6	NUM BIPOL

In order to group these diverse aspects in a meaningful way, we introduce subdimensions, namely "Emotion", "Interruptions", "Responsiveness", "Conventional Politeness", "Face Issues" and "Sentiment" (see Table 1). Each of these subdimensions is represented as an individual row, with each row consisting of square glyphs that represent the individual features (see second column in Table 1). The exact position of these glyphs in the quadrant is described via the index in the third column in Table 1. The underlying feature can be revealed by mousing over the glyphs in the visual interface, for instance the amount of positive or negative emotion is represented by the glyph in position (1,1) in the Discourse Map, the amount of interruptions is captured in position (1,2). The fourth column in Table 1 encodes how the different discourse features are measured. This defines the type of color-coding, a property of Discourse Maps that is discussed in detail in Section 6.5.

6.4.2 Argumentation & Justification

The Argumentation & Justification dimension is situated in the lower right (Southeast; SE) quadrant of the Discourse Map. It contains the subdimensions listed in Table 2: "Information Certainty", "Reason-giving", "Event Modality", "Common Ground" and "Information Exchange". "Information Exchange" is relevant in the Dimension "Argumentation & Justification" because participants in a deliberative process should argue and justify their positions, consequently we expect structures where information is provided, sought or refused. The certainty with which this information is provided is subsumed under the subdimension "Information Certainty": Here we use the scale of Lassiter (2010) which maps expressions of epistemic modality on a scale from 0 (impossible) to 1 (certain).

We further expect argumentative structures, in particular causal argumentation with premises and/or conclusions (subsumed in the "Reason-giving" subdimension). Deontic modals, i.e., those modals that denote how the world should be according to norms or speaker desires, e.g. 'have to' and 'should', are encoded in the subdimension "Event Modality". The "Common Ground" originates in a linguistic concept, whereby interlocutors share an abstract knowledge space (Stalnaker 2002). In German, the Common Ground is frequently referred to via particles, for instance *ja* 'lit. yes', a linguistic category that is highly frequent in spontaneous speech — speakers use these relate themselves or their contributions to the shared knowledge of the discussion partners (Zimmermann 2011).

TABLE 2 Dimension "Argumentation & Justification"

Subdimension	Feature/Measure	Index	Type
Information Certainty	**Epistemic Value**	1, −1	NUM BIPOL
Reason-giving	**Reason**	1, −2	NUM CONT
	Conclusion	2, −2	NUM CONT
Event Modality	**Obligation**	1, −3	BINARY
	Volition	2, −3	BINARY
	External Constraint	3, −3	BINARY
	Permission	4, −3	BINARY
	Alternative	5, −3	BINARY
	Reluctance	6, −3	BINARY
Common Ground	**Common Ground (CG)**	1, −4	BINARY
	Reject CG	2, −4	BINARY
	Activate CG	3, −4	BINARY
Information Exchange	**Information Giving**	1, −5	BINARY
	Elucidation	2, −5	BINARY
	Information Seeking	3, −5	BINARY
	Information Refusing	4, −5	BINARY

As in the Atmosphere & Respect dimension above, the position of the glyphs that represent those features in the Discourse Map are given in the third column of Table 2. For instance, premise units are represented by the glyph in position (1,-2), conclusions are encoded with the glyph in position (2,-2).

6.4.3 Participation

The lower left (Southwest; SW) quadrant of the Discourse Map represents the Participation dimension, a dimension that measures the involvement of individual speakers in the discourse. This is operationalized by looking at the "Equality of Speaker Capabilities" (measured by features that indicate the eloquence of speakers), the "Equality of Speaker Participation" (measured by comparing the number of contributions of one speaker to those of the other interlocutors) and "Topic Comprehensiveness" (measured by the network density of all thematic relations of a speaker turn) (see Table 3). As in the dimensions above, each subdimension is encoded as one row and each feature is represented by one glyph. Again, the position of the glyphs in the Discourse Map is shown in the index column in Table 3.

TABLE 3 Dimension "Participation"

Subdimension	Feature/Measure	Index	Type
Equality of Speaker Capabilities	**Sentence Complexity**	−1, −1	NUM BIPOL
	Maas Index	−2, −1	NUM BIPOL
	Filler Words	−3, −1	NUM CONT
	Stalling	−4, −1	BINARY
Equality of Speaker Participation	**Exp Prob to Speak**	−1, −2	NUM BIPOL
	Moving Gini Index	−2, −2	NUM BIPOL
Topic Comprehensiveness	**Network Density**	−1, −3	NUM BIPOL

6.4.4 Accommodation

Another dimension with a large array of subdimensions is Accommodation, situated in the upper left (Northwest; NW) quadrant in the Discourse Map and detailed in Table 4. In this dimension we capture all linguistic structures that are relevant in negotiation situations, such as instances that signal agreement or disagreement, hint at conditions that need to be fulfilled in order to come to an agreement and are used to achieve some kind of consensus. In total we have five subdimensions: "Condition", "Agreement vs. Disagreement", "Agreement", "Disagreement" and "Arguing vs. Bargaining". In "Condition", we capture conditional discourse relations triggered for instance by 'if ... then' constructions. In "Agreement", we combine information contributed by discourse particles, for instance the agreement information triggered by sentence-initial 'yes', and speech act verbs signaling agreement (e.g. *be-*

fürworten 'to support'). In the subdimension "Disagreement", the information triggered by particles and speech act verbs (e.g. *bestreiten* 'to deny') is combined with conjunctions such as 'instead of' signaling contrastive discourse relations. In "Agreement vs. Disagreement", we set the two measures of "Agreement" (-2,3) and "Disagreement" (-3,4) in relation. On the one hand, we count the absolute number of these two measures (-1,2). On the other hand, we set them in relation (-2,2). In a similar manner, in "Arguing vs. Bargaining", we subsume speech acts of arguing and bargaining (for instance units goverend by 'to justify and 'to resign', respectively). The measures "Negotiation Count" and "Negotiation Relation" describe on the one hand the absolute count (how much is on a scale), and on the other, the relation of "Arguing" vs. "Bargaining" (is the scale tipped to the one or the other side). Note that having count and relation measures together reveals a clearer picture of a phenomenon, i.e., a relation might show a 2:3 scale but only with the count can we distinguish between 20:30 vs. 2000:3000.

TABLE 4 Dimension "Accommodation"

Subdimension	Feature/Measure	Index	Type
Condition	**Condition**	$-1, 1$	NUM CONT
	Consequence	$-2, 1$	NUM CONT
Agreement vs. Disagreement	**Arrangement Count**	$-1, 2$	NUM CONT
	Arrangement Relation	$-2, 2$	NUM BIPOL
Agreement	**Consensus**	$-1, 3$	BINARY
	Agreement	$-2, 3$	BINARY
	Consensus Willing	$-3, 3$	BINARY
	Minimal Consensus	$-4, 3$	BINARY
	Concession	$-5, 3$	NUM CONT
Disagreement	**Opposition**	$-1, 4$	NUM CONT
	Dissent	$-2, 4$	BINARY
	Disagreement	$-3, 4$	BINARY
	Activate Opposition	$-4, 4$	BINARY
	Contrast	$-5, 4$	BINARY
Arguing vs. Bargaining	**Negotiation Relation**	$-1, 5$	NUM BIPOL
	Negotiation Count	$-2, 5$	NUM CONT
	Arguing	$-3, 5$	BINARY
	Bargaining	$-4, 5$	BINARY

After having laid out the linguistic groundwork on which Discourse Maps are based, we now discuss the visualization design in more detail, in particular regarding the modeling and visual representation of different data structures.

6.5 Visualization Design

In order to achieve a suitable visual representation of the data model at hand, we conducted several user studies and sketching sessions, going through a set of eight different prototypes for the Discourse Maps. A selection of five intermediate prototypes is discussed in Section 6.5.1. This section elaborates on the design rationale of the presented visualization and the underlying data structure modeling.

Design Requirements The visual design of such a static, yet complex model has to fulfill a rigid set of requirements. First, this visualization is designed with a strict scheme of data relations in mind. The given hierarchy of dimensions, subdimensions, and measures defines a tight mold which the visual design has to follow. During our design process we experimented with different complexity levels of the visualization and came to realize that this visualization should not try to hide the complexity of the data model, as it is used by analysts as a "brain dump" to rid themselves from remembering the data model and rather focus on the arising patterns for analysis. Hence, a second design requirement was to construct a stable visual mapping that aims at representing all data model relations (taking into account that such a design comes with a learning curve that needs to be absolved). The third design requirement is that this visualization should enable a broad range of analysis tasks through allowing users to define the measures they are interested in focusing on analyzing. Lastly, and most importantly, the visual representation of a single turn should be comparable to the representation of a group of turns to enable comparability across levels of granularity, e.g., topics, speakers, parties, days, etc.

Analysis Tasks Based on the studies we conducted for our requirement analysis, we derived a set of analytical tasks that users intend to perform using the Discourse Maps. These include, most notably, the following tasks:

- Exploration of Measure Relations and Patterns
- Theory-Driven Hypothesis Generation for Expected Relations
- Interactive, Data-Driven Hypothesis Verification
- Comparative Analysis across Turns, Speakers, Parties, Topics
- Refinement of the Deliberation Theory based on Findings

Such an analysis of analytical tasks enabled an effective design of the Discourse Maps and, in turn, led to domain insight and a better understanding of discourse dynamics.

Data Structure Modeling In order to ensure that all features are mapped adequately, we subdivided them into three types.

1. *Numerical Continuous* features are normalized to a scale from 0 to 1 and usually represent relative counts, e.g., the amount of agreement and disagreement particles and speech acts (cf. Table 4, -1,2).
2. *Numerical Bipolar* features are mapped to a scale between -1 and 1 and are typically showing a diverging measure, e.g., the relation between agreement and disagreement particles and speech acts (cf. Table 4, -2,2).
3. *Binary* features are either 0 or 1 and indicate whether an attribute exists or not, e.g., whether a turn contains an agreement particle or speech act or not (cf. Table 4, -2,3).

Note, that these scales are defined on a speaker turn level. When multiple turns are aggregated, the aggregated feature score is mapped back to the same range, with the exception of binary features that are mapped to a continuum from 0 to 1, instead of a discrete scale.

6.5.1 Design Iterations

As previously mentioned, the current visualization design is the result of an iterative process that incorporated the expert feedback into the evolution of the *Discourse Map* prototypes. Figure 2 depicts five out of eight prototypes from the different iterations. Some of the designs mapped a selection of the most important dimensions to the shape of a glyph (e.g., Iterations 1 & 3). Other designs positioned the feature dimensions into a defined structure (e.g., Iterations 4 & 5). Again others used a global visual layout to enhance comparability (e.g., Iterations 2 & 5). However, these designs did not conform to the mental model of the domain experts and, in turn, did not facilitate the externalization of their domain knowledge.

Following our four design requirements, we attempted to find the most suitable visual mapping of the data scheme of our domain experts, while reducing visual complexity and hiding unnecessary information to a second detail level. Iterations 1, 3, 4 & 5, therefore, used a defined glyph structure with up to 12 dimensions to encode the required information (requirement 1). However, our intermediate evaluations showed that these mappings were not sufficient to encode all relations our users care about for the high-level analysis (requirement 2). Increasing the level of visual complexity by encoding more dimensions into the glyph did not scale for some of the designs (e.g., Iterations 1, 3 & 4). In addition, these designs dictated a strict order of the dimensions and were not flexible to accommodate multiple analysis tasks, for example through selecting specific dimensions to focus on (requirement 3).

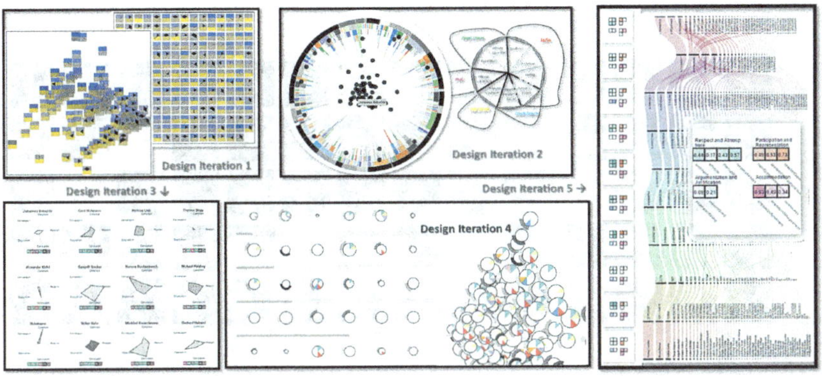

FIGURE 2 Five prototypes from previous design iterations.

Alternative mappings that used the whole screen space to show the relation between feature dimensions (e.g., Iterations 2 & 5) did not allow for comparability across text granularity levels (requirement 4).

Hence, the design of the Discourse Maps as presented here evolved through a long-term design process. After the creation of each prototype, we conducted an expert evaluation, followed by a discussion of design choices and a sketching session. These sketching sessions were usually the starting point for refining a given prototype or, alternatively, beginning a new design iteration. Involving the domain experts into the visualization design process allowed us to incorporate their understanding of deliberation theory into the visualization design and paved the way for creating a (sophisticated) visual encoding that truly externalized their domain understanding, as described in the following section.

6.5.2 Discourse Maps

Given the multimodality of the computed feature set and the derived requirements and tasks, the visual design of our approach has to consider three important principles. First, the visualization needs to preserve and represent the mental model of deliberative communication as defined by political science. Second, the hybrid set of features needs to be mapped onto visual variables that are intuitive and enhance the recognition of the information. Third, the comparability of different aggregation levels needs to be ensured, i.e., the user has to be able to compare the same information across different levels of detail, for instance for a single turn, for individual speakers, for individual topics or for speaker positions.

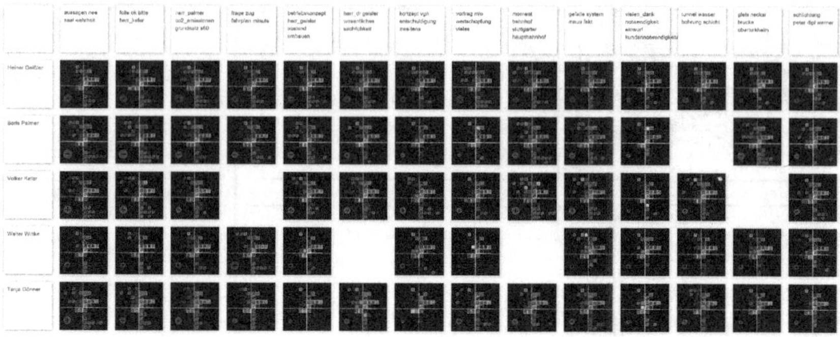

FIGURE 3 *Topics* (columns) by *Speakers* (rows) grid of Discourse Maps sorted to the highest number of turns in rows and columns.

Accounting for all these principles, our approach allows the user to draw inferences regarding the progress of the debate, speaker behavior and argumentative strategies in large amounts of deliberative communication at a glance. Discourse Maps are designed as glyph-based, small multiples that encode all relevant information in an index map, as highlighted in Figure 1. These small multiples can be regard as fingerprints of deliberative communication and are designed to enhance a recognition of the information, in compliance with the design guidelines of Borgo et al. (2013) (DG5: "Justify the choice of outcome measures in terms of their relevance to the objectives of the empirical study"). Hence, important dimensions for the data are highlighted using luminescence and position.

The template for a Discourse Map shown in Figure 1 mirrors the four dimensions of deliberation proposed by our political science partners, with each quadrant representing one dimension: NW (Accommodation), NE (Atmosphere & Respect), SE (Participation), SW (Argumentation & Justification). Each subdimension is represented as a row and each annotation within a subdimension is represented as a small rectangular box, the so-called *feature-glyph*. Each subdimension is dynamically positioned nearer to the center the more often its annotation occurs in the data. In addition, each feature-glyph is positioned nearer to the coordinates the more often it occurs within its subdimension. This dynamic layout generation allows the creation of adaptable Discourse Maps depending on the underlying data. However, the internal layout of a map is stable for a given corpus to avoid confusion and to enable analysts to memorize layouts corresponding to their data. Furthermore, in order to show the average length of each unit of analysis — a turn, we include a small circular icon on the bottom left of the

Discourse Map. This is scaled to the length of the underlying turns and indicates the relative size of the underlying text.

A Discourse Map represents one or more speaker turns, depending on the segmentation of the underlying discourse. For example, Figure 3 shows a *topics X speakers* grid of Discourse Maps, i.e., each Discourse Map represents all turns a certain speaker has said. Such a grid-based segmentation enables the generation of multiple views, alternating the aggregation based on *speakers*, *parties* (speaker positions), as well as, *topics*. Hence, grids such as *topics X parties*, *turns X speakers*, etc., can be created dynamically.

In addition to the dynamic generation of grids for the Discourse Maps, users can interactively select the dimensions, subdimensions, and features they would like to focus their analysis on. This is done through an index map (cf. Figure 1) that allows users to turn individual elements of the map on or off. A feature-glyph that is disabled is rendered in black. Furthermore, other interaction techniques are designed for supporting the analysis process, as described in Section 6.5.4.

6.5.3 Feature-Glyph Design

As described in the previous section, Discourse Maps represent individual measures as feature-glyphs. Each feature-glyph is a small rectangular box that is mapped to certain attributes related to the features presented. Figure 4 illustrates the design of a feature-glyph, mapping three values to a rectangular box.

First, to facilitate the localization, comparison, and distinction of glyphs, we have to take into account different types of data, as described in Section 6.5. These are represented using a shape in the middle of each feature-glyph. The *Numerical Continuous* type is based on frequency counts represented by a simple rectangle □ with no additional lines or

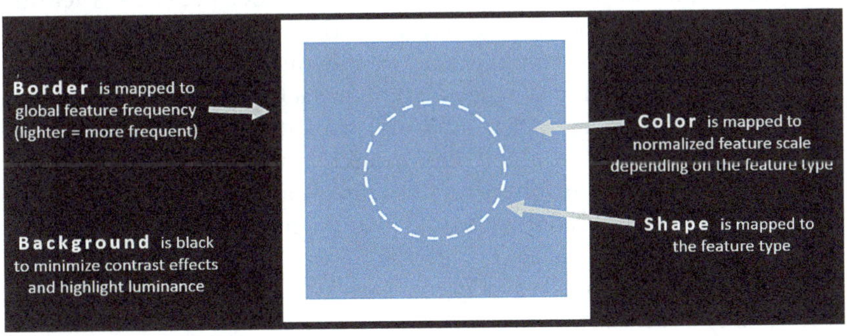

FIGURE 4 Feature-glyph design, utilizing border, color, and shape.

shapes. For *Binary* occurrences (e.g., reason phrase present or not), the rectangle includes a diagonal line. The last type is *Numerical Bipolar* features, where we range from positive to negative values, e.g., for sentiment or emotion words. Since the relation of positive and negative occurrences is relevant, we assume that the normal state is the neutral box and indicate a drift to the positive or negative sides with a plus or a minus sign, respectively.

(a) Binary (b) Num. Continuous (c) Numerical Bipolar

FIGURE 5 Color mappings for the different data types.

Second, the normalized feature value of the particular measure at hand is represented using color. Here, the color scheme (as shown in Figure 5) differentiates between the three data types: *Binary* (a), *Numerical Continuous* (b), and *Numerical Bipolar* (c). These were chosen according to perceptive criteria that highlight the encoded values with the luminescence of the color. All color scales were created using ColorCat (Mittelstädt et al. 2015). An example for the distinction of glyph types by the color scheme is shown here: . Here a sequence of three features is shown, consisting of two *Numerical Continuous* measures, followed by one *Numerical Bipolar* one. As noted above, the aggregation of *Binary* measures results in a continuous numerical scale, which is shown using an interpolation of the two ends of the the binary colormap (Figure 5a), resulting in different shades of purple, e.g., .

Third, the global frequency of each feature is represented by the border color. A white color can be understood as a feature that can be measured for all turns, while a dark gray border indicates a feature that is only present in a few turns within the whole corpus. Note that, throughout the feature-glyph design, we use luminance to indicate noteworthy phenomena. Hence, when a glyph has a black border and a black filling it fades into the background and does not disturb the analysis, e.g., . However, if a glyph has a light border and a dark filling, it will be noticed as an important feature that has a near-zero value for this particular Discourse Map. To compensate for contrast effects potentially caused by a border gradient, we calculate the minimally required number of pixels per glyph based on the model proposed by Mittelstädt et al. (2014).

The overall design of the feature-glyphs is tailored to facilitate their identification and comparison to enable global, as well as, local pattern detection. By using the border to highlight the global feature frequency, we can distinguish important features (i.e., relevant for the discourse at hand) from not so prominent ones. For example, for an instance of the two features *__M__aas __I__ndex* (-2,-1) and *avg. __S__entence __C__omplexity* (-1,-1), we can see that the two features are *Numerical Bipolar*, with a negative value for the MI and a positive value for the SC. Furthermore, we can detect that the SC has been measured for more turns in this particular discourse (shown by the lighter border color) and is, thus, potentially more important for the analysis.

6.5.4 Interactivity

The overall visual workspace around the Discourse Maps is tailored to the exploration and analysis of deliberation patterns across different layers of the discourse. The most basic layer visualizes discourse turns over time. Each turn is ordered sequentially and represented as a feature-glyph. This visualization helps determining deliberative segments within a discourse. In a second layer of analysis, the sequential order is visualized not with respect to the complete discourse but for each speaker separately. With this layer, the deliberative behavior of speakers is compared over time. This visualization supports the identification of deviant behavior of speakers. With the third visualization, as illustrated in Figure 3, patterns of speakers are compared between different topics in a *topics X speakers* grid. The top row shows the different topics, generated with an incremental hierarchical topic modeling algorithm (El-Assady et al. 2018c). Each column represents one speaker, each speaker turn is assigned to one topic. Blank spaces without a Discourse Map show that a speaker did not contribute to a specific topic. This visualization facilitates the detection of topics that are characterized by a particular pattern of deliberation.

Finally, the glyphs can be summarized and aggregated with respect to some given metadata, for instance with respect to different parties, as shown in Figure 6. This level of analysis is used for the case study in Section 6.6, where the deliberative patterns are investigated for the different parties of speakers.

Overall, this interactive segmentation enables users to adjust the discourse granularity and the generation of Discourse Maps to their respective analysis question.

Furthermore, to enable a focused analysis of certain aspects of communication using these complex glyphs, we designed a number of selection and filtering techniques, as well as, details-on-demand (hover to read specific value or click to enlarge the map) interactions. Together with the interactive aggregation of glyphs, the analysis of communica-

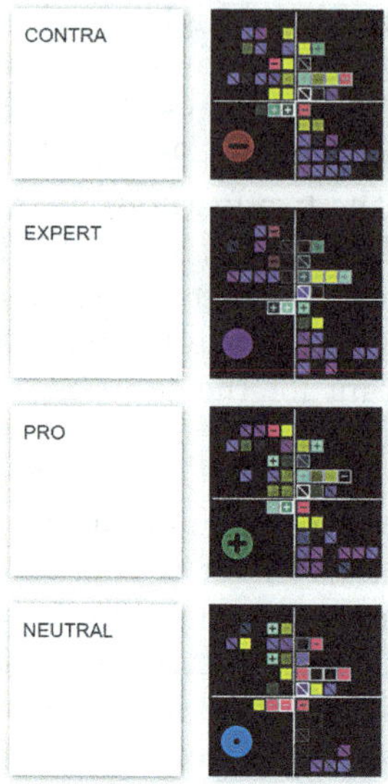

FIGURE 6 Feature-glyphs aggregated to speaker party.

tion dynamics using our system can be utilized to answer a variety of questions with respect to deliberative communication.

6.6 Use Case

In order to showcase that Discourse Maps can be used to analyze discourse where a controversial topic is discussed between multiple interlocutors, we use the transcripts of Stuttgart 21 (henceforth S21),[2] a public arbitration process in the German city of Stuttgart, where a new railway and urban development plan caused a massive public conflict in 2010. The transcribed minutes consist of nine days of sessions, each lasting about seven hours with more than 70 participants. In total, the transcripts contain around 265,000 tokens in about 6,300 speaker turns. The aim of the use case is to show that the different speaker parties exhibit different discourse patterns, in particular regarding their argumentative patterns, their patterns regarding information giving and refusing and patterns of who leads or hinders the discourse.

The first entry point to the analysis of the S21 arbitration is through the analysis of the typical speaker patterns using the *Speaker Profiles*, as shown in Figure 7. This view gives a short biography for each speaker

[2]Until October 2014 the transcripts were publicly available for download at http://stuttgart21.wikiwam.de/Schlichtungsprotokolle. A new, edited version of the minutes can be found here: `http://www.schlichtung-s21.de/dokumente.html`.

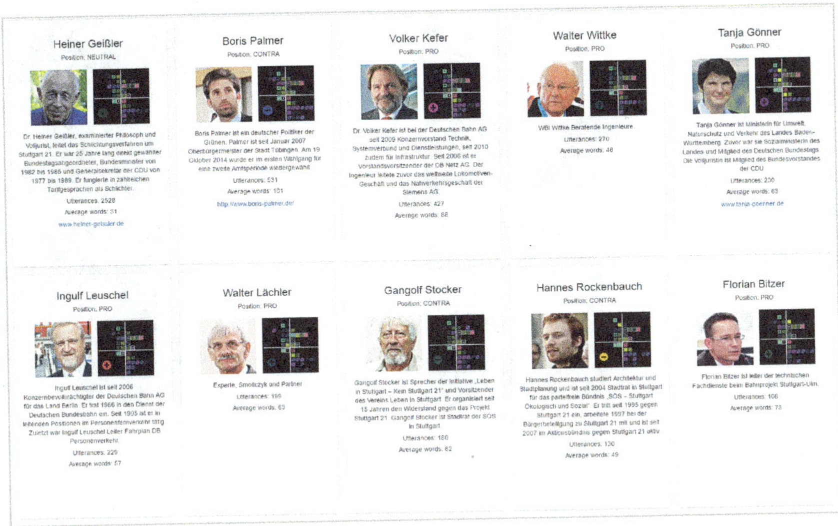

FIGURE 7 S21 *Speaker Profiles* of the speakers with the most turns.

and displays a Discourse Map of their aggregated turns, as a summary to their contributions to the discourse. It also shows the party they belong to, i.e., the group to which their turns will be grouped in further aggregation steps.

There are four speaker parties in the S21 arbitration: the mediator Heiner Geißler (NEUTRAL), the proponents of the S21 project (PRO), the project opponents (CONTRA), and an independent group of experts (EXPERT). In order to allow the comparison of different speaker parties, we aggregate the Discourse Maps of all speakers based on their party affiliation, i.e., the more than 6,300 individual Discourse Maps (one for each speaker turn) are aggregated to only four Discourse Maps (see Figure 8). For comparing features in the discourse, individual glyphs in the Discourse Map are selected.

We first investigate the argumentative structure of the different parties, which we assume to consist of the speaker party's usage of causal, contrastive, conditional and concessive discourse structures across the debate (positions of the individual feature in the Discourse Maps in Figure 8: lower right quadrant: premises (1,-2), conclusions (2,-2); upper left quadrant: consequence (-1,1), condition (-2,1), opposition (-1,2), concession (-4,4). All features are numerical, i.e., the feature-glyphs in the Discourse Map encode the frequency with which argumentative structures occur: The more frequent they occur, the brighter the glyph (for the color mapping see Figure 5).

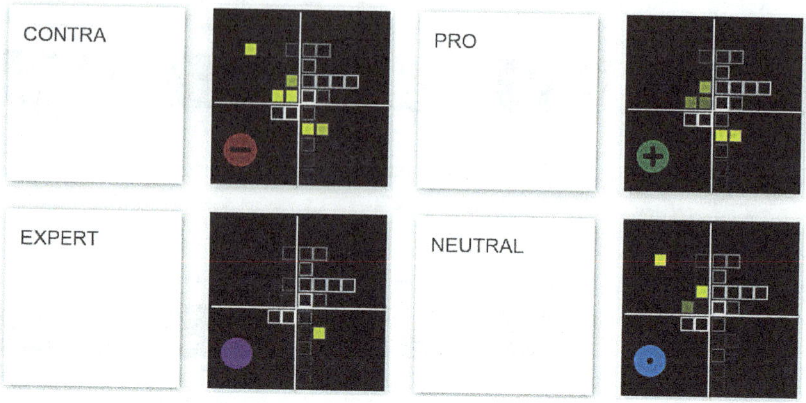

FIGURE 8 Argumentative patterns in S21.

Figure 8 shows that the patterns differ substantially: While the project proponents (PRO) and the project opponents (CONTRA) generally have a high frequency of premises and conclusions (brightness of (1,-2) and (2,-2), respectively), the experts (EXPERT) only employ conclusions (2,-2), the mediator (NEUTRAL) uses none of those patterns. However, he has the highest frequency of oppositions (brightest feature glyph in (-1,2) across the four speaker parties) and concessions in comparable frequency to the opposition (brightness of (-4,4)). Investigating the data more closely, it becomes clear that the mediator tries to come to a conclusion regarding individual points in the debate by either opposing information of individual speakers or conceding to them.

Another important aspect in the context of the S21 arbitration is the degree to which the speaker parties negotiate and accommodate. For the analysis we take into account four features, shown in Figure 9: consensus (-1,3), agreement (-2,3), the negotiation relation (-1,5), and the negotiation count (-2,5). The brighter the glyphs for consensus and the negotiation relation, the more frequent lexical items indicate consensus and negotiation. For instance, the opponents of S21 (CONTRA) have a high frequency of consensus-indicating lexical items and a comparatively lower frequency of negotiation-indicating items. The experts show neither, the proponents only show patterns of negotiation and the mediator shows a low frequency for both consensus and negotiation.

Agreement and the negotiation are bipolar: The redder the glyph, the stronger disagreement and counter-negotiation, the greener the glyph, the stronger agreement and negotiation. The combination of numerical

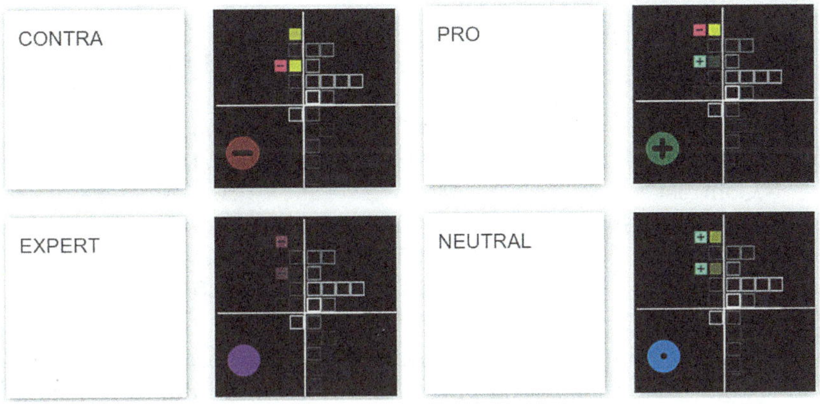

FIGURE 9 Negotiation and accommodation in S21.

and bipolar features allows us to interpret the patterns for the four speaker parties: Whereas the mediator has a high degree of negotiation and accommodation moves, the experts exhibit a comparatively low degree, as is to be expected from their role in the discourse.

6.7 Evaluation

The evaluation is intended to verify that Discourse Maps are a viable means to interpret patterns in large amounts of debate data. To that end we conducted a user study, where we presented the users with different Discourse Maps and a scale as to possible interpretations (e.g. 'Given this Map, rate the following speakers regarding their degree of reason-giving', with '1' for the strongest manifestation of feature X, and '4' for the weakest). The six study participants were Master and PhD students in linguistics or computational linguistics and they each encoded six features for four speakers, resulting in 144 measurements. In the first evaluation, we calculate the deviation from a gold standard rating of a domain expert. Table 5 shows that the average of the participants deviated by 0.041 points in their measurement from the gold standard with a standard deviation of 0.544 points.

In addition to this quantitative feedback, we collected qualitative feedback through semi-structured interviews and expert testimonies. These showed a consensus that although the design of the Discourse Maps visualization is fairly complex, it enables the answering of challenging research questions and the investigation of complex phenomena and hypotheses. Hence, with Discourse Maps we created a specialized expert tool that is tailored to deliberation analysis. Through the strict

TABLE 5 Summary result of the user study for the six measures.

	Average Error	Standard Deviation
Reason	-0.083	0.408
Conclusion	0.000	0.510
Concession	0.208	0.414
Contrast	0.000	0.978
Common Ground	0.000	0.510
Consensus Willing	0.125	0.448
Average	**0.041**	**0.544**

integration of the theoretical dimensions and hierarchy, the experts stated that this visualization became a sort of "brain dump" — reducing the cognitive load of remembering feature relationships and focusing their analysis on the interesting patterns.

Overall, the process of designing such an approach has taught us that the trade-off between the simplicity of the design and the expressiveness of the visualization does not always have to go towards simplicity, especially for tools intended to analyze complex phenomena and targeting expert analysts. Throughout the design process, we were confronted with the feedback that: showing more details in the visualization is desirable, even if that would require certain training in reading the visual encoding. We refer to this as training experts to become literate in reading patterns from the Discourse Maps.

6.8 Discussion and Conclusion

To conclude this paper, we discuss the lessons learned from our collaboration, as well as the limitations of our approach. Lastly, we provide a brief summary and point to future work.

6.8.1 Lessons Learned

Through our iterative design process, as well as the tight collaboration with domain experts, we have learned multiple lessons that are of general interest beyond our concrete use case. The first and most important thing we realized through this process is that a targeted analysis of the users' domain understanding might lead to complex visual encoding to become expressive enough for the problem at hand. According to the user feedback we received, the design of the Discourse Maps had to be tightly aligned to their mental models of the analyzed subject matter, taking into account that the resulting complexity of the visualization will require a training phase and memorization during analysis.

However, through the consistency in the representation on different text-granularity levels, Discourse Maps allowed users to compare single utterances with aggregates based on topics, speakers, etc. This enabled every Discourse Map to serve as a fingerprint of the underlying data. While the dynamic layout generation allows the creation of adaptable Discourse Maps depending on the corpus characteristics, the internal layout of a map is stable for a given corpus to avoid confusion and enable analysts to memorize layouts corresponding to their data.

Lastly, a notable thing to highlight that was useful for designing such an information-dense visual representation is the two-level visual encoding of the data. As described in the paper, we can regard the feature-glyphs as multi-dimensional glyphs ordered in the grid of a Discourse Map. However, the Discourse Maps themselves could also be seen as glyphs, ordered in the grid of the overall layout-canvas as small-multiples. This allows for a data analysis and comparison on two levels of detail and, thus, has been praised by our domain experts as a useful "*overview first, details-on-demand*" technique.

6.8.2 Limitations

As highlighted in Section 6.5.1, this work was a constantly evolving endeavor to search for a suitable visual design, while ensuring an effective visual mapping for the domain problem complexity. We thus considered the most important attributes (i.e., data structure and feature values) to be mapped to the central visual attributes, while taking into account that less important attributes (e.g., size of the underlying text) are mapped to peripheral visual attributes with limited comparability ranges. Such trade-offs were at the heart of every design iterations and are subject to future work.

In particular, limitations include the high visual complexity (remedied by the double encoding of the feature-glyphs, as well as the interactivity, e.g., the ability to enlarge glyphs for a focused analysis); the potentially low visual dynamic range of color mapping (remedied by interactive mouse-over text-popups with the exact feature values, as well as the relative normalization of all color ranges for each feature; and the arrangement of objects to make use of the visual proximity to enhance comparison.

6.8.3 Summary and Future Work

We have presented Discourse Maps, a Visual Analytics approach to analyze conversation dynamics based on the theory of deliberative communication. Our approach is molded to a hierarchical frame of dimensions, subdimensions, and measures determined with respect to a framework informed by questions coming from political science. Discourse Maps are designed in conformity with the guidelines for glyph-based visualizations and enable an interactive, explorative analysis process that can be utilized to form new data-driven hypotheses and verify them. We have showcased the usefulness of our technique via a use case from the S21 arbitration and evaluated the overall approach with quantitative and qualitative studies.

References

Asher, Nick and Alex Lascarides. 2003. *Logics of Conversation*. Cambridge: Cambridge University Press.

Bergstrom, Tony and Karrie Karahalios. 2009. Conversation clusters: grouping conversation topics through human-computer dialog. In *Proceedings of the SIGCHI Conference on Human Factors in Computing Systems*, pages 2349–2352.

Bögel, Tina, Annette Hautli-Janisz, Sebastian Sulger, and Miriam Butt. 2014. Automatic detection of causal relations in german multilogs. In *Proceedings of the EACL 2014 Workshop on Computational Approaches to Causality in Language*, pages 20–27.

Borgo, Rita, Johannes Kehrer, David H. Chung, Eamonn Maguire, Robert S. Laramee, Helwig Hauser, Matthew Ward, and Min Chen. 2013. Glyph-based visualization: Foundations, design guidelines, techniques and applications. In M. Sbert and L. Szirmay-Kalos, eds., *Eurographics 2013 – State of the Art Reports*, pages 39–63.

Bunt, Harry, Jan Alexandersson, Jean Carletta, Jae-Woong Choe, Alex Chengyu Fang, Koiti Hasida, Kiyong Lee, Volha Petukhova, Andrei Popescu-Belis, Laurent Romary, Claudia Soria, and David Traum. 2010. Towards an ISO standard for dialogue act annotation. In *Proceedings of the Seventh International Conference on Language Resources and Evaluation*, pages 2548–2555.

Ceriani, Lidia and Paolo Verme. 2012. The origins of the Gini index: Extracts from *Variabilità e Mutabilità* (1912) by Corrado Gini. *The Journal of Economic Inequality* 10(3):421–443.

Danescu-Niculescu-Mizil, Cristian, Moritz Sudhof, Dan Jurafsky, Jure Leskovec, and Christopher Potts. 2013. A computational approach to politeness with application to social factors. In *Proceedings of the 51st Annual Meeting of the Association for Computational Linguistics*, pages 250–259.

Donath, Judith and Fernanda B. Viégas. 2002. The chat circles series: explorations in designing abstract graphical communication interfaces. In *Proceedings of the 4th Conference on Designing Interactive Systems: Processes, Practices, Methods, and Techniques*, pages 359–369.

El-Assady, Mennatallah, Valentin Gold, Carmela Acevedo, Christopher Collins, and Daniel Keim. 2016. ConToVi: Multi-party conversation exploration using topic-space views. *Computer Graphics Forum* 35(3):431–440.

El-Assady, Mennatallah, Annette Hautli-Janisz, Valentin Gold, Miriam Butt, Katharina Holzinger, and Daniel A. Keim. 2017a. Interactive visual analysis of transcribed multi-party discourse. In *Proceedings of the 55th Annual Meeting of the Association for Computational Linguistics: System Demonstrations*, pages 49–54.

El-Assady, Mennatallah, Rita Sevastjanova, Bela Gipp, Daniel Keim, and Christopher Collins. 2017b. NEREx: Named-entity relationship exploration in multi-party conversations. *Computer Graphics Forum* 36(3):213–225.

El-Assady, Mennatallah, Rita Sevastjanova, Daniel Keim, and Christopher Collins. 2018a. ThreadReconstructor: Modeling reply-chains to untangle conversational text through visual analytics. *Computer Graphics Forum* 37(3):351–365.

El-Assady, Mennatallah, Rita Sevastjanova, Fabian Sperrle, Daniel A. Keim, and Christopher Collins. 2018b. Progressive learning of topic modeling parameters: A visual analytics framework. *IEEE Transactions on Visualization and Computer Graphics* 24(1):382–391.

El-Assady, Mennatallah, Fabian Sperrle, Oliver Deussen, Daniel A. Keim, and Christopher Collins. 2018c. Visual analytics for topic model optimization based on user-steerable speculative execution. *IEEE Transactions on Visualization and Computer Graphics* 25(1):374–384.

Fishkin, James S. and Robert C. Luskin. 2005. Experimenting with a democratic ideal: Deliberative polling and public opinion. *Acta Politica* 40:284–298.

Fuchs, Johannes, Petra Isenberg, Anastasia Bezerianos, and Daniel A. Keim. 2017. A systematic review of experimental studies on data glyphs. *IEEE Transactions on Visualization and Computer Graphics* 23(7):1863–1879.

Gerhards, Jürgen. 1997. Diskursive versus liberale Öffentlichkeit. Eine empirische Auseinandersetzung mit Jürgen Habermas. *Kölner Zeitschrift für Soziologie und Sozialpsychologie* 49:1–47.

Gold, Valentin, Annette Hautli-Janisz, Katharina Holzinger, and Mennatallah El-Assady. 2016. VisArgue: Analysis and visualization of deliberative political communication. *Political Communication Report* 26(1–2).

Gold, Valentin and Katharina Holzinger. 2015. An automated text-analysis approach to measuring deliberative quality. Paper presented at the 73th Annual Meeting of the Midwest Political Science Association, San Francisco.

Gold, Valentin, Christian Rohrdantz, and Mennatallah El-Assady. 2015. Exploratory text analysis using lexical episode plots. In E. Bertini, J. Kennedy, and E. Puppo, eds., *Eurographics Conference on Visualization: Short Papers*, pages 85–90.

Hautli-Janisz, Annette and Miriam Butt. 2016. On the role of discourse particles for mining arguments in German dialogs. In *Proceedings of the COMMA 2016 FLA workshop*, pages 10–17.

Hoque, Enamul and Giuseppe Carenini. 2016. MultiConVis: A visual text analytics system for exploring a collection of online conversations. In *Proceedings of Intelligent User Interfaces*, pages 96–107.

Jekat, Susanne, Alexandra Klein, Elisabeth Maier, Ilona Maleck, Marion Mast, and J. Joachim Quantz. 1995. Dialgue acts in verbmobil. Tech. rep., Saarländische Universitäts- und Landesbibliothek.

Jentner, Wolfgang, Mennatallah El-Assady, Bela Gipp, and Daniel A. Keim. 2017. Feature alignment for the analysis of verbatim text transcripts. In *Proceedings of the EuroVis Workshop on Visual Analytics*, pages 13–17.

Keim, Daniel A. and Daniela Oelke. 2007. Literature fingerprinting: A new method for visual literary analysis. In *Proceedings of the IEEE Symposium on Visual Analytics Science and Technology*, pages 115–122.

Klein, Dan and Christopher D. Manning. 2003. Accurate unlexicalized parsing. In *Proceedings of the 41st Annual Meeting on Association for Computational Linguistics - Volume 1*, pages 423–430.

Landwehr, Katharina and Katharina Holzinger. 2010. Institutional determinants of deliberative interaction. *European Political Science Review* 2:373–400.

Lassiter, Daniel. 2010. Gradable epistemic modals, probability, and scale structure. *Semantics and Linguistic Theory* 20:197–215.

Leshed, Gilly, Diego Perez, Jeffrey T. Hancock, Dan Cosley, Jeremy Birnholtz, Soyoung Lee, Poppy L. McLeod, and Geri Gay. 2009. Visualizing real-time language-based feedback on teamwork behavior in computer-mediated groups. In *Proceedings of the SIGCHI Conference on Human Factors in Computing Systems*, pages 537–546.

Lin, Ziheng, Hwee Tou Ng, and Min-Yen Kan. 2014. A PDTB-styled end-to-end discourse parser. *Natural Language Engineering* 20:151–184.

Mairesse, Francois, Marilyn A. Walker, Matthias R. Mehl, and Roger K. Moore. 2007. Using linguistic cues for the automatic recognition of personality in conversation and text. *Journal of Artificial Intelligence Research* 30:457–500.

Mann, William C. and Sandra A. Thompson. 1988. Rhetorical structure theory: Toward a theory of text organization. *Text* 8(3):243–281.

Marcu, Daniel. 2000. *The Theory and Practice of Discourse Parsing and Summarization*. Cambridge, MA: MIT Press.

McCarthy, Philip M. and Scott Jarvis. 2007. vocd: A theoretical and empirical evaluation. *Language Testing* 24(4):459–488.

Mittelstädt, Sebastian, Dominik Jäckle, Florian Stoffel, and Daniel A. Keim. 2015. ColorCAT: Guided Design of Colormaps for Combined Analysis Tasks. In E. Bertini, J. Kennedy, and E. Puppo, eds., *Eurographics Conference on Visualization: Short Papers*, pages 115–119.

Mittelstädt, Sebastian, Andreas Stoffel, and Daniel A. Keim. 2014. Methods for compensating contrast effects in information visualization. *Computer Graphics Forum* 33(3):231–240.

Mohammad, Saif M. and Peter D. Turney. 2010. Emotions evoked by common words and phrases: Using mechanical turk to create and emotion lexicon. In *Proceedings of the NAACL 2015 Workshop on Computational Approaches to Analysis and Generation of Emotion in Text*, pages 26–34.

Polanyi, Livia, Chris Culy, Martin van den Berg, Gian Lorenzo Thione, and David Ahn. 2004. Sentential structure and discourse parsing. In *Proceedings of the 2004 ACL Workshop on Discourse Annotation*, pages 80–87.

Prasad, Rashmi, Nikhil Dinesh, Alan Lee, Eleni Miltsakaki, Livio Robaldo, Aravind Joshi, and Bonnie Webber. 2008. The Penn Discourse Treebank 2.0. In *Proceedings of the Sixth International Conference on Language Resources and Evaluation 2008*, pages 2961–2968.

Rafferty, Anne N. and Christopher D. Manning. 2008. Parsing three German treebanks: Lexicalized and unlexicalized baselines. In *Proceedings of the ACL 2008 Workshop on Parsing German*, pages 40–46.

Schiller, Anne. 1994. Dmor - user's guide. Tech. rep., Universität Stuttgart, Institut für maschinelle Sprachverarbeitung.

Shahaf, Dafna, Carlos Guestrin, and Eric Horvitz. 2012. Trains of thought: Generating information maps. In *Proceedings of the 21st International Conference on World Wide Web*, pages 899–908.

Sridhar, Dhanya, James Foulds, Marilyn Walker, Bert Huang, and Lise Getoor. 2015. Joint models of disagreement and stance in online debate. In *In Proceedings of the 53rd Annual Meeting of the Association for Computational Linguistics and the 7th International Joint Conference on Natural Language Processing*, pages 116–125.

Stalnaker, Robert. 2002. Common Ground. *Linguistics and Philosophy* 25(5-6):701–721.

Stede, Manfred and Arne Neumann. 2014. Potsdam commentary corpus 2.0: Annotation for discourse research. In *Proceedings of the Ninth International Conference on Language Resources and Evaluation 2014*, pages 925–929.

Versley, Yannick and Anna Gastel. 2013. Linguistic tests for discourse relations in the Tüba-D/Z corpus of written German. *Dialogue and Discourse* 4(2):142–173.

Zarisheva, Elina and Tatjana Scheffler. 2015. Dialogue act annotation for twitter data. In *Proceedings of the SIGDIAL 2015 Conference*, pages 114–123.

Zimmermann, Malte. 2011. Discourse Particles. In P. Portner, C. Maienborn, and K. von Heusinger, eds., *Semantics (Handbücher zur Sprach- und Kommunikationswissenschaft)*, pages 2011–2038. Mouton de Gruyter.

7

Reflected Text Analytics through Interactive Visualization

André Blessing, Markus John, Steffen Koch, Thomas Ertl and Jonas Kuhn

7.1 Abstract

This chapter makes a contribution to an ongoing methodological discussion in the interdisciplinary field of digital humanities. How can techniques from Natural Language Processing (NLP) and Visual Analytics be best exploited to help address research questions from fields like literary studies or history about available text collections? This setup is different from the typical web-scale text mining scenario: (i) The target text corpus tends to be comparatively small and heterogeneous, and often the language and domain characteristics are very different from the development data of standard NLP tools. (ii) The humanities disciplines often take a hermeneutic approach. This means that no concrete analytical target for a given corpus study is specified upfront; projects rather follow an extended process of exploration and refinement of the analytical categories ultimately applied. For both aspects it is important that the expert scholars are in a position to critically examine the tool components and their interplay. The methodological frameworks of NLP and Visual Analytics contain building blocks that can support such a reflected analytical approach very well. However, based on the authors' experience from various digital humanities collaborations, it seems that transparency and flexibility in the applied tool architecture is even more important than in other application contexts.

Visual Analytics for Linguistics (LingVis).
edited by Miriam Butt, Annette Hautli-Janisz and Verena Lyding.
Copyright © 2020, CSLI Publications.

A continuous and open-minded exchange among the collaboration partners is of crucial importance. This chapter discusses these observations in a programmatic way and presents concrete examples of tool combinations from NLP and Visual Analytics that have been beneficial for various digital humanities projects. Emphasis is on questions of cross-disciplinary methodology rather than on technical results within the fields of NLP or Visual Analytics.

7.2 Overview

Advances in the robust modeling of linguistic analysis tasks over the past years and the availability of open access tools have made it possible for non-specialists in NLP to run state-of-the-art models from computational linguistics on their own textual data. Moreover, infrastructural efforts in providing tool components as interoperable webservices (Hinrichs et al. 2010, Bukhari et al. 2013) make it possible to apply complex text analytical processing pipelines assembled from tool components of diverse origin on corpus material from arbitrary sources. Content aspects of larger text collections can thus be aggregated, abstracted, and visualized for systematic exploration, and computational text analysis provides the basis for quantitative corpus studies (Liu et al. 2014, Kim et al. 2017).

However, any combination of text-analytical modules is affected by intricate interaction effects, in particular when they are applied to texts that deviate from the development corpus in any of a number of relevant dimensions (genre, content domain, register, language stage, etc.). Much of the analytical potential lying in the application of available tools cannot be realized without target-specific evaluation, adaptation, and various procedures of meta-analysis. In this chapter, we put a major focus on these steps that recur at various points in the application of complex corpus-analytical pipelines. We discuss visual support for interactive annotation of task-specific data (a key step in transparent and effective tool adaptation) and re-training of models, visualization of inter-annotator agreement, aggregation of results from complex analytical pipelines along different views, and ways of visualizing uncertainty in system predictions. We exemplify our discussions with experiences from text-analytical experiments from several real projects pursuing distinct higher-level objectives.

The rest of the chapter is structured as follows: Section 7.3 discusses adaptable models and the challenges of "not-so-big data". In Section 7.4, we focus on the benefits of combining insights from interactive visualization and computational linguistics research. This is followed by examples that support a reflected interactive text analysis in interdisciplinary collaborations in Section 7.5. A higher-level methodological discussion concludes this chapter in Section 7.6.

7.3 Adaptable Models Supporting Text Interpretation: The Challenges of "Not-so-Big Data"

With the advent of the Information Age, new technologies have gained importance: technologies for collecting, curating and sharing information sources, for preserving, indexing and enhancing them, and for exploring, aggregating, and analyzing the information they carry. This affects not only data collections in the business world, but also throughout academia and in most parts of public life. From the point of view of the emerging field of "Data Science", information comes in different forms: curated structured sources — ranging from official census data to Open Linked Data contributed by user communities (Bizer et al. 2011), numerical data from measurements, such as weather or simulations data (Bruhn et al. 1980), or unstructured data such as images, videos, or documents written in natural language (Kurzhals et al. 2016). Interactive visualization[1] addresses models and methods for supporting human analysts, curators, etc. in the various processes dealing with — often vast amounts of — information.

In the standard "Big Data" view, NLP comes into play (i) as a set of back-end tools for capturing a widespread type of unstructured data and integrating the information it contains with other sources, and (ii) to provide natural language interfaces as a very intuitive front end for information collections. At both ends, NLP techniques are used successfully in today's technologies, ranging from indexing and querying in document retrieval over machine translation to spoken language interfaces. The quality of results as well as the breadth of tasks to which such approaches can be successfully applied has been increasing continuously over the past years. This is in part an effect of the enormous amounts of data available for training effective machine learning approaches, but an important factor is also that providing high quality solutions and continuous improvement is closely tied to the large web companies' business models, so there have been and continue to be considerable investments into research and development.

There are numerous points where specific characteristics of natural language as a means for conveying information might call for interac-

[1]With the term "(interactive) visualization", we refer to visualization as it is defined and used in the research fields of Information Visualization (InfoVis; Card et al. 1999) and Visual Analytics (VA; Keim et al. 2010, Kielman et al. 2009).

tive visualization solutions, e.g., because of intricate interaction effects across model components. It is therefore no surprise that research for text visualization and interactive analysis of text-based information has seen considerable growth during the last years in the visualization community.[2] However, the current standard scenario in web analytics is still to keep the sophisticated analysis pipelines behind the scenes for the user. Preprocessing and intermediate steps such as lemmatization, part-of-speech tagging and parsing are hidden black box components.

This, of course, has the advantage of hiding unnecessary complexities from the analyst, and it is clearly justified in scenarios where the same information is redundantly available from multiple sources. But it reaches its limitations when internals of the black box architecture may be of relevance to the user. This is for instance the case in specialized fields, where the amount of available data for developing reliable models is insufficient, so users have to use approximative modeling solutions.[3] The abundance of web data reflecting mainstream user tasks has made it possible to reach surprising levels of quality even for tasks that were for a long time considered very hard, such as contextually aware Machine Translation in standard domains (Koehn 2009).

But for task variants deviating from the standard, the quality of the available models may degrade considerably. Especially when only relatively small amounts of in-domain data are available, a more interactive approach has a natural place: the underlying model classes need to be adapted, configured, parameterized, or (re-)trained to reach a more adequate behavior (see Sections 7.5.1, 7.5.2 and 7.5.3). Black box approaches are a suboptimal choice in such scenarios, as users provided with more transparent solutions will be able to contribute to improved quality of analysis (Cortez and Embrechts 2013). Interactive visual solutions, synchronized with adaptive modeling architectures, are one way to achieve this transparency (Sacha et al. 2016).

Effective tool support for manual annotation or labeling tasks is of key importance in the digital humanities context (see Section 7.5.4). This is not only so because the best way to evaluate the quality of automatic system components is by comparison against reference data labeled manually by experts. When the target corpus is relatively small or the text sources are not supported by common NLP tools, it is often a

[2] Kucher and Kerren (2015) offer a comprehensive survey on visualization approaches for text visualization (`http://textvis.lnu.se/`).

[3] Another reason for advocating transparency, which we do not address here, is given when the redundant sources of information are not equivalent, but go along with different framings or biases. In this situation, it would be in the interest of the user to make an informed decision about the selection among the sources.

viable option to rely on manual annotation for the central text analysis in a project. Moreover, annotations can of course be used to train or adapt machine learning mechanisms which are commonly employed as part of linguistic (pre-)processing steps. Interactive visualization can support users in the navigation and post-correction of automatic and mixed system output (see Sections 7.5.3 and 7.5.5).

In providing more transparent access to the workings of NLP components, a level of detail has to be chosen that is presented to the user; providing too many tool-specific internals may confuse the user, but potential sources of downstream errors in an analysis pipeline should ideally be accessible (Sacha et al. 2016). The choice of detail is not only influenced by the employed techniques, but also by the level of knowledge and experience of intended user groups. In addition, aspects indicating the quality of results need to be visualized adequately and instantaneously to help users in diminishing issues iteratively on the one hand and to ensure low turnaround times of such iterative assess-and-adapt approaches on the other hand (see Section 7.5.5). This is for example possible by showing uncertainty or confidence information if it is inherently available from automatic methods or if it can be derived in other ways (John et al. 2016).

7.4 Combining Insights from Interactive Visualization Research and Computational Linguistics

There are two "zones" in which the confluence of insights from interactive visualization research and (computational) linguistics can be expected to be particularly fruitful. One can be characterized by the optimistic long-term vision of providing systematic interactive access to the information content conveyed in larger text collections — providing a traceable, scalable characterization of the relevant content of a selected text passage or a collection of related passages. Important intermediate steps towards this vision are aggregation and browsing facilities for linguistic annotations of the text — at a lexical, structural, and semantic level that may be the result of applying a computational model automatically, or possibly an interactive procedure (Mehta et al. 2017, Collins et al. 2007). Many of the contributions in this volume can be viewed as steps on the way towards this goal. (Of course, one need not adhere to the vision of accurate scalable content-based text aggregation, but can view the visualization of text(s) at particular levels of linguistic characterization as a goal in itself.)

The other "zone" of fruitful confluence may seem less obvious at first glance, but it is this zone where, as we will argue, our contribution is mainly headed: one may characterize it by a more skeptical position towards the possibility of providing a single accurate characterization of some text passage's relevant content — even under the hypothetical assumption of perfect analysis components. For instance, in literary studies it is broadly assumed that it is inherent to literary texts that they are "polyvalent", i.e., they bear multiple meanings.[4]

In this zone of methodological challenges, combining interactive visualization research and insights from computational linguistics opens up ways of reflecting on the reliability of a chain of (imperfect) analysis steps within a complex space of approaches towards some higher-level research goals. By applying a certain degree of skeptical scrutiny to all premises that a text analyst takes into account when he or she draws a certain interpretive conclusion, the analyst can reach a more differentiated level of knowledge. Many text-analytical scenarios with long-standing traditions have taken similar approaches when studying mixed collections of textual sources in which neither the reliability of the sources themselves nor of the methods for accessing their information content is fully known upfront: the analysis of a text (source) and a text collection in critical journalism, historiography scholarship or literary studies in the hermeneutic tradition (among others) generally takes a source-critical and method-critical approach: before relying on the implications that a certain text analysis suggests, the journalist or scholar will convince herself — using independent information — that the implications are neither methodological artifacts nor the effect of a problematic source situation. In many cases, it is considered good critical practice to never fully trust an established argumentation for a certain thesis, but keep reflecting on its justification as new theoretical insights, empirical indications, etc., arise.

It is not an easy transition to integrate scalable computational models into the traditional critical/hermeneutic analysis practice, among other things because of the considerable differences in the scholarly cultures and methodological traditions coming together (El-Assady et al. 2016, Hinrichs et al. 2017). Yet we are convinced — and collaborations with scholars from various disciplines show — that the most appropriate way is not to hide all complexities of the modeling approach from the scholars who are to integrate the analysis results in their reasoning. Ideally, the analysis approaches should explicitly take advantage of tentative generalizations across fields of specialization, providing a prototype mode of analysis — marked as such, i.e., not pretending to

[4]Fundamental differences in the research culture in computational linguistics and literary studies are for instance discussed in Hammond et al. (2013).

reach optimal quality. This prototype mode can be the basis of data exploration and critical assessment of limitations, and subsequently the starting point for model adaptation. An effective integration of an imperfect computational model in the justification of a higher-level argument will typically use it as one out of several indications, ideally using independent sources and methods (ultimately, *any* methodology has to be reflected with a degree of skepticism).

In the "not-so-big data" scenario, the analysts are usually advanced specialists in the higher-level questions pursued by the textual analysis, while they are not familiar with technical details of the computational modeling approaches. Hence, the effectiveness of the interactive approach will depend crucially on how well the architecture is designed to draw the specialists' attention to content-related issues that make a difference in the modeling. This is not entirely different from the situation of designing expert-oriented information visualization in other fields of application, but the considerable divergence across a high number of levels of description does certainly make it a challenge that requires careful interdisciplinary coordination.

7.5 Examples of Reflected Interactive Text Analysis in Interdisciplinary Collaborations

In this section, we discuss a number of examples mainly from collaborative projects in the field of digital humanities that the authors have been involved in. The examples illustrate what shape this challenge can take and indicate what solutions may look like that combine interactive visualization and insights from computational linguistics. We believe that it is too early to attempt an exhaustive systematic overview of the problem types for interactive model adaptation (and appropriate solutions) — not least because mostly, a multitude of rather project-specific factors play a role and there is rarely a single point that is the key to an effective overall solution. It can thus be expected that over time, best practices for dealing with certain batches of problems will develop, and hopefully, our discussion in this chapter will provide some input to this development. Rather importantly, we are not aiming at a streamlined optimization workflow for NLP and Visual Analytics tools in general, but the special scenario type of adapting and reflecting tools in the critical/hermeneutic text analysis practice.

7.5.1 Adapting Processing Pipelines to Special Text Collections

As our first example, we discuss adaptable relation/event extraction from a text collection. For text-analytical research that does not regard the linguistic structure itself as the object of study, a typical building block for higher-level analyses lies in the extraction of textual assertions of some predicate or relation (or a reported event). Based on the assertion, one can extract a fact about one or more real-world entities, which are being referred to by names or other referential expressions. A standard example are news reports on appointments in the business news (*Sandy Smith follows Kim Keller as CEO of Marshmallow Inc.*). With an extraction tool that is (i) able to detect alternative lexical expressions of the relevant semantic relation or event type (*hire as*, *appoint for the position of*), and (ii) will take syntactic alternations in argument structure into account (e.g., passive voice: *was hired as*), a systematic study of frequently reported events can be supported with a scalable automatic corpus analysis.

To achieve robust extraction results, the relation extraction is best based on a pipeline of linguistic standard processing steps, such as sentence splitting/tokenization, part-of-speech tagging, named entity extraction, and syntactic parsing (plus, possibly, co-reference resolution). Syntactic parsing will for instance form the basis of mapping arguments in active vs. passive voice realizations. Typically, the processing pipeline has to be adjusted to specifics of the corpus data under consideration. Interactive visual orchestration tools such as WebLicht (Hinrichs et al. 2010, Mahlow et al. 2014) support the flexible setup and application of such a pipeline by non-NLP experts. Extraction studies of limited scope (or studies staying at the level of syntactic structure) can thus be performed by straightforward application of available web services. A subtle methodological issue lies in the question of how well suited the standard pipeline components, which are typically trained on newswire data, are for the content domain, text genre and language stage of the application corpus.[5]

What we address in this subsection are analytical processing pipelines that add a content-oriented analysis step to the conventional NLP chain to satisfy study-specific analytical needs. This is particularly interesting under a methodological angle, trying to establish practices for using flexible, but critically reflected computational devices in the context of text-oriented studies in the humanities.

With supervised machine learning building on the output of the prior processing steps, it is not hard technically to obtain a relatively robust relation extraction component that can be (re-)trained according to

[5]When the tools are used for more than exploratory purposes, the prediction quality on the application data should be evaluated against a sample of independently hand-annotated test data. We will come back to the annotation process in Section 7.5.4.

the analytical needs. A tool of this kind, adapted to the extraction of emigration events from large biographical text collections, is behind the web application "Textual Emigration Analysis" (TEA).[6] The TEA platform was developed in the context of the CLARIN-D[7] project as a showcase of tool interaction and demonstrates ways of aggregating information from the extracted event descriptions and visualizing them under a systematic view that does not follow the original textual presentation of the information (for the extracted emigration events, the countries of origin and destination are used to aggregate information and visualize it on an interactive world map).[8]

The original textual basis for the TEA platform was the collection of all biographical articles in the German Wikipedia. We chose the description of a person emigrating or relocating to a different country as the showcase type of biographical event for this platform, as it is (i) of interest for a variety of broader analytical studies, (ii) occurs relatively frequently, and (iii) can be geographically visualized in aggregated form.[9] There are quite a few linguistic formulations that can be found:[10]

Textual expressions of emigration events in Wikipedia

(a) sie übersiedelte nach Warschau
'she relocated to Warsaw'

(b) Der Weg in die Emigration [...] führte über die Schweiz und England letztlich in die USA.
'The path to emigration [...] led through Switzerland and England, finally to the USA.'

(c) Später ging sie nach Norwegen, wo sie zu den prominentesten deutschen Emigranten gehörte.

---

[6]The platform is available at `http://clarin01.ims.uni-stuttgart.de/tea/`. Blessing and Kuhn (2014) describes technical and methodological details of the approach; a tutorial for web application can be found in `http://clarin01.ims.uni-stuttgart.de/tutorial/tea.html`.

[7]CLARIN is a long-term European initiative to establish an infrastructure of language tools and resources for the humanities and social sciences; Stuttgart is part of a network of CLARIN-D centers in Germany. Principal Investigator for Stuttgart center: Jonas Kuhn (`http://de.clarin.eu/de/`); CLARIN-D is funded by the German Federal Ministry for Research and Education (BMBF) and the research ministry of the state of Baden-Württemberg.

[8]The remainder of this subsection is in part based on text from a translation of Kuhn and Blessing (2017). Kuhn (2019) provides a more detailed methodological discussion of computational text analysis in a Humanities context.

[9]The showcase visualization was developed independent from Schich et al. (2014).

[10](b): from the German Wikipedia entry for Alfred Hauptmann (1881-1948); (c): German Wikipedia entry for Hanna Sandtner, née Ritter (1900-1958).

> 'Later she went to Norway, where she was among the most prominent German emigrants.'

Figure 1 shows the interactive visualization of aggregated results from extraction of the emigration relation (with the mouse pointer over Austria). Countries that are the origin of a relocation to Austria are light red; destination countries of a relocation from Austria are light blue. A table (at the bottom) shows the absolute numbers and the relative distribution among the source and destination countries and provides hyperlinks pointing to a list of the underlying text snippets that formed the basis of the extraction. The snippets are displayed in a pop-up window (labeled "Emigration Details"), and are again linked to the full text source (i.e., the Wikipedia article itself). The hyperlinking makes it straightforward for users, for example, to reassure themselves that there are no errors in the automatic extraction.

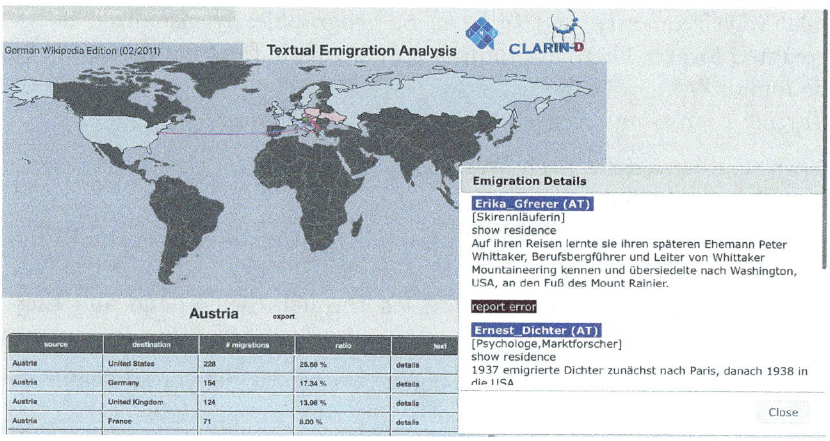

FIGURE 1 Web application "Textual Emigration Analysis": visualization after selecting the Wikipedia-based extraction results for Austria and activating the detailed text instances for migration from Austria to the United States.

It is possible to adapt the system by replacing the emigration relation by some other relation, without having to apply special technical knowledge: the mapping can be retrained by interactively providing some textual examples of the desired relation (for example, the description of the membership of a person in a party or an association). Training is then carried out as a cyclic Active Learning process, as it is known, for example, from the adjustment of email spam filters or trainable face recognition in photo Apps: The interactive system starts

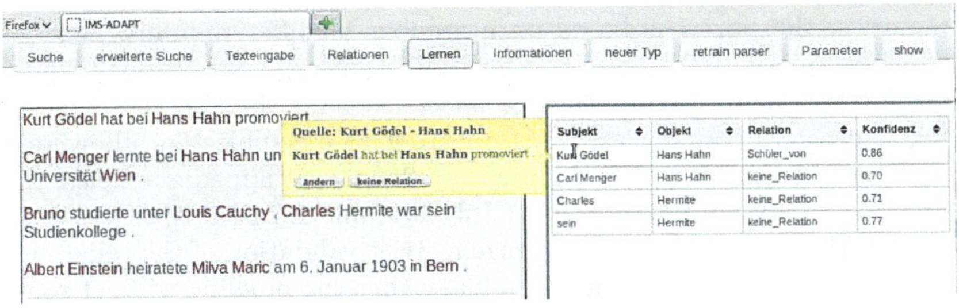

FIGURE 2 Correction step in the interactive (re-)training of a relation classifier for the *(academic) pupil* relation.

out training an initial automatic classifier, which is still very crude; it then applies this classifier to some additional sample texts from a pool of data and displays (a selection) of the predictions to the user, who essentially corrects the system's misclassifications in the result. Figure 2 shows this correction step in the process of training a relation classifier for the *(academic) pupil* relation: based on some initial data, the prelimary predictions (on the right-hand side, shown with confidence scores) are offered for confirmation or rejection. The expanded annotation is then used to train a new generation of the classifier, and the cyclic process is repeated until the automatic analysis results are satisfactory. With this interactive training of the relation extraction, it takes surprisingly little annotation effort to create tools that are at least highly useful for explorative studies.

The TEA web application was originally developed for the collection of all biographical articles in the German Wikipedia. In addition, we collaborated with the Austrian Academy of Sciences to convert the text base of the Austrian Biographical Lexicon (*Österreichisches Biographisches Lexikon*, ÖBL) into a suitable input format. We integrated this collection into the TEA portal as part of an experiment to rapidly transfer the entire analysis pipeline and the aggregation components (Blessing et al. 2015). By comparing the names, dates of birth and death, the person entries from the ÖBL can be heuristically matched against Wikipedia articles (for which in many cases a reference to authority files is available[11]).

Multi-view presentation of analytical results. In the context of the present, largely methodological discussion, we would like to emphasize an aspect of the TEA portal which we believe is typical for the application of relatively complex analysis chains in the digital hu-

[11]Through the Integrated Authority File (*gemeinsame Normdatei*) GND: `http://www.dnb.de/gnd`.

manities: the portal is based on a number of different tools, most of which were originally developed for a different type of text documents; some components were developed specifically for the task at hand using interactive training methods. In order to assemble the full system and make it run robustly on more than 250,000 Wikipedia articles, the interfaces between components apply certain heuristic rules. All this implies that it is difficult to perform a strict validation of the reliability of the full machinery. In fact, it is likely that the pipeline will get some of the less typical cases in the text collection wrong. Yet, the portal presents an invaluable access point for exploring a vast accumulation of information in a systematic way.[12]

What is important for a critically reflected access to the information is that the (limited) reliability of the aggregated information is continuously transparent to the user, that it is straightforward to verify unclear cases, and that erroneous analyses in the data can be immediately reported as they are detected in exploration. To reach these goals, aggregated lists of analysis results or visual aggregations can be linked up with text instances that gave rise to the analysis — a technique which is now commonly applied in transparent tools for text analytics. The presentation of text snippet instances contains a "report error" button, which opens a window with a comment field that users can fill in without losing more than a few seconds during their exploration.

Experience with the TEA showed additional methodological advantages of the aggregation of analytical results along different dimensions: it is particularly beneficial when the ordering principle for the *presentation* of aggregated information is distinct from the principle by which the original text sources were organized. In the case of the emigration relation, it was biographical texts for individual persons that were input to the analysis pipeline; but the visualization of the aggregated results groups the extracted information by countries of origin or destination — a dimension that is neither related to the textual shape of the sources nor the structuring principle of the text collection (person-specific biographies). This has the advantage that systematic errors in the analytical process will not be clustered together in a specific part of the (very large) result space, but they affect results that appear in quite varied places of the presentation — which increases the chance of detecting them. During exploration of the emigration relation ex-

[12]If the process of systematic exploration leads to the insight that a strict quantitative analysis of a detailed question will be beneficial for the high-level question pursued, some additional research and data preprocessing will be required; however, systematically informed exploratory procedures help to support such extra analyses in a very targeted way.

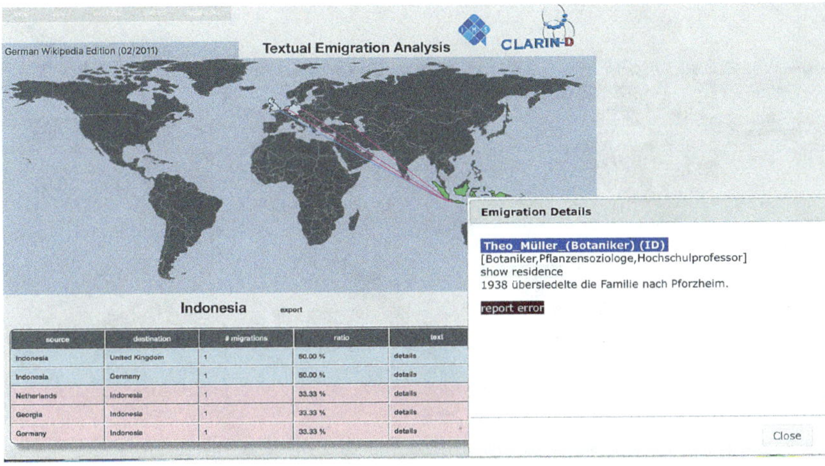

FIGURE 3 TEA portal after selecting Indonesia on the world map and clicking on the table cell for emigration from Indonesia to Germany.

tracted from Wikipedia on the world map, unexpected patterns catch the user's eye. Figure 3 is an example containing a somewhat surprising data point: one may not expect immigration from Indonesia to Germany. By clicking on the table cell, the text snippet for a certain botanist *Theo Müller* is shown, including the sentence "In 1938, the family moved to Pforzheim." One might become skeptical and suspect that the connection with Indonesia is due to some processing error. Following the link to the full Wikipedia entry, it turns out however, that Theo Müller was indeed born in Indonesia and the family moved back to Germany when he was six years old. (Other, similar cases often point to errors in the analysis pipeline.)

The experimental TEA portal includes an additional inspection facility: the text snippet window that pops up when exploring a table cell contains the button "show residences" for each person listed. When the button is clicked, all countries that were detected in the Wikipedia entry for that person are highlighted in the world map (independent of the event that they may be associated with in the biography). This facility is useful to get a quick overview of potential international connections in longer biographical articles; but again, it can be used to detect errors in the text analysis for place and country references (which is based on a number of heuristics to reach a reasonable recall). Figure 4 shows the effect of clicking the "show residences" button for *Theo Müller*, as it appeared in Figure 3. What is very surprising here is the highlighting of the Svalbard archipelago (including Spitzbergen) in the Arctic

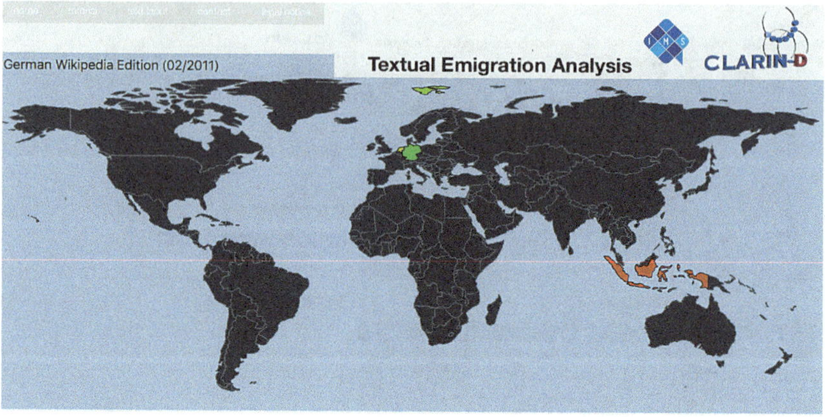

FIGURE 4 TEA portal after selecting all residences for *Theo Müller.*

Ocean — although it could have been a research destination for the botanist. Inspecting the full Wikipedia entry again however, the inclusion of Svalbard turns out to be a system error caused by a heurstic mapping of place names: The botanist Theo Müller authored an article on a nature reserve called "Spitzberg" in Southern Germany,[13] which is incorrectly mapped to "Spitzbergen".

To conclude the observations about the benefit of alternative ordering principles: Multi-view presentation of analytical results is a primary way of inviting the user to adopt a critical position towards the analytical method. (TEA does not aggregate and visualize the temporal dimension of the biographical facts, but this would be an additional view that could be helpful.)

7.5.2 Adaptable Text Categorization on Large Text Collections

As a second example for visual support in interactive text analysis, we present a text filtering/text categorization framework (Blessing et al. 2013) originally devised in the e-Identity project[14] and further developed in the DebateExplorer project.[15] The e-Identity project was a collaboration between computational linguists and political science, which aimed at analyzing a multinational and multilingual corpus of

[13] *Pflanzensoziologische Untersuchungen im Landschaftsschutzgebiet Spitzberg bei Tübingen* [Phytosociological studies in the nature reserve Spitzberg near Tübingen].

[14] Principal Investigators: Cathleen Kantner (lead), Ulrich Heid, Jonas Kuhn, and Manfred Stede (`https://www.sowi.uni-stuttgart.de/abteilungen/ib/forschung/eldentity/`); e-Identity was also funded by the BMBF.

[15] `http://www.debateexplorer.de`

newspaper articles over more than 20 years for the ways in which the public debate about armed interventions appeals to collective identities (such as "we as citizens of the Western world", "us Europeans" etc.).DebateExplorer was a tandem collaboration between academia and data-driven journalism, in which we a tested text-analytical platform using state-of-the-art machine learning routines for text-analytical exploration of large text collections in journalism.[16] The framework developed in these projects addresses a widespread need in scholarly or journalistic research accessing large collections of text documents (such as several running years of full news coverage from newspaper archives or the entire parliamentary proceedings from several years): typically, researchers will be interested in news articles addressing a particular field in politics, society, etc., or some type of event, forming a subcorpus; and on this subcorpus, they will aim to group these articles by more fine-grained content-related distinctions as well as by metadata such as the publication date and the author/speaker. For instance, a researcher may be interested in the news reports and opinion pieces in newspapers from various countries over the course of several years that address wars and armed conflicts (as in the e-Identity project), and aim at a differentiation of whether or not the articles make reference to certain collective identities (such as membership in alliances, religious identities), e.g., testing hypotheses about differences in the public debate across countries (Kantner and Overbeck 2016, Kutter and Kantner 2012, Kantner 2015).

The way studies of this kind typically proceed involves initial corpus exploration, based on some preliminary hypothesis, and then a process of unfolding and narrowing down specific research questions for which the analytical machinery needs to be adjusted. A conventional way of carrying out quantitative corpus studies of this kind makes heavy use of Boolean search terms (often involving morphological variants for the most relevant terms) for filtering the documents to form an appropriate subcorpus, followed by labor-intensive manual annotation (or "coding") work to establish sophisticated keyword profiles that approximate the relevant analytical categories for quantitative studies within the subcorpus. The time-intensive building of effective filters puts natural limitations on flexibility in the process of refining the research question over the course of the study. An additional methodological issue lies in the fact that keyword-based filtering runs a high risk of missing out entire areas of relevance in the space of documents because writers or

[16]Principal Investigator tandem: Jonas Kuhn and Eva Wolfangel (`http://www.debateexplorer.de`); the project was funded by the Volkswagen Foundation.

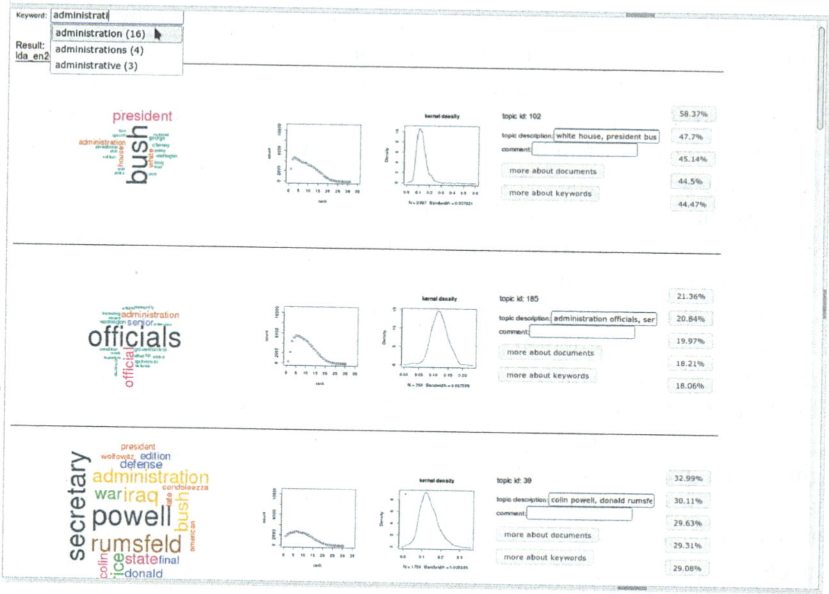

FIGURE 5 The LDA-topic based exploration tool.

speakers use a slightly different wording to refer to the same concepts.

An alternative way of achieving a view on large text collections that differentiates the texts by content areas has gained great popularity not only in text mining, but also in the digital humanities: latent topic models, such as the approach using Latent Dirichlet Allocation (LDA) (Blei et al. 2003). Latent topic modeling is an entirely unsupervised method that can be applied to (large) document collections to detect tendencies among vocabulary items to co-occur in the same document, which is often due to semantic fields, hence the term "topic" (which is however misleading, since the induced clusters rarely form a full match with intuitive semantic groupings). After inducing a topic model with a predefined number of n topics over the full corpus, each document is characterized by a different profile of the various topics contributing to the document; hence, documents dominated by the same latent topic can be assumed to be semantically related. An intuitive grasp of the "meaning" of a topic is typically provided by word cloud representation of the vocabulary items that are most prominent in the typical documents for this topic. Figure 5 includes such word cloud representations of LDA topics (along with additional visualizations from the exploratory framework we discuss below).

Latent topic analysis provides an excellent starting point for explorative corpus analysis, in particular as it does not presuppose any language-specific NLP tools. However, although it is tempting, further quantitative analyses (or fine-grained explorative studies for that matter) should not be based on a putative mapping between certain latent topics and corresponding higher-level analytical concepts (without taking into account the full mixture of weighted topics contributing to a document) — any filtering based on dominant topics is likely to introduce biases to further analyses. In particular, documents that are actually relevant for the target concept but address it in a less typical way would be left out, which may turn the conclusion of an analysis on its head.

To take methodological standards of critical reflection seriously and to effectively ensure that a filter (for selecting the original subcorpus or later for more fine-grained grouping) works according to the theoretical assumptions, a certain amount of manual annotation/coding effort cannot be avoided. Ideally, a representative sample of documents from the original collection should be hand coded for inclusion vs. exclusion in the filtering, to serve as training data for a supervised machine learning classifier.[17] However, representative sampling is non-trivial with a very large base corpus (with an unknown degree of homogeneity) and the need for careful manual annotation is in opposition with the desire to support a flexible unfolding of analytical subquestions clashes. Here, we believe that an interactive approach that combines the strengths of unsupervised and supervised machine learning techniques on the one hand and the expertise of the researcher on the other can provide a solution that is methodologically sound and practical at the same time.

Latent topic-assisted interactive classifier training. At the core of the text classification engine from the e-Identity project is a classical supervised classifier.[18] To ensure rapid adaptability, users can (re-)train the classifier for their own target classes (including the possibility to introduce new ad hoc class labels). The platform supports interactive retraining of versions of a classifier, inspired by the Active Learning paradigm: the predictions of the current classifier can be inspected, including the internal prediction score for each data point (an approximation of the tool's confidence). Buttons for confirming or re-labeling the predictions are used to initiate a new training, based on the original

[17] Alternatively, a (smaller, but still representative) sample of hand-coded data could be used as a validation set for unsupervised techniques, or as a development/tuning set for weakly supervised techniques.

[18] We use the maximum entropy classifier library from the mallet (McCallum 2002) framework.

training data, plus the newly labeled material. It is fairly straightforward for a non-technical user to trim the classifier in a short time frame, by inspecting and correcting low-confidence predictions.

Task 1: Specification of the subcorpus. To address the issue of sampling data points for manual labeling from a large document collection without missing relevant "sub-areas" in the space, the system runs LDA-based latent topic modeling prior to the process of supervised classifier training. It has turned out to be feasible and effective to allow the expert user to explore the topic models and select a number of latent topics that are unioned to form the filter for the original, comprehensive subcorpus. Artifacts from random effects in the unsupervised topic clustering are minimized by inducing a family of distinct LDA-topic models, each with a different number of target topics. Furthermore, the visualization of the induced topic models (including a visualization of parameters relating to the topic distribution, as seen in Figure 5) makes the distribution of topics contributing to a document transparent; hence, the user can develop an intuition that a particular topic tends to be the second- or third-most import topic in a number of document areas and include it in the filtering.

To refer to the topics, keywords that are included in the word clouds are used; the transparent visualization of the interplay of latent topics ensures that users will not draw unwarranted conclusions about direct matches between individual terms and the corresponding topics. Intuitively, the user experiences the topic models as an expansion of a classical keyword-based search which ensures that synonymous ways of referring to a concept (which are easily missed) are automatically included.

Task 2: LDA-feature based document classification. After defining the subcorpus of relevant documents (in a recall-oriented way, i.e., rather being overly inclusive than risking to miss certain documents), the researcher can use the interactive document browser to start the interactive training process for more fine-grained study-specific text classifiers. The originally induced latent topic models are used as features in the supervised classifier; thus, the supervised training on a relatively small set of labeled data can take advantage of generalizations captured in the topics induced on the large corpus.

Practical experience shows that in the interactive labeling of training data, the transparent topic-based pre-structuring of the document space helps to avoid systematic "blind spots," i.e., areas for which no manual labeling is performed because early versions of the classifier already reach reasonable confidence — but some of the predictions are in fact incorrect. This tends to happen when there are documents in the subcorpus that share certain properties with the majority classes, but are special in some other dimension that is outside the focus of attention in annotation. The annotation workflow we advocate works against this risk: to sample data points for annotation, the user defines some highly relevant keywords characterizing the target category (e.g., *court*, *criminal*, *law* for legal debates). Each keyword is used to filter the latent topics in the model, giving rise to a few relevant topics. Now, the user selects for manual annotation at least (i) one highly ranked document for this topic, (ii) one low-ranking document, and (iii) one document from the middle ground. This introduces not just the typical and completely atypical documents into the interactive annotation procedure, and increases the chance that "special areas" are detected over the course of bootstrapping more and more confident classifiers.

An empirical study (Dick et al. 2015) which compared a bag of word to our LDA-feature based classifier showed that the our system performs on the same level. The Max entropy algorithms in both settings allowed a rating of each classified instance by a confidence value. The evaluation showed that in our LDA-based setting the falsely classified instances have a lower confidence level then in the bag-of-words (BoW) based approach. This is very helpful in an active learning context, also it helps to tune the system if high precision is required by increasing the confidence threshold.

7.5.3 Visualization Techniques for Making a Classifier Transparent

A more comprehensive approach to the opening up of a machine-learning classifier for transparent adaptation (as discussed in Section 7.3) is presented in Heimerl et al. (2012): here, users create classifiers that can be seen as representing the other end of the spectrum of techniques letting users steer and adapt such Machine Learning techniques by offering more insights into the internal configuration of a model. The approach was developed in a subproject of the DFG Priority Program "Scalable Visual Analytics"[19], to help with recall-biased retrieval scenarios as encountered in patent analysis and search for state of the art scientific literature. The approach presented is subsequently different from the other projects presented in this chapter, because it does not explicitly address a task in the digital humanities. However, it is a good example to describe how transparent adaptation setups could

[19]Principal Investivators: Thomas Ertl and Hinrich Schütze; subproject "Scalable Visual Analysis of Patent and Scientific Document Collections" funded by the German Research Foundation (DFG); `http://www.visualanalytics.de/`.

look like if complex methods such as machine learning based ones are to be made transparently adaptable by users. In its originally presented version, the approach can be used to classify documents according to user-defined binary criteria. For this purpose a straight-forward BoW-based model was used and a linear support vector machine (lSVM; Vapnik 1998) served as the classification mechanism. While the used features can be easily replaced by other, more sophisticated linguistic feature vectors to assist in other classification tasks, the approach offers interactive visual views that are tailored to users with no or little expertise in machine learning and linguistic processing so that they can understand and assess the state of a lSVM, its uncertainties, and the immediate impact of annotations to future training rounds.

As opposed to the idea of more opaque classification approaches, such as they can be integrated, e.g., into VarifocalReader (see Section 7.5.5), this approach trades the flexibility of switching classification models for a much more detailed level of insight into a specific classification mechanism and a higher level of control in adapting and training the method for users. If VarifocalReader resembles an interactive visual approach that is close to the black box model, the document classification approach of Heimerl et al. can be seen as representing one close to a "glass-box" model (Bertini and Lalanne 2009).

The central view depicts a simplification of the support vector machine's state in order to achieve this high level of user-control. Here the data items to be classified, in this case documents represented by the weighted word vectors are depicted in the form circular glyphs, as can be seen in Figure 6a. Since it is not possible to show the state of a high-dimensional classifier directly (Sacha et al. 2017), a simplified two-dimensional representation is offered to users that reflects the two classes of the classifier model, represented with blue and red backgrounds, with its decision border in the middle. In Figure 6a the gray circular glyphs are the ones that have no label yet, whereas the purple glyphs represent the training documents. All glyphs placed in the red area are classified as non-relevant and the blue one holds all documents that are classified as being relevant according to a user's definition.

The distance of the glyphs from the decision border directly reflects the uncertainty or confidence of the classifier's prediction: the further away documents are placed from the decision border, the higher the confidence of the prediction and vice versa. In the y-direction, the documents are laid out based on the first principle component of the 100 documents closest to the decision border. The intended effect of this approach is twofold. Firstly, it offers a direct visual impression of how well the classifier model can separate the documents. Secondly, users

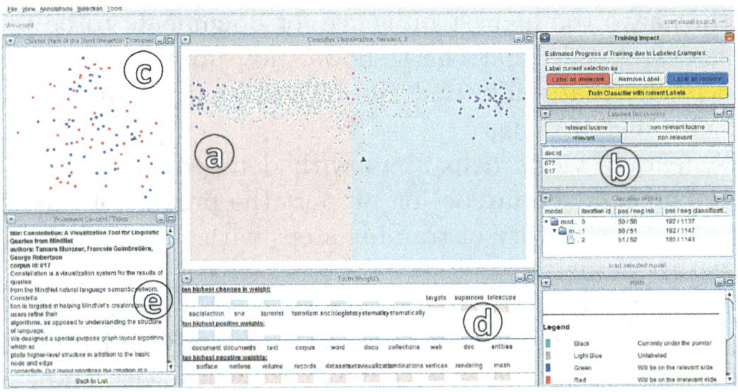

FIGURE 6 The interactive desktop for visual classifier training consists of multiple linked views that provide analysts with insights on the data and the classifier's state.

can immediately identify documents where the uncertainty of the prediction is high and which might therefore might be good candidates to inspect and label in order to refine the classification model in a subsequent training iteration.

If users choose to add additional labels for refining the classifier, a new model is automatically computed in the background. This model is used to offer direct visual feedback on how a labeling action would influence future classification models. To achieve this, newly labeled instances are shown with their respective class label (red or blue triangle glyphs in Figure 6a), instances that would change the predicted class as consequence are shown as red or blue circular glyphs. (Re-)Assigning labels for future training steps can be accomplished through the control panel shown in Figure 6b. If users have relabeled one or several instances, a new classification model can be trained based on all available labels. This leads to an update of the views showing the new classification model.

In addition, to this main view, other different views help users in finding suitable candidates for labeling and provide more insights into the current state of the model. The view shown in Figure 6c shows a two-dimensional projection of the 100 most uncertainly predicted documents of the currently displayed classifier. The distance of glyphs here indicates the similarity of documents in their high-dimensional vector-space representation. As a consequence, closely placed glyphs with different predicted class memberships are good candidates for closer inspection, since one would expect them to have the same class. The bar charts depicted in Figure 6d show those dimensions of the document vectors that have the highest influence for documents to be predicted one of classes. A third bar chart shows those dimensions of the classification model that underwent the biggest changes through the last round of classifier training.

Supplementary views help users with detailed information on inspected documents (Figure 6e) or support the process of classifier creation by offering a history of training steps with possibilities to switch back to earlier models.

This high level of control in steering the creation of a classifier has a number of benefits but also some risks. A user study indicated that it is possible to achieve very good classification results with fewer labeling actions than a perfect labeler using an active learning approach based on uncertainty sampling (Settles 2011). At the same time, users learn much about the data set itself through the many interactive exploration methods that are available for inspecting and assessing the classification model and the data instances. This is certainly interesting for the "not too Big Data" case. A drawback can be the time that is required for visual inspection of instances as opposed, for example, to an active learning approach where the system decides on the instances that should be labeled next by users. However, this freedom avoids the problem of missing important data items which would have probably never been shown to users due to the effects of automatic selection of labeling candidates. Additional risks arise with empowering non-ML-expert users to perform arbitrary labeling and training actions. Of course, the latter makes it possible to create classifiers that do not work as intended, even if this becomes quickly obvious through interactive visual assessment. Overall, users emphasized their higher trust and confidence in the results of the proposed visual interactive system as opposed to a black box approach.

7.5.4 Annotation Support

As should be clear from various parts of our discussion so far (and as we pointed out, e.g., in Section 7.5.2), one has to make a clear methodological distinction between exploratory usages of text analytical models or tools and strict quantitative studies. In the former case, failure to meet the exact modeling assumptions inherent to the tool may not defeat the purpose of data exploration (although, as we pointed out, it is important to make users aware of potential issues). In the latter case, even seemingly miniscule deviations from assumptions may cause substantial biases in more complex tool pipelines.

Whenever the results of corpus-based text analysis are used to make some substantial argument for a higher-level thesis, it is therefore crucial to validate the appropriateness of the tools applied for the specific dataset. Typically, this involves independent hand annotation of a test set taken from the target corpus, following the annotation guidelines of the original tool's development data. So, annotation methodology is one of the most central parts of critically aware text analysis in the digital humanities. But since there is a substantial literature on this — and there are many known connecting points between computational (or corpus) linguistics and visualization research —, we only indicate some details from our experience in interdisciplinary project contexts. The typical workflow for manual annotation in a text analysis context is well supported by adaptable generic tools such as WebAnno (Yimam et al. 2013), which for instance supports parallel annotation by multiple annotators.

Facsimile text visualization for annotation: CRETAnno. Tool support for text annotation in (corpus) linguistics has generally attempted to (i) provide easy access to the information relevant to making annotation decisions (e.g., often the relevant prior discourse context), and (ii) facilitate an uncluttered visualization of the information added by the annotation (e.g., a graphical representation of the syntactic structure). In addition, practical considerations, such as re-usable, generic tool components, play a role. Our experience in the CRETA project[20] revealed an aspect that is largely irrelevant in linguistic annotation work, but quite important in a number of digital humanities contexts in which the material aspect of texts plays a role: annotators get an awkward feeling when the text is not presented in the shape that is familiar from the original source or a standard edition. An annotation procedure that reflects the typical text reception by professional readers should hence be based on a facsimile view of such an edition. Textual visualization tools that are used to support annotation tasks for various different text types should thus ideally allow the user to switch between different views. The CRETAnno annotation tool, which is used in a broad range of disciplinary contexts, e.g., for annotating entity mentions, provides such capabilities. Figure 7 shows how a parliament debate and a medieval text are displayed.

Comparing spans of free textual annotation. A second specific visualization need that arose from annotation work in interdisciplinary

[20]The "Center for Reflected Text Analytics" (CRETA) is an interdisciplinary collaboration involving humanities disciplines such as literary studies, linguistics and philosophy, political science, and computational linguistics and visualization. Principal Investigators: Jonas Kuhn (director), Manuel Braun, Thomas Ertl, Cathleen Kantner, Catrin Misselhorn, Sebastian Pado, Nils Reiter, Sandra Richter, Achim Stein, and Claus Zittel (`http://www.creta.uni-stuttgart.de`).

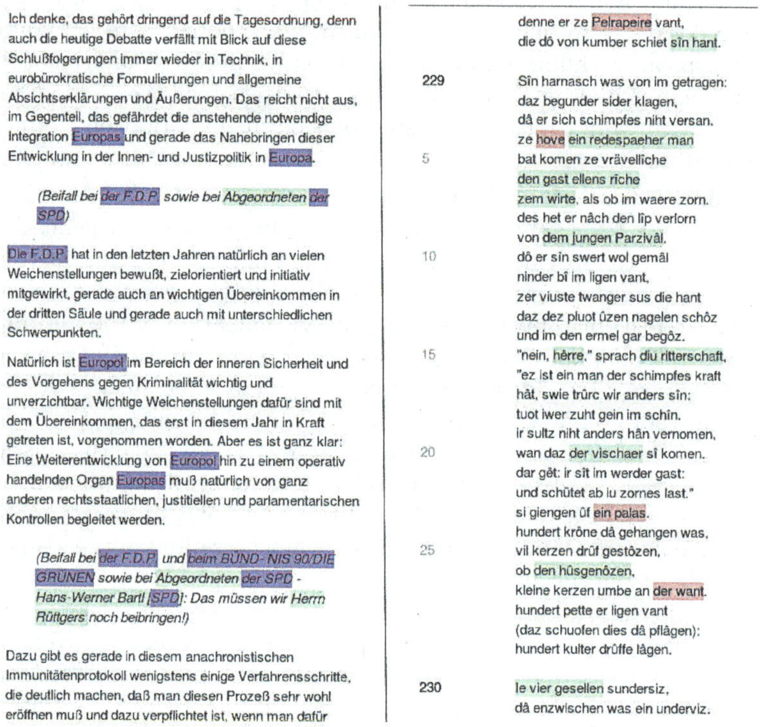

Ich denke, das gehört dringend auf die Tagesordnung, denn auch die heutige Debatte verfällt mit Blick auf diese Schlußfolgerungen immer wieder in Technik, in eurobürokratische Formulierungen und allgemeine Absichtserklärungen und Äußerungen. Das reicht nicht aus, im Gegenteil, das gefährdet die anstehende notwendige Integration Europas und gerade das Nahebringen dieser Entwicklung in der Innen- und Justizpolitik in Europa.

(Beifall bei der F.D.P. sowie bei Abgeordneten der SPD)

Die F.D.P. hat in den letzten Jahren natürlich an vielen Weichenstellungen bewußt, zielorientiert und initiativ mitgewirkt, gerade auch an wichtigen Übereinkommen in der dritten Säule und gerade auch mit unterschiedlichen Schwerpunkten.

Natürlich ist Europol im Bereich der inneren Sicherheit und des Vorgehens gegen Kriminalität wichtig und unverzichtbar. Wichtige Weichenstellungen dafür sind mit dem Übereinkommen, das erst in diesem Jahr in Kraft getreten ist, vorgenommen worden. Aber es ist ganz klar: Eine Weiterentwicklung von Europol hin zu einem operativ handelnden Organ Europas muß natürlich von ganz anderen rechtsstaatlichen, justitiellen und parlamentarischen Kontrollen begleitet werden.

(Beifall bei der F.D.P. und beim BÜND- NIS 90/DIE GRÜNEN sowie bei Abgeordneten der SPD - Hans-Werner Bartl [SPD]: Das müssen wir Herrn Rüttgers noch beibringen!)

Dazu gibt es gerade in diesem anachronistischen Immunitätenprotokoll wenigstens einige Verfahrensschritte, die deutlich machen, daß man diesen Prozeß sehr wohl eröffnen muß und dazu verpflichtet ist, wenn man dafür

denne er ze Pelrapeire vant,
die dô von kumber schiet sîn hant.

229 Sîn harnasch was von im getragen:
daz begunder sider klagen,
dâ er sich schimpfes niht versan.
ze hove ein redespaeher man
bat komen ze vrävelîche
den gast ellens rîche
zem wirte, als ob im waere zorn.
des het er nâch den lîp verlorn
von dem jungen Parzivâl.
dô er sîn swert wol gemâl
ninder bî im ligen vant,
zer viuste twanger sus die hant
daz dez pluot ûzen nagelen schôz
und im den ermel gar begôz.
"nein, hêrre," sprach diu ritterschaft,
"ez ist ein man der schimpfes kraft
hât, swie trûrc wir anders sîn:
tuot iwer zuht gein im schîn.
ir sultz niht anders hân vernomen,
wan daz der vischaer sî komen.
dar gêt: ir sît im werder gast:
und schütet ab iu zornes last."
si giengen ûf ein palas.
hundert krône dâ gehangen was,
vil kerzen drûf gestôzen,
ob den hûsgenôzen,
kleine kerzen umbe an der want.
hundert pette er ligen vant
(daz schuofen dies dâ pflâgen):
hundert kulter drûffe lâgen.

230 Ie vier gesellen sundersiz,
dâ enzwischen was ein underviz.

FIGURE 7 CRETAnno: text view for annotating parliament debates (on the left) and the medieval verses of Wolfram von Eschenbach's epic *Parzival* (on the right).

FIGURE 8 CRETAnno: annotation comparison view. The bottom part shows the annotations of all annotators as span, which allows a quick comparison. Selected annotations are additionally highlighted in the upper text view.

projects is concerned with textual target spans. While certain text annotation tasks go along with very clear-cut guidelines for the beginning and the end of a relevant unit (e.g., named entity annotation), many of the content-oriented annotations (or codings) that are relevant in text analysis for political science or literary studies can hardly be operationalized in a way that ensures strictly unique token spans — even among two annotators sharing the same interpretive intuition. As a consequence, some annotation/coding initiatives refrain from marking the relevant text span for a content annotation at all, and rather add the annotation as an attribute of a higher-level unit (such as the paragraph, chapter or article). The chances of reaching relatively high inter-annotator agreement at the unit level are of course increased with this approach — however at the cost of discarding important information about each annotator's justification of a certain interpretive decision.

Our policy has been to encourage annotators to mark the exact text spans that carry a relevant interpretive content (and ideally work towards a clearer operationalization of the span selection). Rather than only calculating inter-annotator agreement on the spans chosen by multiple annotators, we provide a visualization of the parallel decision (see Figure 8), which can be very informative for the different interpretive strategies and for the reconciliation process.

7.5.5 Visual Support for Close and Distant Reading

An observation in Section 7.5.4 was that the form of presentation of the textual material plays an important role for integrating computational modeling components in higher-level questions from within the humanities. In this section, we address visual support for the idea of "scalable reading",[21] i.e., switching back and forth between an aggregate view on text(s) in "distant reading" (Moretti 2000, 2013), and classical "close" reading.

Some high-level text analysis tasks, for example, as they are carried out as part of digital humanities efforts, have rather focused goals either through a restriction of text sources or research questions. At the same time they aim to achieve verifiable high-quality results in order to ensure valid scientific interpretation. Interactive visualization lends itself to support the analysis of such text corpora in many ways, since it can offer different perspectives on them. In this way close and distant reading can be supported, ideally both within one system. The number of approaches realizing such visualization support is growing (Jänicke et al. 2015).

With VarifocalReader (Koch et al. 2014), we suggested an approach for close and distant reading of single text documents. In addition, it facilitates manual and automatic annotation in a manner that allows for their iterative refinement. The approach was developed as part of the "ePoetics" project that dealt with the analysis of German poetics. In this project, a team of researchers from literary studies, computational philology, Visual Analytics, and computational linguistics explored analytical perspectives on a corpus of poetics, i.e., theoretical writings on literature from several centuries.[22] VarifocalReader is therefore tailored to support larger, book-sized texts. It can be seen as an example for a versatile interface that fosters "round-trip" adaptation of classification and other text analysis tasks. The approach is close to the black box model in that internal mechanisms of text processing steps remain opaque, and only effects of iterative improvement are conveyed to the users.

VarifocalReader's characterizing feature is the parallel representation of different hierarchic levels of texts, starting from the overview level of the whole text to a sentence-level view at the highest resolution as shown in Figure 9. Intermediate levels such as pages, paragraphs and chapters can be shown as well. All views of these levels are linked to each other, whereas in higher levels the clipped section shown in the next lower level is indicated. Users can navigate and explore texts and contained annotations quickly by scrolling within each of the shown hierarchical levels. Scrolling higher levels results in a very high scroll

[21] See e.g. Denbo and Fraistat (2011), Weitin (2013), Mueller (2014).

[22] Principal Investigators: Sandra Richter (lead), Thomas Ertl, Jonas Kuhn, and Andrea Rapp; ePoetics was funded by the BMBF.

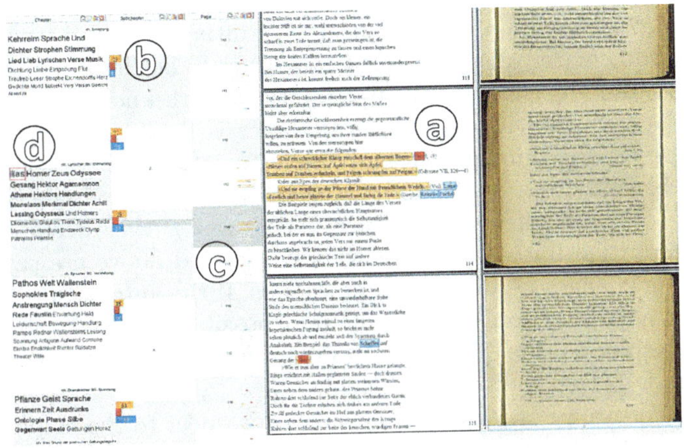

FIGURE 9 Emil Staiger's *Grundbegriffe der Poetik* divided (from left to right) into layers showing chapters (with word clouds), subchapters (with bar charts), pages (with bar pictograms), lines of text, and scanned images of the actual pages.

speed and scrolling lower levels in a lower scroll speed.

The lowest, sentence-based level, shows the text directly (Figure 9a). Annotations that are made either manually or automatically are shown in a straightforward manner by highlighting annotated tokens with a background color other than white. All levels above the lowest level show aggregated representations of the text. Users can choose from three different aggregation views. One option is to get a summary of available annotations in the form of a bar chart based on the level granularity of the respective layer (Figure 9b). If this is for example applied to the subchapter level, then summaries for each subchapter are shown. The second view shows a pictogram-based representation where the text is simplified to straight lines and annotations to small colored subsections within these lines (Figure 9c). This depiction helps to quickly grasp the distribution of annotations as it occurs within the corresponding level of detail. The third view shows word clouds that characterize the sections of the next lower level of abstraction (Figure 9d). The word clouds offer additional navigation hints within texts: clicking a word highlights its occurrences similar to annotations in texts.

With its navigation and browsing features, which are based on SmoothScroll (Wörner and Ertl 2013), VarifocalReader offers a suitable interface for carrying out manual annotations which can then be used as training data for supervised machine learning methods. The success of such a training step and the resulting automatic annotation can be immediately displayed in the interface to be checked and refined by users interactively with the possibility to start a new training round with the corrected labels. VarifocalReader is flexible with respect to the type of text mining task and the automatic method that is used in the backend to solve it, as long as the user-corrected labels can be used to improve the method. In order to assess the effects of training/adaptation both annotation views described above are capable of depicting changes between training rounds. If the automatic procedure delivers a form of confidence value it is possible to indicate it using a suitable color palette. This helps users to quickly navigate to uncertain automatic results for assessing them.

The versatility of VarifocalReader with respect to the employed automatic analysis technique is an advantage of the approach making it possible to plug in different supervised techniques. However, this design also has drawbacks. Only the effects of training steps are observable by users without providing further insights into the state of the underlying machine learning approach.

The VarifocalReader approach has been developed in particular for analysis of large single text documents. It obviously cannot be applied easily to huge text corpora. However, the underlying idea of helping users judging the effects of a supervised machine learning method through offering by an interactive visual representation is transferable to other scenarios as well. Creating a combination of visual navigation aids and different visual levels or perspectives of access to annotations can be assembled into powerful Visual Analytics approaches to create or adapt supervised machine learning techniques quickly.

7.6 Discussion

We have presented a number of text-analytical scenarios for which it has turned out beneficial to provide interactive visual support accompanying complex computational modeling solutions. Our emphasis was on scenarios that call for a high degree of transparency in the analytical tool chain — as is common for the research practice in the (digital) humanities, for various reasons: research typically follows an evolving hermeneutic process, which makes it important to rapidly adapt existing computational solutions to new questions and base corpora; the combination of analytical results from systematic computational analysis with findings based on quite different methodologies and practices — including for instance aesthetic considerations — makes a critical reflection of the provinence of results even more important than in methodologically homogeneous contexts; and last but not least, the standard NLP tools available tend to be less reliable when they are applied outside the standard domain of newswire or mainstream web data, calling for a validation of the model performance. However, although the conventional web search scenario as discussed in Section 7.3 tends to work well with a black box approach, the more transparent methodology we discussed in the chapter could also give users in a classical Web Analytics setup more entry points for developing a critically reflected picture of the interconnections brought out by analytics tools. In fact, we believe that some of the findings from extensive interdisciplinary exchanges between data scientists and critical content specialists prominent in digital humanities research form a good basis for developing best practices in critically reflected analytics in general.

We note a few specific technical lessons from the cross-disciplinary projects: An aspect of appropriate tool offerings that tends to be underestimated among computer scientists regards the entry threshold to trying out a technical solution. Since the benefits of a given computational approach will not be obvious to potential users, it makes a considerable difference when the tool is offered as an entirely platform independent web application, without the need to install additional software and is accessible from any place (Hinrichs et al. 2010). With such a web service approach, large servers running in the background will also enable processing of large data volumes. Also, the multiuser environment of a web services makes it very natural to approach text analysis as collaborative work. On the downside, the web interface puts limitations on the functionality that can be straightforwardly provided, e.g., complex graph-annotations as overlay of a text view cannot easily be realized. Thus, for more advanced tools, classical software solutions have a place too.

One may also ask at a more abstract methodological level what are the lessons learned for a systematic approach to interactive visualization in complex text-analytical scenarios. A natural objective would seem to be to head for generic technical frameworks that offer catalogues of alternative modules for aggregation, analysis and visualization that one merely needs to plug together to create a project-specific solution. It clearly turns out that at least now, such a "library" approach is not feasible. The actual adaptation needs to accommodate the specifics of a given project require a degree of flexibility that would be prohibitive to anticipate in a non-technical generic framework — especially when the high standards of validity of model application are taken seriously. This suggests that for the coming years, effective user-centered solutions for interactive text analytics continue to require a substantial effort.

Yet, experience from interdisciplinary collaborations across a wide range of text-analytical target disciplines (ranging from literary studies and philosophy to political science, in particular in the CRETA project) shows that there *are* synergy effects that can be exploited when the fields engage in an open-minded exchange. The transparent toolbox approach, which puts the humanities scholar or social scientist in a responsible position, opens up connecting points across text-oriented disciplines that, we believe, have rarely been exploited in the past:[23] there is a great overlap of methodological needs (and potential insights) regarding descriptive, "lower-level" text analysis steps that form the basis of interpretations independent of the discipline-specific higher-level theories and working assumptions — especially the ones that are not in the classical core interest of linguistics, e.g., the identification and grounding of expressions referring to relevant entities, such as persons or places.[24] Cross-disciplinary exchanges show that while different text disciplines place their respective initial emphasis on seemingly divergent aspects of descriptive text analysis (suggesting the need for a discipline-specific agenda), it often turns out that many of the issues *are* relevant across the various fields — it is just a question of prioritization (which may in part be the effect of traditional placements of emphasis that a corpus-oriented computational approach may override). For example, the textual attribution of perceptions or propositional attitudes to actors may seem a relatively straightforward building block of text analysis outside of narratology in literary studies (where subtle questions of point of view and focalization are prominent), but the more subtle aspects of attribution do play a role in non-literary text interpretation too.

A comprehensive and methodologically diverse approach to text analysis, crucially supported by interactive visualization for transparent access to the model architecture, may thus contribute to new synergies across fields.

[23] In the past, there have of course been methodological "turns" in specific fields in the humanities and social sciences that have led to the reception of insights and methodologies across disciplines. But these seem to have occurred in infrequent waves and were often not accompanied by a feedback into the field of origin (and with a data-oriented validation of the implications that the methods have for the two fields).

[24] This task has been at the center of interdisciplinary conceptualization studies in CRETA and forms the core of the data set for the CRETA unshared task ("CUTE"; Reiter et al. 2017).

Acknowledgements

The work reported and discussed in this paper was supported in a number of funded projects. We are grateful to the German Federal Ministry for Research and Education (BMBF), the research ministry of the state of Baden-Württemberg, and the Volkswagen Foundation for their support. The authors would like to thank their collaborators in the various projects; the discussions and practical exchanges have contributed substantially to the approaches we discuss here.

References

Bertini, Enrico and Denis Lalanne. 2009. Surveying the complementary role of automatic data analysis and visualization in knowledge discovery. In *Proceedings of the ACM SIGKDD Workshop on Visual Analytics and Knowledge Discovery: Integrating Automated Analysis with Interactive Exploration*, pages 12–20.

Bizer, Christian, Tom Heath, and Tim Berners-Lee. 2011. Linked data: The story so far. In A. Sheth, ed., *Semantic Services, Interoperability and Web Applications: Emerging Concepts*, pages 205–227. Hershey, PA: IGI Global.

Blei, David M., Andrew Y. Ng, and Michael I. Jordan. 2003. Latent dirichlet allocation. *Journal of Machine Learning Research* 3:993–1022.

Blessing, André, Andrea Glaser, and Jonas Kuhn. 2015. Biographical data exploration as a test-bed for a multi-view, multi-method approach in the digital humanities. In *Proceedings of the First Conference on Biographical Data in a Digital World 2015*, pages 53–60.

Blessing, André and Jonas Kuhn. 2014. Textual emigration analysis. In *Proceedings of the Ninth International Conference on Language Resources and Evaluation*, pages 2089–2093.

Blessing, André, Jonathan Sonntag, Fritz Kliche, Ulrich Heid, Jonas Kuhn, and Manfred Stede. 2013. Towards a tool for interactive concept building for large scale analysis in the humanities. In *Proceedings of the 7th Workshop on Language Technology for Cultural Heritage, Social Sciences, and Humanities*, pages 55–64.

Bruhn, J.A., William E. Fry, and Gary W. Fick. 1980. Simulation of daily weather data using theoretical probability distributions. *Journal of Applied Meteorology* 19(9):1029–1036.

Bukhari, Ahmad C., Artjom Klein, and Christopher J.O. Baker. 2013. Towards interoperable bioNLP semantic web services using the SADI framework. In C. Baker, G. Butler, and I. Jurisica, eds., *Data Integration in the Life Sciences*, pages 69–80. Heidelberg: Springer.

Card, Stuart K., Jock D. Mackinlay, and Ben Shneiderman. 1999. *Readings in Information Visualization: Using Vision to Think*. San Francisco, CA: Morgan Kaufmann.

Collins, Christopher, Sheelagh Carpendale, and Gerald Penn. 2007. Visualization of uncertainty in lattices to support decision-making. In K. Museth, T. Möller, and A. Ynnerman, eds., *Proceedings of the 9th Joint Eurographics / IEEE VGTC Conference on Visualization*, pages 51–58.

Cortez, Paulo and Mark J. Embrechts. 2013. Using sensitivity analysis and visualization techniques to open black box data mining models. *Information Sciences* 225:1–17.

Denbo, Seth and Neil Fraistat. 2011. Diggable data, scalable reading and new humanities scholarship. In *Second International Conference on Culture and Computing (Culture Computing)*, pages 169–170.

Dick, Melanie, André Blessing, and Ulrich Heid. 2015. Automatische Verfahren zur Bewertung der Relevanz von Dokumenten für geisteswissenschaftliche Forschungsfragen. Paper presented at the 2. Jahrestagung der Digital Humanities im deutschsprachigen Raum.

El-Assady, Mennatallah, Valentin Gold, Markus John, Thomas Ertl, and Daniel Keim. 2016. Visual text analytics in context of digital humanities. In *1st IEEE VIS Workshop on Visualization for the Digital Humanities as part of the IEEE VIS 2016*, pages 1–10.

Hammond, Adam, Julian Brooke, and Graeme Hirst. 2013. A tale of two cultures: Bringing literary analysis and computational linguistics together. In *Proceedings of the NAACL 13 Workshop on Computational Linguistics for Literature*, pages 1–8.

Heimerl, Florian, Steffen Koch, Harald Bosch, and Thomas Ertl. 2012. Visual Classifier Training for Text Document Retrieval. *IEEE Transactions on Visualization and Computer Graphics* 18(12):2839–2848.

Hinrichs, Erhard, Marie Hinrichs, and Thomas Zastrow. 2010. Weblicht: Web-based lrt services for german. In *Proceedings of the ACL 2010 System Demonstrations*, pages 25–29. Association for Computational Linguistics.

Hinrichs, Uta, Mennatallah El-Assady, Adam James Bradely, Stefania Forlini, and Christopher Collins. 2017. Risk the drift! stretching disciplinary boundaries through critical collaborations between the humanities and visualization. In *2nd IEEE VIS Workshop on Visualization for the Digital Humanities as part of the IEEE VIS 2017*, pages 1–10.

Jänicke, Stefan, Greta Franzini, Muhammad Faisal Cheema, and Gerik Scheuermann. 2015. On close and distant reading in digital humanities: A survey and future challenges. In R. Borgo, F. Ganovelli, and I. Viola, eds., *Eurographics Conference on Visualization (EuroVis) – STARs*, pages 83–103.

John, Markus, Steffen Lohmann, Steffen Koch, Michael Wörner, and Thomas Ertl. 2016. Visual analysis of character and plot information extracted from narrative text. In J. Braz, N. Magnenat-Thalmann, P. Richard, L. Linsen, A. Telea, S. Battiato, and F. Imai, eds., *Computer Vision, Imaging and Computer Graphics – Theory and Applications*, pages 220–241. Heidelberg: Springer.

Kantner, Cathleen. 2015. National media as transnational discourse arenas: The case of humanitarian military interventions. In T. Risse, ed., *European Public Spheres: Politics Is Back*, pages 84–107. Cambridge: Cambridge University Press.

Kantner, Cathleen and Maximilian Overbeck. 2016. Religiöse Identitäten als Diskursblocker. In I.-J. Werkner and O. Hidalgo, eds., *Religiöse Identitäten in politischen Konflikten*, pages 173–191. Wiesbaden: Springer VS.

Keim, Daniel, Jörn Kohlhammer, Geoffrey Ellis, and Florian Mansmann, eds. 2010. *Mastering the Information Age: Solving Problems with Visual Analytics*. Goslar: Eurographics Association.

Kielman, Joe, Jim Thomas, and Richard May. 2009. Foundations and frontiers in visual analytics. *Information Visualization* 8(4):239–246.

Kim, Minjeong, Kyeongpil Kang, Deokgun Park, Jaegul Choo, and Niklas Elmqvist. 2017. TopicLens: Efficient multi-level visual topic exploration of large-scale document collections. *IEEE Transactions on Visualization and Computer Graphics* 23(1):151–160.

Koch, Steffen, Markus John, Michael Wörner, Andreas Müller, and Thomas Ertl. 2014. VarifocalReader – In-depth visual analysis of large text documents. *IEEE Transactions on Visualization and Computer Graphics* 20(12):1723–1732.

Koehn, Philipp. 2009. *Statistical Machine Translation*. Cambridge: Cambridge University Press.

Kucher, Kostiantyn and Andreas Kerren. 2015. Text visualization techniques: Taxonomy, visual survey, and community insights. In *Proceedings of the 8th IEEE Pacific Visualization Symposium*, pages 117–121.

Kuhn, Jonas. 2019. Computational text analysis within the humanities: How to combine working practices from the contributing fields? *Language Resources and Evaluation,* https://doi.org/10.1007/s10579-019-09459-3.

Kuhn, Jonas and André Blessing. 2017. Die Exploration biographischer Textsammlungen mit computerlinguistischen Werkzeugen – methodische Überlegungen zur Übertragung komplexer Analyseketten in den Digital Humanities. In A. Z. Bernad, C. Gruber, and M. Kaiser, eds., *Europa baut auf Biographien. Aspekte, Bausteine, Normen und Standards für eine europäische Biographik*, pages 225–257. Wien: new academic press.

Kurzhals, Kuno, Markus John, Florian Heimerl, Paul Kuznecov, and Daniel Weiskopf. 2016. Visual movie analytics. *IEEE Transactions on Multimedia* 18(11):2149–2160.

Kutter, Amelie and Cathleen Kantner. 2012. Corpus-based content analysis: A method for investigating news coverage on war and intervention. *International Relations Online Working Paper Series* 2012(1):1–38.

Liu, Shixia, Xiting Wang, Jianfei Chen, Jun Zhu, and Baining Guo. 2014. TopicPanorama: A full picture of relevant topics. In *Proceedings of the IEEE Conference on Visual Analytics Science and Technology*, pages 183–192.

Mahlow, Cerstin, Kerstin Eckart, Jens Stegmann, André Blessing, Gregor Thiele, Markus Gärtner, and Jonas Kuhn. 2014. Resources, tools, and applications at the CLARIN Center Stuttgart. In J. Ruppenhofer and G. Faaß, eds., *Proceedings of the 12th Edition of the Konvens Conference*, pages 11–21.

McCallum, Andrew Kachites. 2002. MALLET: A Machine Learning for Language Toolkit. `http://mallet.cs.umass.edu`.

Mehta, Hrim, Adam Bradley, Mark Hancock, and Christopher Collins. 2017. Metatation: Annotation as implicit interaction to bridge close and distant reading. *ACM Transactions on Computer-Human Interaction (TOCHI)* 24(5):35.

Moretti, Franco. 2000. Conjectures on world literature. *New Left Review* 1:54–66.

Moretti, Franco. 2013. *Distant Reading*. London/New York: Verso.

Mueller, Martin. 2014. Shakespeare his contemporaries: Collaborative curation and exploration of early modern drama in a digital environment. *Digital Humanities Quarterly, The Alliance of Digital Humanities Organizations* 8(3).

Reiter, Nils, André Blessing, Nora Echelmeyer, Markus John, Steffen Koch, Gerhard Kremer, Sandra Murr, Maximilian Overbeck, and Axel Pichler. 2017. CUTE: CRETA UnShared Task on Entity References. In *Digital Humanities im deutschsprachigen Raum 2017: Abstracts*, pages 19–22.

Sacha, Dominik, Hansi Senaratne, Bum Chul Kwon, Geoffrey Ellis, and Daniel A. Keim. 2016. The role of uncertainty, awareness, and trust in visual analytics. *IEEE Transactions on Visualization and Computer Graphics* 22(1):240–249.

Sacha, Dominik, Leishi Zhang, Michael Sedlmair, John A. Lee, Jaakko Peltonen, Daniel Weiskopf, Stephen C. North, and Daniel A. Keim. 2017. Visual interaction with dimensionality reduction: A structured literature analysis. *IEEE Transactions on Visualization and Computer Graphics* 23(1):241–250.

Schich, Maximilian, Chaoming Song, Yong-Yeol Ahn, Alexander Mirsky, Mauro Martino, Albert-László Barabási, and Dirk Helbing. 2014. A network framework of cultural history. *Science* 345(6196):558–562.

Settles, Burr. 2011. Closing the loop: Fast, interactive semi-supervised annotation with queries on features and instances. In *Proceedings of the Conference on Empirical Methods in Natural Language Processing*, pages 1467–1478.

Vapnik, Vladimir Naumovich. 1998. *Statistical Learning Theory*, vol. 1. New York: Wiley.

Weitin, Thomas. 2013. Thinking slowly. Reading literature in the aftermath of big data. *LitLingLab Pamphlet* #1:1–17.

Wörner, Michael and Thomas Ertl. 2013. Smoothscroll: A multi-scale, multilayer slider. In G. Csurka, M. Kraus, L. Mestetskiy, P. Richard, and J. Braz, eds., *Computer Vision, Imaging and Computer Graphics – Theory and Applications*, pages 142–154. Heidelberg: Springer.

Yimam, Seid Muhie, Iryna Gurevych, Richard Eckart de Castilho, and Chris Biemann. 2013. Webanno: A flexible, web-based and visually supported system for distributed annotations. In *Proceedings of the 51st Annual Meeting of the Association for Computational Linguistics: System Demonstrations*, pages 1–6.

8

An Interactive Visualization of the Historical Dictionary of Bavarian Dialects in Austria

Alejandro Benito-Santos, Antonio Losada, Roberto Therón, Eveline Wandl-Vogt and Amelie Dorn

8.1 Introduction

In this chapter we discuss the goals, motivations and other particularities of a visual exploratory analysis tool for historical dictionaries of the Bavarian dialects in Austria. As an input data set we employ the digitized version of the Historical Dictionary of Bavarian Dialects in Austria (*Wörterbuch der bairischen Mundarten in Österreich* or WBÖ), an initiative started in 1963 which compiles more than five million paper slips collected during the years 1911–1998 in different areas of current Austria, the Czech Republic, Hungary and northern Italy. In the 1990s these paper slips started to be progressively digitized, becoming part of the Database of Bavarian Dialects (DBÖ) and in 2010 nearly 32,000 records related to plant names were made available online on the DBÖ electronically-mapped (dbo@ema) platform.[1] In more recent efforts, the project "exploreAT!: Exploring Austria's Culture Through the Language Glass", which this work is part of, started in 2015. Its aim is "to reveal unique insights into the rich texture of the German Language, especially in Austria, by providing state of the art tools for

[1] https://wboe.oeaw.ac.at.

Visual Analytics for Linguistics (LingVis).
edited by Miriam Butt, Annette Hautli-Janisz and Verena Lyding.
Copyright © 2020, CSLI Publications.

exploring the unique collection (1911–1998) of the Bavarian Dialects in the region of the Austro-Hungarian Empire", and it has originated other publications in conference proceedings that we encourage the reader to review: Therón and Wandl-Vogt (2016) and Dorn et al. (2016).

As previously mentioned, this project has generated interesting studies by humanities scholars from different backgrounds beyond lexicography, such as historians, sociologists or anthropologists, as it can provide answers not only related to this particular field but also present clear pictures of the society at the time a certain dictionary was compiled (Dorn et al. 2016). By relating lexicography to other disciplines, fostering this historical, cultural and sociological inquiry, lexicography itself can greatly benefit by questioning its impact, validity and role over the course of time.

Among the many definitions for the concept of a dictionary provided by several authors over the years, one was taken under special consideration in our research: "A lexicographical product which shows interrelationships among the data." (Nielsen 2008). Consequently, one of the goals of our tool is to serve the purposes of a variety of scholars and also the general public curious to explore the interrelationships of the lemmas found in the dictionaries under study in an easy and fun way. In order to fulfill this initial requirement, we base our tool on a set of well-defined computational tasks: **Spatio-temporal analysis**, **fast full-text search** and **social network analysis (SNA)**, which are exposed to the end user by means of data visualization. All these computational tasks serve the ultimate purpose of browsing, exposing, projecting and exploring these interrelationships by applying well-known data visualization techniques. Thus, the role of data visualization is specially important in our approach, given the profile of such end users, which is expected not to be necessarily technical or academic. This means end users might not know — or even want to know — the inner workings of any of the aforementioned computational techniques, but still want to benefit from the advantages these techniques can bring to their activity. Data visualization proved to be effective in reducing the cognitive load involved in the exploration tasks and also in lowering the user's level of digital mastery needed to operate the proposed tool resulting from our research.

Elaborating on this topic, the two first computational tasks are employed because of obvious reasons given the matter of study: spatial analysis is needed given the inherent relationship there is between a dialect and the geographical area where it is — or was — spoken. Furthermore, the historical component of the set of dictionaries under study inevitably calls for a temporal analysis solution, preferably linked to the former one. A need for a fast, potent full-text search feature is also desirable, as one of the most repeated tasks performed in a dictionary is precisely searching for words. The last computational task that we incorporate in our prototype, SNA, is of the utmost importance as it can provide great insights on the relationships between the various lemmas by making the structural and relational patterns in the data apparent to the user's eyes. The detection of these patterns is key to providing a comprehensible overview of the evolution of the language and its strong connections to the folklore and society of a certain time and place.

Finally, we present our tool in a web-application format. In an inherently collaborative environment like digital humanities (DH), we consider crucial the creation of web-ready systems able to run in the browser, by employing open web standards and adopting adequate software methodologies oriented towards this aim, in order to ensure a correct exposure, dissemination and verification of scientific productions.

8.2 Related Work

The increasing availability of computational resources has generated a great amount of academic and non-academic DH-related studies and work in recent times (Rodighiero 2015). In this section we provide a general overview of the many influences this academic work has received, specially those related to the visualization of temporal change of natural language and other lexicographic features. This project also looks upon other work that, even though not always related to the study of lexicography or linguistics, presents important findings related to the mapping and representation of other cultural features in maps, graphs or a combination of both.

One of the first attempts to create a digital edition of a dictionary that could be explored visually makes intensive use of scroll lists and a network analysis of hyperlinks. At the core of this work resides an ad hoc search engine with potent natural language processing and string search capabilities that allow end users to launch fuzzy searches in order to detect misspellings and alternative spellings of headwords (Manning et al. 2001). In our study we place searching capabilities at the core of the architecture that supports the proposed pilot tool.

There are other approaches that present different visual alternatives for exploring dictionary data in order to highlight and detect diachronic change patterns in natural language, and more specifically, in corpora related to historical dictionaries (Therón and Fontanillo 2015). This work presents a visual solution to detect, explore and comprehend changes in the meaning of headwords in the course of time by employing an interactive branched timeline. This paper is part of a larger system that does not only add a temporal dimension to the data, but also other spatial and geographical characteristics that allow richer representations in the form of animated maps, which allow experts to draw conclusions on cultural aspects not necessarily linked to the information contained in the text. The paper adds a series of guidelines useful for the decision making process that takes part during the conception of visual text analytic tools, specially oriented towards the correct validation of results, which we replicate in our study in Sections 8.7 and 8.7.3.

In recent years, desktop software has been progressively replaced by web applications that can be run by computers in an Internet browser. Data visualization is a field specially susceptible to adopting these techniques, and much of the academic work done these days is ready to be run on the Web. This is the case for a linguistics-related visualization study, on which the authors propose a visual solution for the identification of recurrent coincidences in synchronous lexical associations within the CLICS[2] database (Mayer et al. 2014). Furthermore, the artifacts resulting of their investigation were designed specifically to run on the Web and finally made available for the general public in an interactive web application. As a consequence, their work urged us to adopt a web-ready strategy since the very first stages of our research.

The main aim is simple yet innovative: to identify tendencies in the usage of certain works referring to the same concepts in different languages across time. As a solution, they present a web application with three, two-way linked views that enables geographical, textual and network analyses to be performed at the same time. Network analysis is achieved by means of a force-directed graph in which nodes represent the different concepts and connecting edges their coincidences in meaning (Figure 1). The database sample managed by the visualization holds more than 300,000 words, covering 1,280 different concepts and so it makes their tool a good example on how to deal with high-density graphs resulting of linguistic data. In a first attempt, the authors claim that 45,667 colexification cases were found, which generated a graph with 1,280 nodes and 16,000+ edges, too big to be effectively visualized as a whole. This problem is solved by applying community detection algorithms and other clustering methods to the graph, enabling smaller, more manageable separate visualizations without losing perspective on the data. While this solution is valid for certain types of analysis, it

[2] `http://clics.lingpy.org/`.

is also true that it handicaps the rest of the analysis process, as the system is only capable of showing partial, precalculated snapshots of the available data, increasing the difficulty of forming a clear mental image of the whole. This problem, that is acknowledged by the authors at the end of their paper, applies in a similar way to our domain. In our case we propose a top-down approach to explore the data, in which the spatial and temporal projection of subsets resulting from textual queries lead the analysis task, serving as an entry point to the more computationally demanding network analysis.

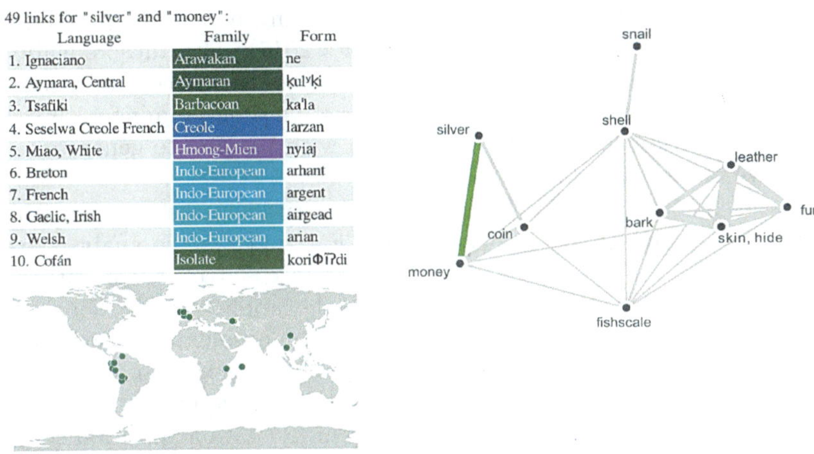

FIGURE 1 Prototype proposed by Mayer et al. (2014) showing a system with three linked views: force-directed graph (right), terms list and geographic map.

The software methodology employed to build the prototype resulting of this research is iterative, user-centered and guided by experts. This model, proposed by authors in the field of DH (Bernard et al. 2015) is highly successful and of proven efficiency in this discipline. In the first stages of development, small prototypes are created, showcasing certain functionality related to a portion of the total data. The aim behind this practice is to give the different stakeholders involved greater insight on the available information. These prototypes are validated by experts in formal meetings and their feedback is incorporated in the next stage, either to modify the existing prototypes or to create new ones. Following their practices, we created six small prototypes over the course of this research that led to the final one, that is presented in Section 8.6.

The workflow proposed by the pilot tool is deeply influenced by work of data visualization experts (Keim et al. 2008), also called the *visualization mantra*: "Analyze first, show the important, zoom, filter and analyze further, then details on demand." (Shneiderman 1996) This workflow has proven to behave specially well with massive data sets such as the ones employed in our research: "[...] current and especially future data sets are complex on the one hand and too large to be visualized straightforward on the other hand." (Keim et al. 2008)

In order to implement these precepts in the particular case of our pilot tool, and given the large size of the input data sets, we received strong inspiration from previous work on the construction of multiple linked-view visualization systems employing a reactive paradigm (Facca et al. 2005, Kelleher and Levkowitz 2015). The authors elaborate in their work on the design and development of pieces of software that combine elements from functional reactive programming with the Model View Controller (MVC) paradigm with the aim to generate responsive and reusable visualizations.

As a consequence of the analysis of the cited works, we note the importance of designing a cohesive workflow that fits the analysis expectations of the end users. This point is stressed by some authors (Wanner et al. 2016). Also important is the application of heuristic methods and data-mining techniques that condense expert knowledge and that are able to extract the adequate information from structured and non-structured natural language texts. In our approach we apply similar heuristic, semi-assisted techniques in the data acquisition stage (see Section 8.5) to extract spatiotemporal traits from the input texts.

8.3 Problem Description

In order to define the problem of analyzing a dictionary, one of the first tasks the team had to do was to reflect on the definition of the word "dictionary" itself. Furthermore, if this problem is to be tackled by visual means, in which human psychology plays an important role, the task becomes even more important. Hence, we must analyze the possible user profiles of the hypothetical software solution who could be scholars or curious citizens willing to explore the data. For this task, we reviewed several definitions of the dictionary according to different authors, until we could find one definition that semantically aligned with our data visualization approach. As we introduced in the first section of this chapter, modern, data-oriented definition of the dictionary particularly affected the development this research (Nielsen 2008). This definition, however, diverts from what resides in popular consciousness, which according to other authors is closer to the idea of an "alphabetically ordered collections of words accompanied by their respective meanings, which are presented to the final user in paper form." (Bergenholtz 2012)

This juxtaposition between the old and the new proved to be highly relevant in our problem and immediately led to the following questions: What are the characteristics of a visual exploration tool for dictionaries that divert from old representations of traditional dictionaries while keeping its most basic, primal operations — look up and browsing — at the core? In case this is feasible, how can it *look and feel* like a dictionary to novel users and still make the advantages supposedly provided by the application of computational methods readily obvious? And finally, how is this system supposed to represent the interrelationships among lexicographic data for it to allow inquiry of historical, cultural and linguistic nature? The pilot tool that we introduce in the next section tries to give answers to these questions by not confronting the two given definitions but rather making them complementary, keeping in mind that the old must not be left behind, and the new must be looked at with a high dose of skepticism. The artifacts we deal with in this research are the result of decades work of dozens of lexicographers, which contain an invaluable and vast source of knowledge that needs to be properly analyzed, shared and exposed. On the other hand, this fact makes data representations of these artifacts harder to deal with digitally than recent work. Moreover, if the number of entries reaches the order of millions, then the problem falls into the category of *Big Data*, posing new challenges that need to be overcome.

Furthermore, dealing with historical data has other disadvantages that affected the progression of our study at certain times. We often found data stored in old databases and modeled in out-of-date formats. In our case, some of the digital assets that we managed were more than 10 years old, which technologically speaking, is an enormous amount of time. This data had to be translated into newer standards that aligned exactly with our research needs. Even though ongoing efforts of migrating this data to platforms such as the Semantic Web (Wandl-Vogt and Declerck 2013) exist, this process is highly painstaking and will take several years and effort to be completed but surely will motivate new and richer forms of dictionary exploration once it is completed.

8.3.1 Questioning the Current Model — Research Aims

As we have seen in previous sections, many of the tools dealing with this kind of data sometimes abuse lists of ordered words that are presented in a computer screen. These representations can be linked to the popular definition of dictionary, and they lack many usability and design patterns that can immensely reduce the system's analysis capabilities. Large lists usually denote weak information crafting and data preparation techniques, as many other more engaging and effective visual alternatives exist for the same purpose (Hightower et al. 1998). According to other authors (Therón and Fontanillo 2015), it is therefore necessary to stress the importance of drifting away from these old conceptions and providing more adequate visual solutions that exploit the benefits of employing computer-assisted methods.

The whole process of compiling a historical dictionary and the set of artifacts resulting from the lexicographers' work over the course of this task must be thoroughly examined in order to create smart tools that are able to expose relevant information according to the users' needs at all times. Hence, the final purpose itself of these artifacts must be hardwired in the data formats that are managed by the tools that allow accessing the dictionary. In this new implementation of a dictionary, given the radically higher capabilities of a computer, the information should be projected in not only one but multiple dimensions, often at the same time, enabling completely new ways of exploration for academics and the general public. In our case, we scrutinize these artifacts in order to design the behavior of computational methods able to not only expose them when necessary, but also create new ones that add value to the data.

A Big Data flow for the dictionary

Data flows and formats encode rules that model the problem domain and they must be specially crafted for the visualizations that make use of them. After analyzing in-browser tools from previous studies, we were able to identify three different categories according to the way they interact with underlying data. This classification supports the data modeling choices taken in our tool and it is explained hereafter:

1. The approach that appeared more often is the following: A initial load of all available data is performed. The data is transferred from a remote location to the user's browser (transfer times vary depending on the amount of available data or latency, amongst other factors). Once the transfer is complete, algorithms adapt the data and input it to the presentation layer, which changes its state. The algorithms can be tuned and rerun as many times as necessary, providing great flexibility in transforming the data. This approach usually fails to respond in interaction times when these calculations are too expensive but it is the more appropriate when the volume of data is of small or moderate size.

2. In a similar approach, the visualization data structures are created in a previous stage and served along with the data in load time. This is the strictest approach, as the user's actions are limited by the pre-computations applied to the data in the first step but it scales better to bigger data volumes.
3. A combination of the two previous approaches. The most expensive computations are run before the application loads and the others are left to be performed in run time. This is a more flexible, complex approach but it may not be suitable for all the situations, for example, when the problem imposes that these expensive computations are re-run very often.

In our case, fast string querying fell into the category of expensive computation and proved one of the biggest challenges. When performing these searches the interface responsiveness should not be negatively affected. Given the amount of data that we managed, it was not possible to follow any approaches derived from 1 on the one hand, as it is not feasible to perform a memory loading and browsing of the whole dataset. On the other hand, solutions exclusively based in 2 would require to precalculate in advance data structures for all the sets of elements resulting of all possible string queries, which is also not realistic.

Since the aim of our research was to create a system that performed in interaction times and is able to continuously fix the user's mental state in the interface with the lowest possible latency, we identified the following desirable characteristics for our tool:

1. Expensive operations must be calculated in advance. This involves text indexing and generation of summaries using binning and/or clustering algorithms.
2. An overview of the dictionary must be provided at first.
3. Zoom level and filter must affect the underlying metrics and data structures to enable progressive access to the data is allowed, which in turn will modify the views state as explained in 1.
4. Given the volume of data, some data structures and metrics must be calculated in run time, depending on the user's actions and cannot be precalculated.

Considering these constraints, we decided to provide a general overview of the dictionary by employing the spatial and temporal projections of the data, due to of their obvious relation to the study of dialects (Wandl-Vogt 2010). We did not build, however, a similar overview based on the more complex SNA analysis that we employ in other parts of the tool. Whereas it is true that it can reveal interesting structural patterns in the data, we did not want to give it a primary role in our solution. There are many possible types of network analysis that can be done to analyze interconnections between elements in the dictionary, but they would require a more concise understanding of the problem that escaped the aims of our research.

For these reasons, visual network analysis is relegated in the interface to a secondary level. Its complexity is of the simplest kind and its role serves the purpose of introducing network analysis to novel users. While its inclusion certainly adds some value to the proposed analysis (see Sections 8.7 and 8.7.3), we could not rely at first on such a simple network analysis task to lead the exploration, specially when its validity was yet to be proven. As a consequence, we preferred to remain skeptical towards SNA and offer it as a details-on-demand task that can reveal new exploration pathways and iterations of the proposed workflow as seen in other approaches (Mayer et al. 2014).

8.4 Input Data Sets

8.4.1 TUSTEP

TUSTEP[3] is a scientific text processing suite created in the 1960s at the Center for Data Processing of the University of Tübingen (Germany). It is closely linked to the study of the German language and the humanities. Despite its longevity as a piece of technology, it is still employed nowadays by many academics in the field of German studies. More recently the suite adopted the XML standard to store texts and it exposes a text-only interface that supports string-based queries written in the XQuery language.[4] This query language allows the retrieval of records matching certain search criteria inside a collection of XML documents. DBÖ project data — roughly two million records — is stored in this format and it serves as one of the starting points for our work. Whereas we did not use TUSTEP directly in our research, we employed the files this suite manages in order to create more complex datasets adequate to our needs.

8.4.2 Dbo@ema

The paper slips introduced in the previous section were the main artifacts resulting of the lexicographers' field work developed in the different population centers spread across the Austrian territories during the 20th century. It worked in the following way: Questionnaires about different themes were delivered amongst the sample population. By

[3] `http://www.tustep.uni-tuebingen.de/tustep_eng.html`.

[4] `https://en.wikipedia.org/wiki/XQuery`.

means of these questionnaires, the respondents were asked to answer a series of questions about the specific words that they used to refer to certain concepts. Once completed, the questionnaires were collected and complemented with personal interviews. At the end of the process, these usages were accounted for in paper slips, in which the word appeared along with its definition and intended meaning. They normally contained handwritten notes and even drawings for the purpose of obtaining the highest possible degree of disambiguation in the future, if necessary. The slips were finally stored with the original answers, sorted and made available for consultation to other academics. Figure 2 shows an image of a sample paper slip and a questionnaire. On the bottom-right, the digitized XML version of the paper slip is featured.

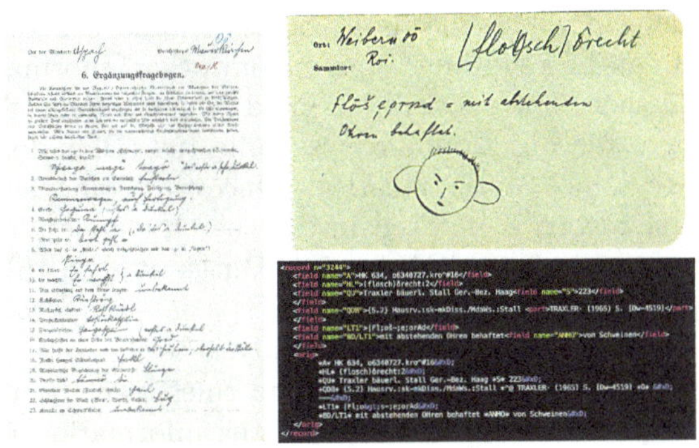

FIGURE 2 Left: A scan of a questionnaire used in Upper Austria (circa 1920). Top right: A paper slip with handwritten notes and a drawing defines the word *floschorecht* ('big-eared'). Bottom right: Detail of the TUSTEP record related to the paper slip presented on the left. The field "BD/LT1" holds the original meaning written by the collector: *mit wegstehenden Ohren behaftet* ('affected by protruding ears').

8.5 Data Acquisition: An Hybrid Approach

8.5.1 Extracting Dimensions

During the design and implementation process of the different micro-prototypes built over the first stages of the research, we realized the two data sets introduced in the previous section were both lacking necessary features for their correct visual representation in a browser application. XML, and particularly MySQL representations did not adapt well to our research purposes of performing fast string searches in the dictionary. In order to circumvent this problem, it was necessary to build a new data set by combining the former two, which enabled the information to be consumed and indexed by a text search engine. At the end of this conversion process, the search engine hosted a new multidimensional data set that could interact with the proposed linked-view system. In this section the process of combining these two data sets is described.

Due to its completeness and larger number of records, the XML format is used as primary data set, whereas the MySQL database is employed as supporting or secondary data set that adds the geographical information to the records of the former. In Figure 3 two entries from each data set are depicted. In the upper image, the XML-TUSTEP record shows one the different fields associated with a lemma. Specially interesting is the "QDB" field — standardized source —, which contains the source in which the usage of the lemma can be found. The number 1913 can be read on it apart from other information such as the original author. The subfield "O" holds the toponym that refers to the place where the questionnaire was collected (Blaindorf, a municipality in the region of Styria, Austria). Once this coincidence has been found, the first record is indexed in the search engine along with the spatial information in GeoJSON format (Butler et al. 2016),[5] creating a new document that holds all the required spatial, temporal and textual dimensions that will drive the visual analysis task.

For this task a set of initial heuristic rules were coded in a semi supervised script that extracted in turn the information from the two data sets and compounded the final entry in JSON format that was finally consumed by a search engine. When this set of rules could not automatically resolve the exact coordinates for a toponym, the team of experts supervising the work had to input a record number manually or desist and index the record without geographical information.

Spatial dimension

The numbers show that 1,861,878 records, which account for 80% of the total, contain standardized toponyms. The remaining 20% or 322,459 records, do not possess any hints referring to the place the questionnaires were collected due to errors in the process of digitization, or missing information in the originals. Knowing the exact causes why this information is missing is a research question in itself which is beyond the scope of our work. For the records that do contain a toponym, we retrieve the correspondent GeoJSON string that is indexed by the search engine with the rest of the processed XML record it belongs to.

[5] `https://www.rfc-editor.org/info/rfc7946`.

```
<record n="447">
  <field name="A">HK 869, z8690113.kro^#8</field>
  <field name="HL">(Hals)zapfen:1</field>
  <field name="QU">Blaindorf Stmk. Fabiani</field>
  <field name="QDB">{3.5g02} uFeistritzt.:mOSt. <part>FbB.FABIANI· (u.1913) [SFb.]</part>
    <field name="O">Blaindf. St.</field>
  </field>
  <field name="NR">4L7: Gaumen</field>
  <field name="LT1">H;olsz-abfrl [D2]</field>
  <orig>
    *A* HK 869, z8690113.kro^#8&#xD;
    *HL* (Hals)zapfen:1&#xD;
    *QU* Blaindorf Stmk. Fabiani&#xD;
    *QDB* {3.5g02} uFeistritzt.:mOSt. *^@ FbB.FABIANI· (u.1913) [SFb.] *O* Blaindf. St.&#xD;
    ===&#xD;
    *NR* 4L7: Gaumen&#xD;
    *LT1* H;olsz-abfrl [D2]&#xD;
    ===&#xD;
  </orig>
</record>
```

1)

```
id,nameKurz,nameLang,sort,bearbeitungsgebiet_id,gemeinde_id,gis_ort_id,namensvarErl,behoerde,quellen,ort_verzeichnis
_id,originaldaten,freigabe,checked,wordleiste,druck,online,publiziert,anmerkung,trust,menschkurz,OKZ,autokurz
16650,Blaindf.,Blaindorf,999999,2,995,15887,,,NULL,1,NULL,0,1,0,0,1,0,NULL,3,Blaindf.,15091,Blaindf.
```

2)

FIGURE 3 1: A record, 447, found in an XML-TUSTEP file, referring to the lemma *Halszapfen* ('palatin uvula'). In the field QDB the temporal (1913) and spatial (Blaindf. St.) dimensions can be found. 2: CSV representation of the MySQL entry containing the spatial coordinates for "Blaindorf". Notice how the toponyms employed in both records sensibly differ.

Temporal dimension

Another different set of heuristic rules was created in order to automatize the extraction of the temporal dimension from each of the TUSTEP-XML records. Strings defining dates are extracted and correctly formatted to be consumed by the search engine. Although some of the dates found represent periods of time, we decided to work only with the starting year of the intervals in this stage of the research process. The current prototype does not provide a visual treatment of the precision and accuracy of the data, and it is one of the challenges the visual exploration tool will try to overcome in its future versions.

Import results

In Table 1 we present a final recount of all the documents indexed by the search engine resulting from the combination of the two data sets. Despite only a small percentage of the final indexed records contained spatial and temporal information, the pilot tool adopts design principles to give this subset a major importance in the analysis task. In our approach this information serves as a supporting data subset for the others lacking any of the other dimensions and helps the analyst to complete data gaps.

TABLE 1 Recount of records according to the spatial and temporal dimensions that could be extracted in the data acquisition stage. InputN: Number of input records, IndexN: Number of successfully indexed records, S+T: Spatial and temporal, S: Spatial only, T: Temporal only, N: None.

InputN	IndexN	S+T	S	T	N
2,206,227	95.3%	9.8%	32.4%	26.6%	31.1%

8.6 Pilot Tool

This section presents the proposed visual analysis tool. As mentioned in previous sections, the main idea behind the design of the tool is to achieve a top-down workflow that implements the precepts of the visualization mantra (Keim et al. 2008), allowing a type of exploration that drives the user from the generalities to the particularities of the dictionary. In a similar approach to work by other authors (Anselin et al. 2002), we also propose a dynamic multiple linked-views exploration system for multivariate dictionary data. We expand and adapt work on the reactivity of web applications and visualization systems by some authors (Facca et al. 2005, Kelleher and Levkowitz 2015) and introduce the component of the search engine as a data-management entity that plays the role of predictable state container often seen in these approaches.

When the prototype performs its initial data load, it presents a general spatiotemporal overview that serves as starting point for the exploration. Once this data is analyzed, a series of actions to be performed by the user is expected. Through the reception of the events of zooming, filtering and panning, the system will continuously adapt the state of the linked views to new data resulting of these events in order to reflect the user's mental state and reduce the cognitive load of analyzing the two million records data set. The prototype supports three types of filtering, implemented by means of different UX and visualization techniques, that arise from the requirements set at beginning of the research: Spatial, temporal and textual. The user progressively modifies a combination of these filters in an iterative, continuous refinement process employing the technique known as "brushing and linking" (Keim 2002).

8.6.1 Notes on the Architectural Model

The general schema of the system is depicted in Figure 4. In this web-ready, reactive architecture, the client first receives and renders HTML content from the application server, which is transmitted on first load. The client and the search engine, as we explained in the previous section, employ the lightweight data exchange format JSON. According to his authors, this data format is more flexible and works better than XML in web environments, and it is key to achieve low-latency interfaces such as the one proposed in our study (Bray 2014). Since only the required information to transform the views is transmitted from the search engine to the client with each action, and given the resolution of results is managed by the logic implemented in the controllers and the search engine, the size of the transmitted chunks is effectively reduced to the order of the hundreds of bytes. Only the specific parts of the visualizations that are affected by changes in the responses are rendered again, leaving the rest of the interface untouched. This practice saves computational resources and therefore enhances the overall performance of the system, allowing us to achieve the targets set related to the overall responsiveness of the tool.

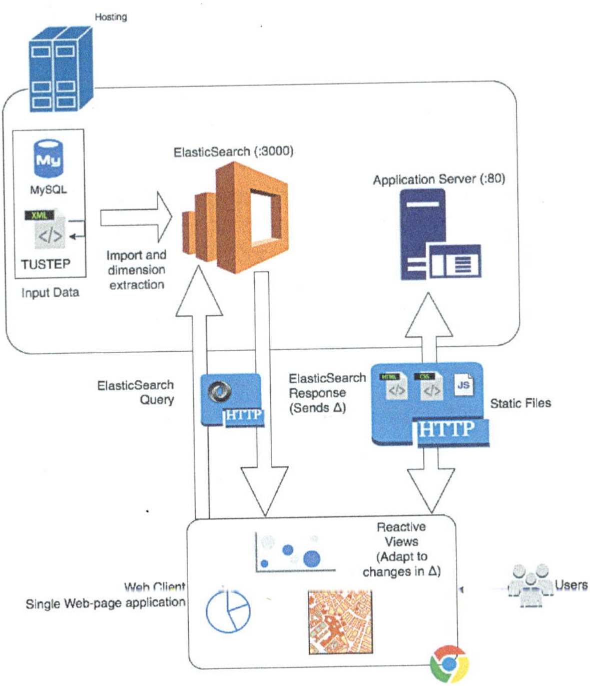

FIGURE 4 Web architecture.

8.6.2 A Search Engine for the Dictionaries

As we anticipated in previous sections, a key feature of the pilot tool to implement was the full-text search that XQuery supported. Also, another important software requirement was to build a web-ready piece of software able to run in browsers. For these reasons, the chosen data storage and search engine was the open-source, Apache-licensed ElasticSearch documental search engine. Despite its short lifetime, ElasticSearch has become a strong software alternative in real-time analysis of human-readable, machine-generated computer logs. Given the similarity of these formats to those employed in our context and taking previous work of other DH practitioners as example (Hauswedell and Wevers 2015), ElasticSearch presented itself as a suitable solution for indexing and querying our data.

The results of this addition were promising. With more than two million different indexed documents, the search engine adapted very well to work in a web environment, acting as a predictable state container in the context of the reactive paradigm that we employ in our tool. Along with its strong text search capabilities, the search engine offers the possibility to obtain summaries of the response data sets by using *aggregations*.[6] These summaries are condensed in special data structures called *buckets* that, upon receipt, are processed by data controllers which in turn trigger the necessary changes in the linked-view system. The calculation of these metrics is embedded at the core of the search engine and it can be programmed by supplying appropriate data-modeling schemas that were designed by our team, thus it is extremely fast in comparison to other simpler alternatives previously explained.

In Figure 5 a sample JSON query request is depicted. It is divided into two fundamental parts: The textual query establishes the criteria the members of the result set should match and the aggregation specifies how the results should be structured within the buckets. In this case the response will aggregate results by two of the dimensions incorporated in the data acquisition stage: time and space. A sample response for this request is shown in Figure 6. In our example the search string controls the amount of data that is visualized, whereas the aggregations manage the resolution in which the results are given. We implemented pieces of software (controllers in MVC) that manage and adapt this resolution automatically.

---

[6] `https://www.elastic.co/guide/en/elasticsearch/reference/current/search-aggregations.html`.

```
"{
  "aggs": {
    "ortMain": {
      "geohash_grid": {
        "buckets_path": "years",
        "field": "gisOrt",
        "precision": 3
      },
      "aggs": {
        "years": {
          "date_histogram": {
            "field": "startYear",
            "interval": "365d",
            "time_zone": "Europe/Berlin",
            "min_doc_count": 1
          }
        }
      }
    },
    "yearsMain": {
      "date_histogram": {
        "field": "startYear",
        "interval": "365d",
        "time_zone": "Europe/Berlin",
        "min_doc_count": 1
      },
      "aggs": {
        "ort": {
          "geohash_grid": {
            "buckets_path": "years",
            "field": "gisOrt",
            "precision": 3
          }
        }
      }
    }
  },
  "query": {
    "bool": {
      "must": [
        {
          "exists": {
            "field": "startYear"
          }
        }
      ]
    }
  },
  "size": 0
}"
```


FIGURE 5 String query to ElasticSearch buckets requesting to receive the response structured in buckets.


```
▼aggregations: Object
  ▼ortMain: Object
    ▼buckets: Array[175]
      ▼[0 … 99]
        ▼0: Object
            doc_count: 14248
            key: "u296"
          ▶years: Object
          ▶__proto__: Object
        ▼1: Object
            doc_count: 11931
            key: "u23h"
          ▶years: Object
          ▶__proto__: Object
        ▼2: Object
            doc_count: 11575
            key: "u2e8"
          ▶years: Object
          ▶__proto__: Object
        ▶3: Object
        ▶4: Object
        ▶5: Object
```


FIGURE 6 The response to the previous request takes less than 250ms for a search space of 2 million sources.

8.6.3 Visual Interface

The prototype resulting from our research offers a multidimensional visual analysis tool of the textual features extracted in the data-acquisition stage, plus time and space, which give a general overview of the data subsets resulting of the operations of in a continuous refinement cycle.

The exploration is centered in the spatial dimension of the data and it serves as an entry point to the others. Furthermore, maps are less intimidating and generally work better in psychological terms than other artifacts, because they allow an incremental access to the information and provide meaningful and easy-to-remember visual structures (Good and Bederson 2002).

In Figure 7 a screenshot of the prototype interface is presented, showing all its views, of which only the first three will be available at first. The network analysis area is hidden or displayed dynamically depending on the stage of the workflow the user is at.

1. **Spatial view:** Here the data with available coordinate information is projected. It supports the panning, zooming and filtering by selecting specific visual elements on the map.

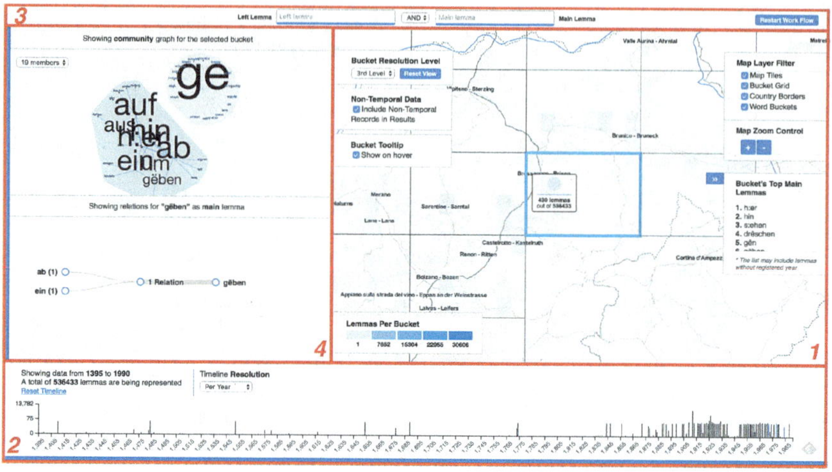

FIGURE 7 Proposed interface, featuring 1) Map spatial projection, 2) Temporal projection or timeline, 3) Textual search bar, 4) Network analysis area.

2. **Timeline:** This histogram is linked to the spatial view and makes a representation of the records with temporal information (projected over the y-axis).
3. **Textual search bar:** This element collects the text queries performed by the user. It employs instant search or "Search as you type": In this technique filtering is performed on each user keystroke, leaving out of the current selection the documents that does not match the search criteria.
4. **Network analysis area:** This area shows the graph representations of the networks present in the current selection. It helps the user to identify patterns and hidden connections between lemmas in a certain geographical area. Closing the linked-view cycle, this view relates to the timeline and textual search bar and permits a fast tuning of the temporal and textual filters.

Spatial view

The map is the main view and it leads the analysis process as orography and general terrain layout play a fundamental role in the study of dialects. Maps are no longer static pieces of art, but rather they have evolved into complex interactive artifacts, in which different data is presented according to the users' choices during the exploration process. For this purpose we implemented in this view several visual components as seen in Figure 8.

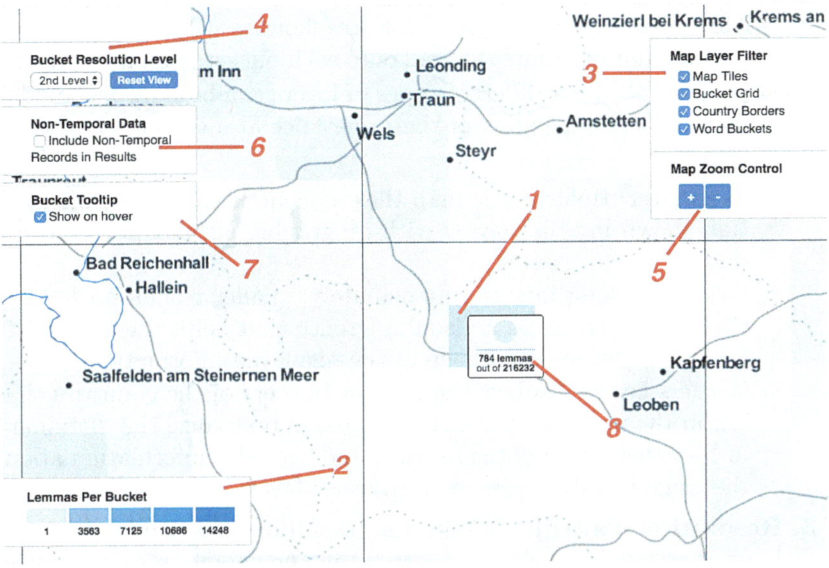

FIGURE 8 Detail of the map view. 1. Geohash/spatial bucket representation, 2. Scale, 3. Layer control, 4. Data resolution control, 5. Zoom control, 6. Control to include/exclude of elements without temporal information, 7. Control to show/hide the bucket summary view, 8. Tooltip.

1. Spatial aggregations: The spatial aggregations of results are represented by means of a geocoding system called geohash[7] that divides the territory in equal parts in a way that they can be indexed and searched as text, making it suitable for documental search engines as ElasticSearch. In Figure 8 we see the representation of the geohashes for a certain portion of terrain, colored in different tonalities of blue, according to the scale depicted in area 2. When the user clicks in one of these representations, the zoom level adjusts to the size of the geohash and the resolution automatically adapts to the new situation. Simultaneously, the network analysis area is presented on the left of the screen. This form of simple visual spatial clustering still allows for fast pattern recognition but can be run substantially faster than other more computationally expensive approaches such as Voronoi or k-Means tessellation. Moreover, the efficacy of these other patterns in the specific case of our research still needs to be confirmed. We considered that the creation of visual patterns (any patterns) was good enough for this first version and therefore we picked the simplest and fastest approach.

---

[7]http://geohash.org/.

2. Scale: Each geohash representation follows a color scale that encodes the amount of results that fall onto each bucket (Figure 8, area 2).

Layer control: Four different types of layers can be shown or hidden upon user request depending of their relevance at a current step of the workflow.

1. Tiles layer: Holds static map tiles. It contextualizes the information shown in other layers with orographic, urbanistic and other data.
2. Grid layer: Outlines the immediately smaller resolution level of the data. It serves as a visual reference that helps users to create a hierarchical mental image of the displayed information.
3. Borders layer: Displays the current borders of the countries that fall in the map viewport. It helps to contextualize the dictionary in historical and political terms, and provides information about the origins of data presented in other layers.

3. Resolution control: Despite the resolution selection being modified automatically according to changes in the zoom, an extra control is enabled to augment or decrease it upon user request. This triggers actions in the controllers that send new requests to the search engine to adjust data resolution. In Figure 9 the view is shown before the user selects the new resolution. The operation of the control triggers a new request in the format shown in Figure 5. When the search engines responds, the view adapts to this change showing the desired resolution (Figure 10).

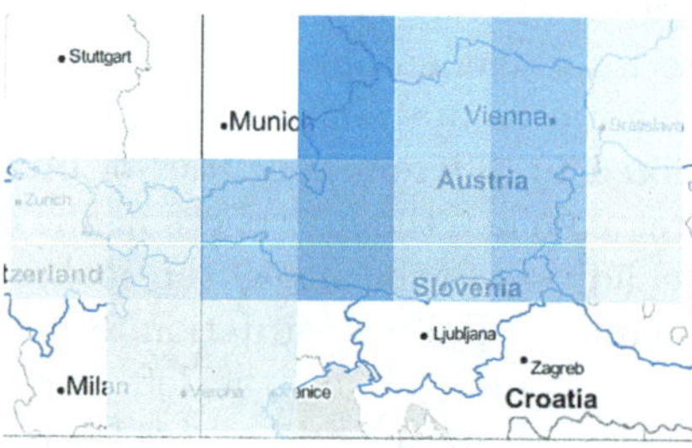

FIGURE 9 Lowest possible resolution level.

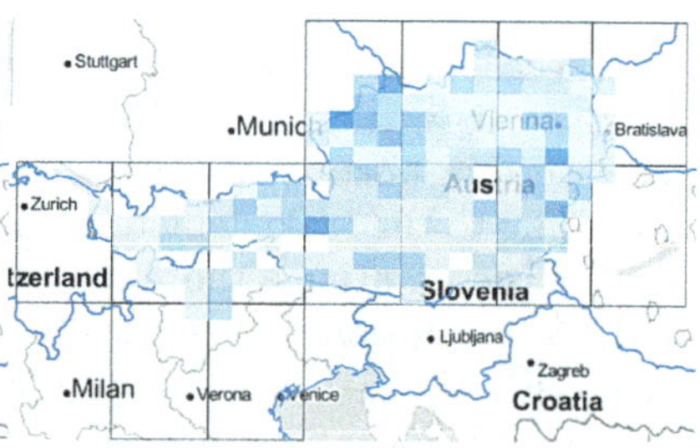

FIGURE 10 Immediately higher resolution.

4. Zoom control: A change in projection is commonly used in maps. This action triggers a resolution change so the available information is presented gradually to the user.

5. Include non-temporal data: Different subsets of the data according to the number of dimensions that could be extracted from the text in the data acquisition stage exist. By default, the prototype projects on the map and timeline the records that hold spatial and temporal information. Once the control is operated by the user, the displayed subsets are now disjoint, and thus it can occur that a representative of a document does not have a counterpart on the timeline. This might be useful in some types of research tasks that do not necessarily rely on an analysis of the temporal dimension and it can help the user to create a hypothesis about the origin of certain undated sources based on information obtained in other parts of the visualization system in a "connect the dots" fashion.

6. Tooltip: When hovering on any bucket representation, and following the last part of the visualization mantra, an informative view is displayed with specific details about the exact number of records that fall into that particular area (Figure 8, area 8). Simultaneously, correspondent representations of these records on the timeline are highlighted. This is a simple and effective solution that helps the user to identify other dimensional traits of a set of entries.

Timeline

This histogram lays out the data along the y-axis, which encodes the temporal information of all the records in the result set under analysis (Figure 11).

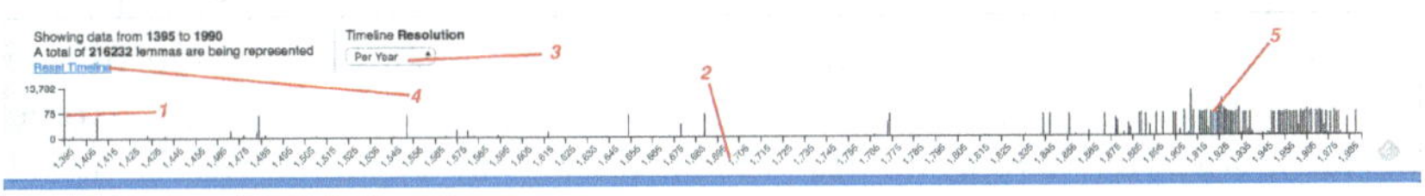

FIGURE 11 Detail of the timeline: 1) Scale, 2) X-axis, representing time, 3) Resolution change control, 4) Explanatory text and reset function, 5) Histogram bars.

The timeline supports filtering of elements by the action of brushing, triggering changes in the spatial view (Keim 2002). It is also possible to change the resolution and highlight the selected elements on the map by the action of hovering. Timelines are entry-level visualizations that adapt well to all levels of digital literacy, and they can be seen in many of the works commented in Section 8.2.

Textual search bar

String queries are used to perform textual filtering of the data. The search engine processes these queries and returns documents matching the input criteria specified by the input query, written in *Lucene*[8] syntax

[8]`https://lucene.apache.org/core/2_9_4/queryparsersyntax.html`.

tax. The string queries run on the original "HL" field (main lemma or headword), and allows separate searches on its prefix and lexeme parts. This is particularly important in the German language because it makes extensive use of compound words (as Mark Twain wittily notes in his 1880 essay *The awful German Language*). In the case of this dictionary, lemmas are often presented in their original form or accompanied by signs that denote the original pronunciation of the term. The two criteria can be combined by means of the logical operators "AND" and "OR". More expressiveness can be included in the queries, for instance by making use of the Levenshtein distance fuzzy operator, which is particularly useful in the study of dialectal linguistic phenomena (Heeringa 2004).

Network analysis area

Previously in this chapter we pointed out the possibility to create visual structures oriented towards the analysis of social networks. These structures can be generated in run time capable of unveiling domain-specific connections in the data impossible to identify by employing other types of analysis (temporal or spatial). By using the pilot visualizations presented below, the user is going to be able to refine the initial parameters of the next iteration according to the newly discovered evidence presented in the former.

Force-directed graph: This is the first type of visual representation presented to the user to perform network analysis. Each node of the graph represents a single lemma, which can appear as a prefix or lexeme in the headwords found in the result data set. The size of the label linearly maps to the frequency of such lemma as seen in abstract word cloud text representations (Heimerl et al. 2014, Wanner et al. 2016). Edges connecting two lemmas indicate that a headword composed by the connected lemmas is present on the analyzed network. Edge width encodes the number of sources for the headword, employing a polylinear scale. The reading direction is given by the arrows at the end of the sides of the edge. Consequently, disconnected nodes in the graph denote that a certain lemma appears only as lexeme of a word. Finally, the user can trigger new textual searches by selecting a node, action that would start a new iteration of the workflow.

Community analysis: Given the usually large size of the analyzed networks, the network is partitioned by running a community detection algorithm on the graph. Communities are groups of nodes in a network "within which the connections are dense but between which they are sparser" (Newman 2004). This method is successfully employed by other authors in the visual detection of colexification patterns and other linguistic phenomena and reduces the cognitive load involved in the process of cluster identification (Mayer et al. 2014). As these communities had to be calculated in real time when the user demands this operation, we chose an algorithm that performs very fast in browsers without compromising accuracy (Blondel et al. 2008, Orman et al. 2011).

In Figure 12 we provide a screenshot of the network after applying the algorithm to entries found in the geohash "u20". It can be noticed how the different communities are outlined by means of a colored convex hull of the nodes that conform each community. When two or more communities overlap, they form new, darker colors that promote the rapid identification of areas of confluence. Communities with a population under the network's average are hidden by default for clarity's sake, although they can be displayed at user request by operating the relevant control at the top of the view. As displayed in Figures 12 and 13, the graph is presented for the current selection. A combined string query can also be launched from a community. It searches for occurrences of any of the members in other parts of the map, expanding the result set to include other geographical areas.

FIGURE 12 Default state of the graph. Communities with populations below the average of the displayed set are hidden by default.

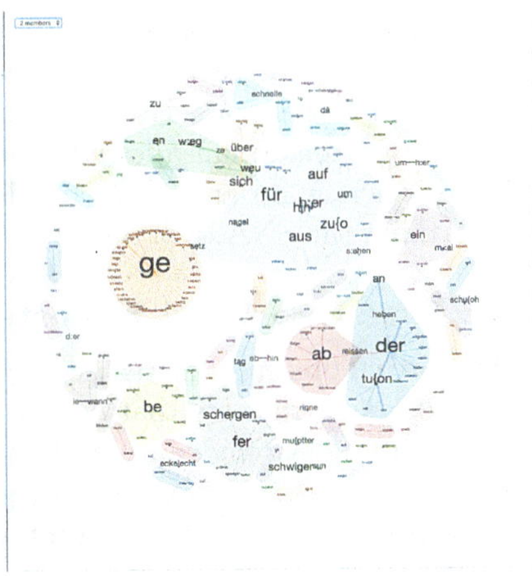

FIGURE 13 The same graph with a less restrictive filtering applied. Smaller communities appear now on the visualization.

Tree representation: When a certain graph node catches the user's attention, a more specific visualization can be activated on demand. The tree graph represents a slice of the network that only includes lemmas connected to the one represented in the selected node. This visualization, which is in turn linked to the timeline using highlighting, displays the exact number of connections between nodes and allows triggering new textual searches in a similar manner as seen in the force-directed graph.

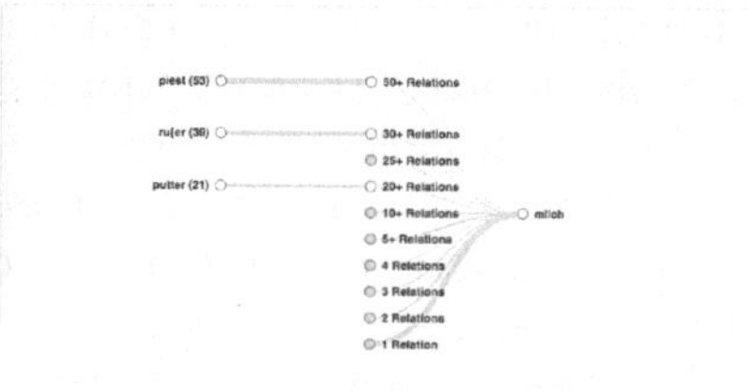

FIGURE 14 The tree visualization shows the lemma *milch* ('milk') positioned as lexeme. Combinations are shown on the left.

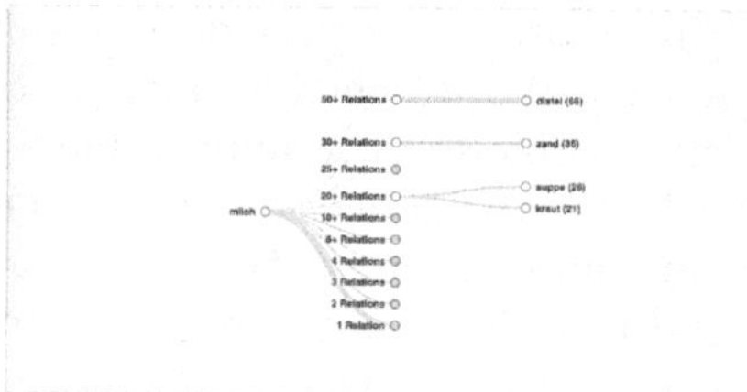

FIGURE 15 The lemma acting as prefix of the compound word. The user can switch between the two views by clicking a designated button.

Original record

On certain occasions, it is interesting to access the original TUSTEP record if the information available in the visualizations is not enough to confirm or deny a certain hypothesis. Once the map resolution has reached the maximum allowed level, the user can access this information by clicking on any of the displayed buckets, action that instead of performing the SNA, will display the information in a pop-up window.

8.7 Use Cases and Experts Feedback

This section presents the results of a short test session performed by the team of lexicographers that collaborated in this research. The two use cases that were found during the session demonstrate the advantages of the proposed workflow in the free exploration of the dictionary and its ability to facilitate the extraction of different kinds of knowledge.

8.7.1 Color Term Usage

At the beginning of the session, the participants chose to base the exploration on the usage of colors through the language. Colors form an integral part of our lives and are also a prominent topic spanning across several academic disciplines. Moreover, color concepts play an important role in the representation of cultural knowledge (Deutscher 2010). In this case, they looked for common referents and associations of red (*rot*) with other terms, as this practice can provide insight on the cultural ramifications of such color (Deutscher 2010). In order to

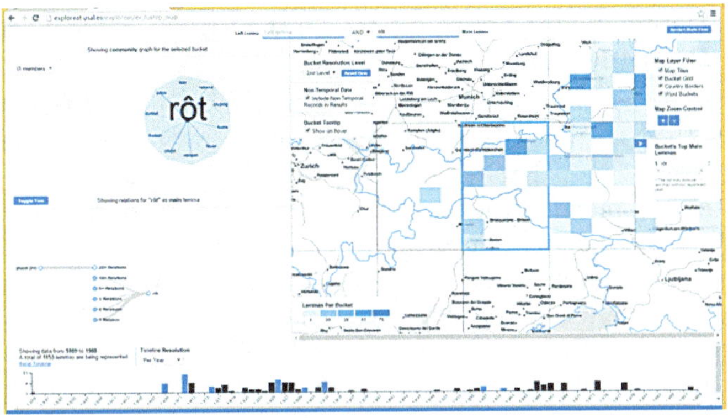

FIGURE 16 Visual output of the color term *rôt* ('red') in compound words and its possible referents.

do this, they looked for the presence of red (*rot*) in compound words such as *weinrot* ('wine red') or *blutrot* ('blood red') and compared the results obtained for different regions. As a first step, the color term *rôt* (note the pronunciation mark on the "o") was manually entered in the lexeme input box, while the prefix input box was intentionally left blank. Non-temporal data was selected to be included in the results since temporal analysis was not considered relevant in this case. Then, the spatial view presented the results returned by the search engine, showing an even spatial distribution of the query results. Finally, they selected a bordering area between modern Italy and Austria containing 272 sources to perform the SNA.

Figure 16 shows the visual output for *rôt* ('red') and its referents as found in our data. The tree visualization shows that the color red is linked to a variety of different concepts. The relations plot revealed that most compounds start with *blut/pluôt* (a pronunciation of 'blood'), *pluôtrôt* ('blood red'), or *brenn/prinn* ('burning'), *prinnrôt* ('burning red'). The experiment was repeated for other regions, and the participants could verify these results held the same for all of them, meaning that the term "red" is most typically associated with concepts of blood (*blut*) and fire-related terms (*prinn/glos/glut*) across different regions and times. Other results included *glos/glut/feuer/blutig/fuchs* ... ('glow'/'smolder'/'fire'/'bloody'/'fox' ...) to varying degrees across different regions, fact that could not lead to any significant conclusions.

8.7.2 Using Fuzzy Searches to Find Similar Headword Pronunciations

This second use case expands the work flow by centering the attention on one of the top combinations of red found in the previous example: the lemma *prinn*. The participants launched a new textual query by using the contextual menu of the particle, which returns results of headwords containing this particle at the beginning of the compound word. In addition, they opted to add fuzzy parameters to the search query in order to analyze a different kind of phenomenon.

Variations in the pronunciation and written representation vary greatly among dialect areas. On the segmental level, vowels are a particularly prominent example of showing high variability. Fuzzy searches are therefore particularly well suited to tackling such queries and have also been employed by other authors (Manning et al. 2001). When the search term was modified to "prinn∼", obtained results included lemmas that varied in maximum one character from the input term. In turn, SNA was launched for the region of Vienna, producing intriguing results (see Figure 17).

The network visualization showed the network with the different communities detected by the algorithm which are dominated, as expected, by terms matching the fuzzy query. At first sight, the users' attention is drawn to the more populated communities of *prenn* and *prunn*, which are not connected and therefore appear distant in the force-directed graph, *repelling* each other. This is not the case, however, for the *prinn* community, which is connected to the *prenn* node by two different paths: *h-eiss* ('hot') and *rôt*. At the top of the visualization appears yet another particle, *trenn* ('to separate'), which is less tightly connected to *prenn* than the previous one, having only one lemma in common, *sch<äre* ('scissors').

The original sources of the records displayed confirm there is a reason why *prenn* and *prinn* appear closer in the graph: *prenn/prinn h-eiss* ('very hot') and *prenn/prinn rôt* ('burning red') are manifestations of the same underlying word form, both meaning the same. On the other hand, the team of experts stated that they could not find any semantic coincidences between *prenn* and *trenn*, because the introduction of the fuzzy character modified in this case the lexical root and thus the origin of these two words was completely different. This comment also confirmed the validity of the chosen visualization, which placed the node farther apart than it did with the lemma *prinn*.

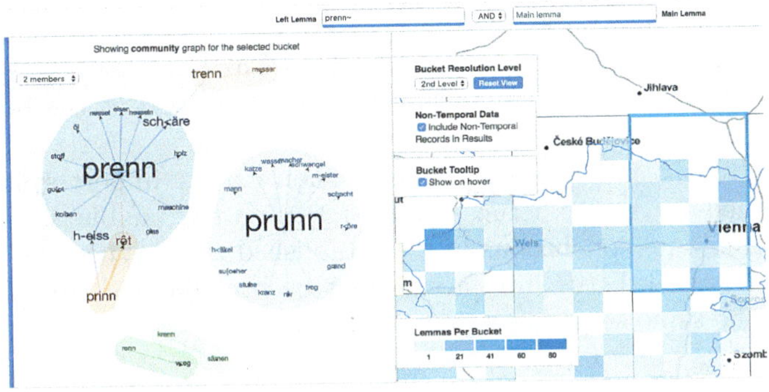

FIGURE 17 Visual output of the color term *rôt* ('red') in compound words and its possible referents.

8.7.3 Experts Feedback

By employing the proposed development methodology explained in Section 8.2, at the end of each iteration joint meetings were held in which the experts' feedback was collected to be incorporated in the next stage. The pilot tool presented in this chapter is the result of the last iteration, which also ended with a series of tests. In this last tests round, eight different experts with various backgrounds (although all of them held positions related to e-Lexicography), used the pilot tool in sessions with a maximum duration of 30 minutes. No constraints on the usage of the tool were particularly imposed on the testers, and they were asked to use the tool to freely explore the dictionary in the way they preferred. After completion of these sessions, they were asked to provide a list of strengths and weaknesses found in the application. Listed below are the ones that appeared most often:

We received positive feedback on the general purpose of the pilot tool related to the new perspective it gives to the data, which was radically different from the one traditional text-only tools provide. However, the importance of incorporating more refined and specific workflows that mimic their daily research tasks was also stressed. This refers, for example, to the generation of network graphs based on other available parameters found in the records, such as the sense of the word or pronunciation.

A major drawback was found in the inability of the pilot tool to provide more detailed metrics about the result sets managed at the different iterations of the workflow. Whereas it is true that part of these details can be obtained on demand (for example by hovering the mouse over the spatial buckets), a more specific, configurable visualization showing the distribution of the response documents according to one or more variables was marked as necessary. This feature would facilitate the fine-tuning of the selected parameters employed at the beginning of each iteration.

Finally, the inclusion of a work session export/import system was underlined by the experts. Many of them were unable to reach to any meaningful conclusions in the established time. When the window browser is closed, the interface cannot be brought back to that state unless the same steps are repeated again.

8.8 Discussion and Future Work

DH prove a highly interesting field for the application of classic computational techniques in novel ways. The necessity to create open standards, methods and frameworks able to adequately direct this experimentation has become an academic imperative. Envisioning new interactive and plastic techniques capable of managing the increasing volume of data related to humanistic studies and foster knowledge extraction has become a core component of data visualization in recent years and will be the origin of many of the future applications of this discipline.

This work draws attention to the key role of data visualization in enhancing the accessibility to computational methods usually employed in linguistics. Furthermore, we put into practice a novel architecture specially oriented towards the analysis of big data sets and the creation of responsive visualizations in the web using open standards. The software methodologies and paradigms adopted during the conception of the pilot tool proved to be very successful, and the alternation of micro-prototypes and testing sessions with the team of lexicographers involved in this investigation contributed greatly to the suitability and usefulness of the resulting software. Additionally, the reactive paradigm proved to adapt well to the inclusion of the search engine as a state manager although and we felt it was good enough for a first attempt. However, in future research they will have to be more tightly connected in order to create more complex interfaces, such as adding more logic to the controllers that allow a complete exploitation of the search engine capabilities.

We identified other possible lines of work that arose over the course of this research. Visual treatment of uncertainty would have a tremendous impact on the study of cultural evolution and the dating and classification of dictionary entries with missing information. The study of the past is, by definition, uncertain and in consequence some of the sources in the study could not be dated accurately by automatic means, while others presented incomplete or missing information. Incorporating elements that are able to transmit this uncertainty and lack of information in visual terms to the user, as showcased in previous work (Barthelmé 2010, Dasgupta et al. 2012), will suppose one of the most important challenges in future investigations.

Regarding the network analysis capabilities, we noticed certain degree of detachment (in interface terms) between the elements in the SNA area (and more specifically, the graph nodes) and their counterparts on the map. This fact made the establishment of a direct visual correspondence difficult for some of the participants and as a consequence, the multidimensional nature of the sources was at times hard to grasp. We also noticed this problem arose more often in medium/large sized computer screens. A common solution for this issue implies merging the two representations, creating a new visualization that allows spatial and network analysis to be performed using the same visual elements and areas of the screen, as seen in other famous visualizations.[9] Moreover, time could also be brought into this same view as other authors have attempted in their work (Grossner and Meeks 2014). This could enable more self-contained and effective forms of dynamic network analysis and novel ways to represent the temporal uncertainty that is present in some of the sources.

The analysis of massively populated graphs still needs to be addressed in future versions of the tool. When the number of nodes analyzed reaches the order of thousands, the amount of edges displayed on screen grows exponentially, producing the unwanted, so-called *hairball graphs* and impeding the extraction of knowledge. A common approach to solve this issue involves clustering the data in order to create a more intelligible representation. Although we looked into possible alternatives, more work is needed to be done in conjunction with the team of lexicographers collaborating in this research in order to find a combination of algorithms able to produce meaningful results. If these questions are to be solved, SNA will be promoted to a first-class element in our analysis, placed at the same level of time and space. This addition will open new doors to more complex and exciting ways of multivariate analysis.

References

Anselin, Luc, Ibnu Syabri, and Oleg Smirnov. 2002. Visualizing multivariate spatial correlation with dynamically linked windows. In L. Anselin and

[9]`http://www.tom-carden.co.uk/p5/tube_map_travel_times/applet/`.

S. Rey, eds., *New Tools for Spatial Data Analysis: Proceedings of the Specialist Meeting*. Santa Barbara, CA: Center for Spatially Integrated Social Science, University of California, Santa Barbara. CD-ROM.

Barthelmé, Simon. 2010. *Visual uncertainty (a bayesian approach)*. Ph.D. thesis, Université Paris Descartes.

Bergenholtz, Henning. 2012. What is a dictionary? *Lexikos* 22(1):20–30.

Bernard, Jürgen, Debora Daberkow, Dieter Fellner, Katrin Fischer, Oliver Koepler, Jörn Kohlhammer, Mila Runnwerth, Tobias Ruppert, Tobias Schreck, and Irina Sens. 2015. VisInfo: A digital library system for time series research data based on exploratory search – a user-centered design approach. *International Journal on Digital Libraries* 16(1):37–59.

Blondel, Vincent D., Jean-Loup Guillaume, Renaud Lambiotte, and Etienne Lefebvre. 2008. Fast unfolding of communities in large networks. *Journal of Statistical Mechanics: Theory and Experiment* 2008(10):P10008.

Bray, Tim. 2014. The javascript object notation (json) data interchange format. Tech. rep., `https://tools.ietf.org/html/rfc7159`.

Butler, Howard, Martin Daly, Allan Doyle, Sean Gillies, Stefan Hagen, and Tim Schaub. 2016. The GeoJSON format. `https://www.rfc-editor.org/info/rfc7946`.

Dasgupta, Aritra, Min Chen, and Robert Kosara. 2012. Conceptualizing visual uncertainty in parallel coordinates. *Computer Graphics Forum* 31(3):1015–1024.

Deutscher, Guy. 2010. *Through the Language Glass: Why the World Looks Different in Other Languages*. New York: Henry Holt & Company.

Dorn, Amelie, Eveline Wandl-Vogt, Jack Bowers, and Thierry Declerck. 2016. The colour of language! Exploiting language colour terms semantically for interdisciplinary research. Poster presented at the Fourth Progress in Colour Studies Conference.

Facca, Federico M., Stefano Ceri, Jacopo Armani, and Vera Demaldé. 2005. Building reactive web applications. In *Special Interest Tracks and Posters of the 14th International Conference on World Wide Web*, pages 1058–1059.

Good, Lance and Benjamin B. Bederson. 2002. Zoomable user interfaces as a medium for slide show presentations. *Information Visualization* 1(1):35–49.

Grossner, Karl and Elijah Meeks. 2014. Topotime: Representing historical uncertainty. In *Digital Humanities 2014: Book of Abstracts*, pages 181–182.

Hauswedell, Tessa and Melvin Wevers. 2015. Reporting the Empire: The branding of Metropolises and Empire in the Pall Mall Gazette 1870-1900. In *The Second Digital Humanities Benelux Conference: Book of Abstracts*, pages 78–80.

Heeringa, Wilbert J. 2004. *Measuring Dialect Pronunciation Differences Using Levenshtein Distance*. Ph.D. thesis, University of Groningen.

Heimerl, Florian, Steffen Lohmann, Simon Lange, and Thomas Ertl. 2014. Word cloud explorer: Text analytics based on word clouds. In *Proceedings of the 47th Hawaii International Conference on System Sciences*, pages 1833–1842.

Hightower, Ron R., Laura T. Ring, Jonathan I. Helfman, Benjamin B. Bederson, and James D. Hollan. 1998. Graphical multiscale Web histories: a study of padprints. In *Proceedings of the Ninth ACM Conference on Hypertext and Hypermedia: Links, Objects, Time and Space – Structure in Hypermedia Systems*, pages 58–65.

Keim, Daniel A. 2002. Information visualization and visual data mining. *IEEE transactions on Visualization and Computer Graphics* 8(1):1–8.

Keim, Daniel A., Florian Mansmann, Jörn Schneidewind, Jim Thomas, and Hartmut Ziegler. 2008. Visual analytics: Scope and challenges. In S. J. Simoff, M. H. Böhlen, and A. Mazeika, eds., *Visual Data Mining: Theory, Techniques and Tools for Visual Analytics*, pages 76–90. Berlin, Heidelberg: Springer.

Kelleher, Curran and Haim Levkowitz. 2015. Reactive data visualizations. In D. L. Kao, M. C. Hao, M. A. Livingston, and T. Wischgoll, eds., *Visualizaton and Data Analysis 2015*, vol. 9397 of *SPIE Proceedings*, page 93970N.

Manning, Christopher D., Kevin Jansz, and Nitin Indurkhya. 2001. Kirrkirr: Software for browsing and visual exploration of a structured Warlpiri dictionary. *Literary and Linguistic Computing* 16(2):135–151.

Mayer, Thomas, Johann-Mattis List, Anselm Terhalle, and Matthias Urban. 2014. An interactive visualization of crosslinguistic colexification patterns. In *Proceedings of the LREC 2014 Workshop VisLR: Visualization as Added Value in the Development, Use and Evaluation of Language Resources*, pages 1–8.

Newman, Mark E.J. 2004. Analysis of weighted networks. *Physical review E* 70(5):056131.

Nielsen, Sandro. 2008. The Effect of Lexicographical Information Costs on Dictionary Making. *Lexikos* 18(1):170–189.

Orman, Günce K., Vincent Labatut, and Hocine Cherifi. 2011. On accuracy of community structure discovery algorithms. *Journal of Convergence Information Technology* 6(11):283–292.

Rodighiero, Dario. 2015. Representing the Digital Humanities Community: Unveiling The Social Network Visualization of an International Conference. *Parsons Journal of Information Mapping* 7(EPFL-ARTICLE-208934).

Shneiderman, Ben. 1996. The eyes have it: A task by data type taxonomy for information visualizations. In *Proceedings of the IEEE Symposium on Visual Languages*, pages 336–343.

Therón, Roberto and Laura Fontanillo. 2015. Diachronic-information visualization in historical dictionaries. *Information Visualization* 14(2):111–136.

Therón, Roberto and Eveline Wandl-Vogt. 2016. New trends in digital humanities. In *Proceedings of the Fourth International Conference on Technological Ecosystems for Enhancing Multiculturality*, pages 945–947.

Wandl-Vogt, Eveline. 2010. Point and find: The intuitive user experience in accessing spatially structured dialect dictionaries. *Slavia Centralis* 2(2010):35–53.

Wandl-Vogt, Eveline and Thierry Declerck. 2013. Mapping a traditional dialectal dictionary with linked open data. In I. Kosem, J. Kallas, P. Gantar, S. Krek, M. Langemets, and M. Tuulik, eds., *Electronic Lexicography in the 21st century: Thinking Outside the Paper: Proceedings of the eLex 2013 conference*, pages 460–471.

Wanner, Franz, Wolfgang Jentner, Tobias Schreck, Andreas Stoffel, Lyubka Sharalieva, and Daniel A. Keim. 2016. Integrated visual analysis of patterns in time series and text data – Workflow and application to financial data analysis. *Information Visualization* 15(1):75–90.

9

Visual Analytics for Parameter Tuning of Semantic Vector Space Models

THOMAS WIELFAERT, KRIS HEYLEN, DIRK SPEELMAN AND DIRK GEERAERTS

9.1 Introduction

In the past decades, a wide range of statistical techniques have been developed for the corpus-based modeling of the semantic similarity between words and word uses (see Turney and Pantel 2010 and Baroni et al. 2014 for an overview and comparison of different models). At the SemEval competitions, different models have proven to be state-of-the-art for different tasks, such as synonymy extraction, lexical substitution, word sense disambiguation and word sense induction. All of these semantic similarity models heavily rely on tuning different parameters and experimenting with different types of models. Comparing differently parameterized models is commonly done using task-specific F-scores on a gold standard. However, such an evaluation is not well suited to analyze the effect of parameter settings on specific items (error analysis), nor to explore the task-independent properties of models. What these classification tasks have in common is an optimal classification or gold standard, usually provided by the competition's organizers, which participants have to use to evaluate their models against. Model performance is subsequently reported in the form of measures like precision and recall or both combined in an F1-score. What these measures

Visual Analytics for Linguistics (LingVis).
edited by Miriam Butt, Annette Hautli-Janisz and Verena Lyding.
Copyright © 2020, CSLI Publications.

can not tell however, is what went actually wrong. Error analysis remains a manual effort that can only be done by digging into the model, which is challenging when the model is a black box. Moreover, when comparing different models, precision scores do not tell which part of the data was classified correctly. In theory, it could even be possible that two competing models both attain a precision of 50%, without having any overlap in the data they classified correctly.

Distributional semantics is also used for purposes where an a priori categorization is not available. Word Sense Induction (WSI), as token-level distributional models are called in Computational Linguistics, belongs to the family of unsupervised modeling. In the context of task based computational modeling evaluation however, it is rather treated as a Word Sense Disambiguation task with predefined senses as a gold standard and thus supervised for evaluation purposes. When using unsupervised word sense induction for lexical semantic purposes, there is no alternative to manually going through the occurrences of the target word to see the semantic patterns, if any, unveiled by the model. Treating these models as Word Sense Disambiguation requires that the output is additionally submitted to a clustering algorithm. This additional processing layer renders these models even more opaque.

As a complementary tool to F-scores for categorization tasks, or in the case of unsupervised learning, as a proper evaluation tool, we propose a Visual Analytics approach that visualizes semantic similarity matrices directly, regardless of whether other evaluation methods are available. It allows us to explore and compare interactively how differently parametrized models affect the semantic similarity between single items of interest or groups with specific properties. The tool consists of three levels in which the different models can be selected (1), compared (2) and inspected (3), each level and function in the spirit of Shneiderman's Visual Information Seeking Mantra (1996): "Overview first, zoom and filter, then details-on-demand". The idea is that on each level, the user can filter and select models/tokens of interest for a detailed investigation. According to Keim et al. (2010) a trade-off exists between the insights that can be gained from automatic analysis versus (manual) explorative analysis where Visual Analytics could be the integration of both to get more optimal solutions. We argue that this is the case for our problem: automated statistical measures to evaluate each single model exist. However, these scores are not capable of telling the researcher what is going on from a linguistic point of view, nor do they provide a realistic option to look at the data points and analyze the errors in the context of the model that is being investigated.

For the Visual Analytics tool we propose, we will use a hybrid approach with manually assigned word sense labels for the case study. This way, we aim at showing the output of the model and the separation of the word senses as directly as possible, without having to add an extra layer by applying, for instance, k-means clustering, yet introducing an easily observable structure. The ultimate goal of this semantic modeling is of course to be able to separate senses automatically and unsupervised; the manually assigned sense labels are nothing more than the intermediary step to achieve this. Baroni and Lenci (2011) argued that "[t]o gain a real insight into the abilities of Distributional Semantic Models to address lexical semantics, existing benchmarks must be complemented with a more intrinsically oriented approach, to perform direct tests on the specific aspects of lexical knowledge captured by the models." We believe that Visual Analytics can be part of this "more intrinsically oriented approach"; we want to facilitate parameter optimization by visual means. It should also be stressed that this tool is not designed towards a broad audience, but is rather a complementary tool for (linguistic) researchers to visually inspect models that have been generated by different kinds of models for the vector representation of word meaning.

The remainder of this chapter is structured as following: first we briefly introduce the distributional semantic algorithm and the data used for the case study. Apart from explaining the algorithm, we also explain how high-dimensional similarity data can be turned into 2D coordinates, allowing to create visual representations from similarity data. Next, we go through the three levels or layers of the visualization tool and illustrate by means of screenshots and detailed descriptions how the researcher-user, interested in exploring semantic similarity data, can take advantage of our approach. The last section provides a general discussion and some conclusions.[1]

9.2 Distributional Semantic Algorithm and Data

This section forms a brief introduction to the algorithm for token-level distributional semantic models and for the data we use to train and test the different models in the case study. The explanation of the distributional algorithm is merely meant to provide a full understanding of the case study we present, but is in our opinion not required to grasp the visualization part of the study. For the case study we are focusing on

[1]At this point, it should be noted that a static textual description (including screenshots) can never recreate the user experience of a truly interactive visualization framework. Therefore, we strongly encourage the interested reader to also take a look at the actual tool as it is shared online: `https://tokenclouds.github.io/LeTok/`.

this specific type of model, nevertheless all sorts of (semantic) models which can be represented as a distance/similarity matrix can fairly easily be plugged into the visual framework on two conditions. First these models have different parameters that can be varied and second, the data points can, after applying dimension reduction, be represented in two dimensional space rendering an x- and y-coordinate for each data point.

9.2.1 Token-level Algorithm

Distributional Semantic Models, Word Space Models or Semantic Vector Spaces exist in many flavors and varieties. We will very briefly explain here an adapted version of one of the earlier models, namely Schütze's (1998) bag-of-words model. This model is no longer considered state-of-the-art in distributional semantics, but its intuitive ideas make it attractive for lexical semantic purposes and to use it as a generic baseline model to experiment with. One of the main problems with token-level models is that constructing token vectors with raw co-occurrence frequencies will lead to data sparsity. Suppose a training corpus contains 10,000 different word types, meaning a first-order co-occurrence matrix has 10,000 columns, and that we use a context window of 10 words (a symmetrical window of 5-5 around the target). This would mean that in a best case scenario 10 cells out of 10,000 (0.1%) of the vector would be filled with actual frequencies and the other 99.9% with zeros, and thus be very sparse, making vector comparison mathematically intractable. Schütze's insight is that we can overcome this problem by moving on to so-called second-order co-occurrences. These second-order co-occurrences are the type-level context features of the (first-order) context words co-occurring with the token. This way, we still model the tokens by their "co-occurrences", but these are no longer the direct collocates. Note that the first-order model still has to be created to construct the second-order model.

Following Schütze, for each token we normalize the frequencies by the number of context words for that token:

$$o_i^{\vec{w}} = \frac{\sum_{j \in C_i^w}^{n} \vec{c_j}}{n}$$

where $o_i^{\vec{w}}$ is the token vector for the ith occurrence of word w and C_i^w is the set of n type vectors $\vec{c_j}$ for the n context words in the window around that i^{th} occurrence of word w. However, this summation means that each first-order context word has an equal weight in determining the token vector. Yet, not all first-order context words are equally informative for the meaning of a token. In a sentence like "While walking to work, the teacher saw a dog barking and chasing a cat", *bark* and *cat* are much more indicative of the meaning of *dog* than for instance *teacher* or *work*. In a second, weighted version, we therefore increased the contribution of these informative context words by using the first-order context words' association measures with the target word. The association value of a word w and a context word c_j can now be seen as a weight $weight^w_{c_j}$. In constructing the token vector $\vec{o^w_i}$ for the ith occurrence of noun w with $weight^w_{c_j}$, we now multiply the type vector $\vec{c_j}$ of each context word by the weight $weight^w_{c_j}$, and then normalize by the sum of the all weights:

$$\vec{o^w_i} = \frac{\sum^n_{j \in C^w_i} weight^w_{c_j} * \vec{c_j}}{\sum^n_j weight^w_{c_j}}$$

When this procedure has been repeated for each token, we get a token by second-order co-occurrence matrix. By computing the cosines between these token vectors, we obtain a similarity matrix.[2] This similarity matrix is subsequently the starting point for visualizing the models, but not before some further processing, described in the following sections.

9.2.2 Training Data

To get sufficiently high token frequencies for the target words, we made use of the British National Corpus (BNC), a balanced corpus of (British) English, composed of different sources to create frequency vectors for our models. The BNC is a 100 M word corpus which is widely used as a benchmark for evaluating Natural Language Processing tasks, including word sense induction (see for instance Rapp 2003, Brody and Lapata 2009, and Lau et al. 2012). It is large enough to be used as a training set for a data intensive algorithm such as the token-level distributional semantic model we describe. The version of the BNC we used was lemmatized and Phart-of-Speech tagged with the CLAWS7 tagset (Wynne 1996).

9.2.3 Testing Data

We use the test data from the SemEval 2010 task *Word Sense Induction & Disambiguation Task* (Manandhar et al. 2010) – a shared task for computational semantic analysis systems. From the SemEval test data, we selected 17 English nouns (*air, body, campaign, chip, class, community, field, flight, gas, house, idea, mind, moment, officer, road,*

[2]For the more thorough, full explanation on how the weighted Schütze bag-of-words model works, we would like to refer the interested reader to the first sections of Heylen et al. (2015).

television, threat) and 8 verbs (*apply, deny, insist, introduce, lay, lie, operate, reveal*), based on the number of occurrences included in the data: 100 $< n <$ 300 occurrences. This lower bound is to make sure that a reasonable number of items is left in case there are empty token vectors. For the upper bound however, the motivation is twofold: first, we found out experimentally that around 300 items is the upper limit of the variation the dimension reduction algorithm of our choice (Non-metrical Multidimensional Scaling or NMDS) can handle with our type of data. Second, retaining too many items in the samples results in very cluttered plots which would hamper the interpretation. Furthermore, using more than 300 items is unlikely to contribute "new" information to the plots. When one is confronted with a larger amount tokens, we would advise to turn to samples of a similar size and visualize (and thus evaluate) these separately. Next, the SemEval test data provides exactly one sentence before and after the sentence containing the target word, making its window ideal for these purposes. Each target token has been annotated with a sense label derived from OntoNotes (Hovy et al. 2006), allowing to quickly visually verify the distinguished senses in each model. The OntoNotes word senses rely on a 90% inter-rater agreement to create a high-quality language resource. OntoNotes turns the often too finely grained WordNet (Miller 1995) senses into a tree structure which is cut off at a granularity level where different senses can still be reliably distinguished by human annotators.

9.2.4 Parameter Space

As distributional models exist in many configurations and are by definition parameter-rich, the parameter space could be virtually infinite and exponentially increases the number of models that can be created with all possible combinations of parameter settings. We want to give a brief overview of the parameter settings that were varied for our case study. Table 1 shows how first and second-order co-occurrences are combined leading up to 192 different models in total. The table's symmetry is slightly distorted by the models where the first-order co-occurrences are not weighted. Even though we have stretched this parameter space even further, by using more than one association measure for the first-order weighting, we opt here to only show one possibility for this specific parameter, namely positive pointwise mutual information (PPMI). The reason for this is that adding hundreds of extra models does not contribute to the leveled Visual Analytics approach we want to show and could cause more harm than good by introducing extra noise into the visual space.

For the second-order weighting scheme, we use three additional mea-

TABLE 1 Parameter variation.

1'order		10L-10R				20L-20R				40L-40R			
	weight	none	ppmi			none	ppmi			none	ppmi		
2'ord.	scheme		2L-2R	4L-4R	7L-7R		2L-2R	4L-4R	7L-7R		2L-2R	4L-4R	7L-7R
2L-2R	dice	001	017	033	049	065	081	097	113	129	145	161	177
	LLR	002	018	034	050	066	082	098	114	130	146	162	178
	ppmi	003	019	035	051	067	083	099	115	131	147	163	179
	tscore	004	020	036	052	068	084	100	116	132	148	164	180
4L-4R	dice	005	021	037	053	069	085	101	117	133	149	165	181
	LLR	006	022	038	054	070	086	102	118	134	150	166	182
	ppmi	007	023	039	055	071	087	103	119	135	151	167	183
	tscore	008	024	040	056	072	088	104	120	136	152	168	184
7L-7R	dice	009	025	041	057	073	089	105	121	137	153	169	185
	LLR	010	026	042	058	074	090	106	122	138	154	170	186
	ppmi	011	027	043	059	075	091	107	123	139	155	171	187
	tscore	012	028	044	060	076	092	108	124	140	156	172	188
10L-10R	dice	013	029	045	061	077	093	109	125	141	157	173	189
	LLR	014	030	046	062	078	094	110	126	142	158	174	190
	ppm	015	031	047	063	079	095	111	127	143	159	175	191
	tscore	016	032	048	064	080	096	112	128	144	160	176	192

sures as an alternative to PPMI (Niwa and Nitta 1994), which is the de facto standard association measure for semantic vector space models (Jurafsky and Martin 2018:Chapter 15). Alternatives we will consider are log-likelihood ratio (LLR) (Dunning 1993), t-score and Dice coefficient (diceM). We do not intend to draw conclusions on any of these measures as the preferable option, but they are merely introduced because they have been considered and tested within distributional semantics (see for instance Lapesa and Evert 2014 for such a large-scale comparison) as an alternative to positive pmi. There are extensive studies on the different pros and cons of each of these measures (see for instance Bullinaria and Levy 2007), which are not a point of discussion in this chapter.

The models have both been named and numbered. Model #018 from Table 1, named "air.n.10-10.weightsBNC-4-4pospmi.2-2.LLR", contains tokens of the noun *air* and a 10-10 window left and right of the target has been used to collect context words. In other words: the bag-of-words for each type has size 20. These 20 context words have been weighted with information from the BNC (in the visualizations referred to as "BNCweights"), namely the positive pointwise mutual information ("pospmi" or "ppmi") constructed with a 4-4 window. These context words are in their turn weighted with by the second-order co-occurrences (co-occurrences of co-occurrences) within a 2-2 window and scored with log-likelihood ratio (LLR).

9.3 From High-dimensional Space to Visualization

The output of a "traditional" distributional model is a similarity matrix (or its inverse, a distance matrix), which is n-dimensional with n being the number of items modeled. To visualize high-dimensional space in a 2D visualization, we need a dimension reduction technique. The standard algorithm to reduce these kind of similarity matrices is Kruskal's Non-metric Multidimensional Scaling (Kruskal 1964), which tries to preserve the individual distances between the items. Its success rate is calculated as stress, the algorithms inability to preserve the original distances in the scaled version, for which a cost function tries to minimize the former. The question that remains is: at which point the stress value is low enough to assure the reduced spatial representation of high-dimensional space is accurate enough to be trusted?

The goodness of fit is a complex problem in the case of NMDS. Kruskal provided some guidelines to make a basic interpretation of the stress values: higher than 20% is poor, between 10% and 20% is fair and lower than 5% is considered good. Experiments with sizable (250-300 items) semantic dissimilarity data however showed us that a stress value lower than 20% is rare if the number of dimensions is set to 2. There are two straightforward strategies to cope with these high stress values: 1) increase the number of dimensions in the MDS and 2) reduce the variation in the data. For the first option, is possible to use the scree plot[3] to make an informed decision, which is called the "elbow method".[4] This entails looking for the point where adding extra dimensions is no longer justified by the decline of the stress value, which can often (but not always) be visualized in a scree plot, the so-called elbow. However, as we will still be visualizing high-dimensional space on a flat, 2D display, this might not be the optimal strategy. Using more than two dimensions in a visualization creates additional interpretation difficulties when the third dimension can not be visualized as such, for instance on a 3D-wall or through a virtual reality headset. Moreover, the high-dimensional space is not necessarily better represented in 2D than in 3D as this one, extra dimension still means throwing away the majority of 250 to 300 dimensions. We performed all dimension reduction operations in R.[5] The result of the MDS are the 2D coordinates which form the basis for the data frame we plug into the visualization.

[3]A scree plot is a decreasing function, which in this case shows the stress level to the number of dimensions.

[4]The elbow method is a typical technique from cluster analysis.

[5]isoDMS from the *MASS* package, 10 iterations with a random initiation, initMDS, from the *vegan* package to avoid getting stuck in a local optimum. The result with the lowest stress value is retained as the solution.

Furthermore, we should note that when the axes remain unlabeled it means the first dimension is represented on the x-axis en the second on the y-axis. Unlike the dimensions of Principal Component Analysis (PCA) for instance, it not possible to interpret the NMDS dimensions or put meaningful labels on the axes.

Setting this aside, the way this chapter and the case study is set up forces us to stay agnostic about the exact implications for the remainder of this chapter, besides integrating the above mentioned stress levels in the visualization. Dimension reduction is not only a complex problem, but also an entire field of its own. Therefore, we opted to use the de facto standard, long established algorithm. Another, more cutting-edge algorithm is briefly touched upon in the discussion section, but not used in the visualization. The reason for this is two-fold: first, we have introduced a number of statistical measures which express the quality of the different models. These measures are consequently used to back up the visual structures that are generated by the dimension reduction. Second, introducing more than one dimension reduction algorithm for the visualizations would broaden the focus of this study, which is visually comparing and evaluating a large number of different semantic models, towards the difference between the dimension reduction algorithms. Undoubtedly, this is material for a thorough evaluation, but this evidently falls entirely outside the field of (Visual) Linguistics proper.

9.4 Leveled Visualization Tool

The large number of different models pose a new challenge to visualize in a user-friendly, yet structured way. Rather than randomly browsing through different models, we created a layered visualization with 3 levels: the top one (Level 1) showing all available models in a standard scatterplot which enhances selection on visual and formal criteria, a middle layer (Level 2) which visualizes up to 9 previously selected models in a so-called scatterplot matrix and at the lowest level (Level 3), again an interactive scatterplot to fully explore individual models and visualizing the individual data points in all its details, including the metadata encoded in the data frame.

The tool is written with D3.js,[6] a JavaScript framework for data visualization, making it accessible in any modern-day web browser and easily shareable online. The visualization tool was designed to be data independent, meaning that any data frame derived from similarity data, fulfilling the minimal requirements can fairly easily be plugged in. These minimal requirements entail that each data point has a unique ID, x-

[6] https://d3js.org.

and y-coordinates and a text field along with a number of optional and further unspecified numerical and categorical variables or features (aka parameter settings).

Before moving on, there are two important remarks we would like to make. First, the case study below focuses on the noun *air* and does not touch upon the other nouns and verbs from the SemEval test set, because each target noun or verb is studied independently, in separate sessions with different contexts. We would like to point out however that the target word was chosen arbitrarily and not because the data fits the models better with the noun *air*; we even turned a blind eye to the question whether this is the case. Our tool should allow to study any target word, as long as enough and appropriate models have been created.

Secondly, this case study is just scratching the surface of what could be done with the tool. As translating visual features and interactions to a textual description eats up a lot of space, we have been forced to focus on a limited number of models/tokens/parameters. As a result any explanation or exploration is far from comprehensive in the sense that it is fairly easy to come up with a virtually endless list of new features that could be added to the visual representations. However, this should not pose a problem as the constant interaction between user, data and visuals is key to the process of Visual Analytics.

9.4.1 Related Work

Related studies includes Le and Lauw (2016) who visualize high dimensional semantic similarity data from document-based topic modeling with a neighborhood regularization network, to preserve the distance in the lower dimensional representations. The dimension reduction aspect relates to our study, but the study focuses exclusively on the probabilistic topic model to model document-level semantics, while we are interested in distributional token-level semantics.

Cao et al. (2010) turn to multifacet visualization to visualize document relationships in a graph network while Zhao et al. (2012) use a graph representation to facilitate discourse analysis, including a keyword-in-context opportunity to browse through the nodes underlying the linguistic analysis. The former studies are exclusively document-based and while their multifaceted approach is definitely inspirational to ours, these visualizations rely on graph relationships which are not present in our data.

Heimerl et al. (2012) collect user input to train a classifier in order to facilitate document search in large text corpora. One of the goals in this study is to let domain experts improve the supervised learning without the need of technical skills to optimize the parameters for the actual learning. Similarly to our work, they want to give the user an insight in the black box of an algorithm. The main difference, however, is that our visualization tool should be (re)usable or easily adaptable to any kind of data, while the user is expected to have intrinsic knowledge about both the data and the algorithm he or she has applied to generate the similarity matrix.

9.4.2 First Level: Model Selection

The highest level in the tool provides a structured overview of the models that have been created by looping over all possible combinations of parameters. It sticks to the basic structure we use for visualizing the semantic similarity data, namely a scatterplot. To make a representation of the models themselves, we performed a symmetric Procrustes analysis (Mardia et al. 1980, Peres-Neto and Jackson 2001) on the 2D coordinates of the models in R.[7] Procrustes compares two matrices by rotating one of them until it resembles the target matrix best. The so-called sum of squared distances between the rotated matrix and the target is then used to express this resemblance. This measure is subsequently used to construct a new similarity matrix which, in its turn, can be fed to the NMDS dimension reduction algorithm, resulting in 2D coordinates for each model and thus form the input for a scatterplot of models. The different parameters can be visually coded in the scatterplot, either through color and shape (categorical variables) or size (numerical variables), giving a visual insight in how models with different settings behave vis-à-vis each other. To create a clear visual distinction between the glyphs that represent models (Level 1) and those that represent actual tokens (Level 2 and 3), we are using a "wye" symbol for the first and standard circles for the latter as their default representation.

Returning to the *air* example, we can now visualize which influential parameters can be defined. In Figure 1 the top row (white) buttons control the selection of both visual parameter and glyphs (the models in this case). In contrast, the second row of (blue) buttons controls the selection of the visual features: color, shape and size. If we select first order-weighting to be color-coded, we get the picture in Figure 2. This very simple visual coding immediately shows the effect of weighting first-order context words: the weighted models (in orange, green and red) are quite well separated from those (in blue) which use raw frequencies. This kind of observation is probably insufficient to draw any

[7]The procrustes function is part of the *vegan* package.

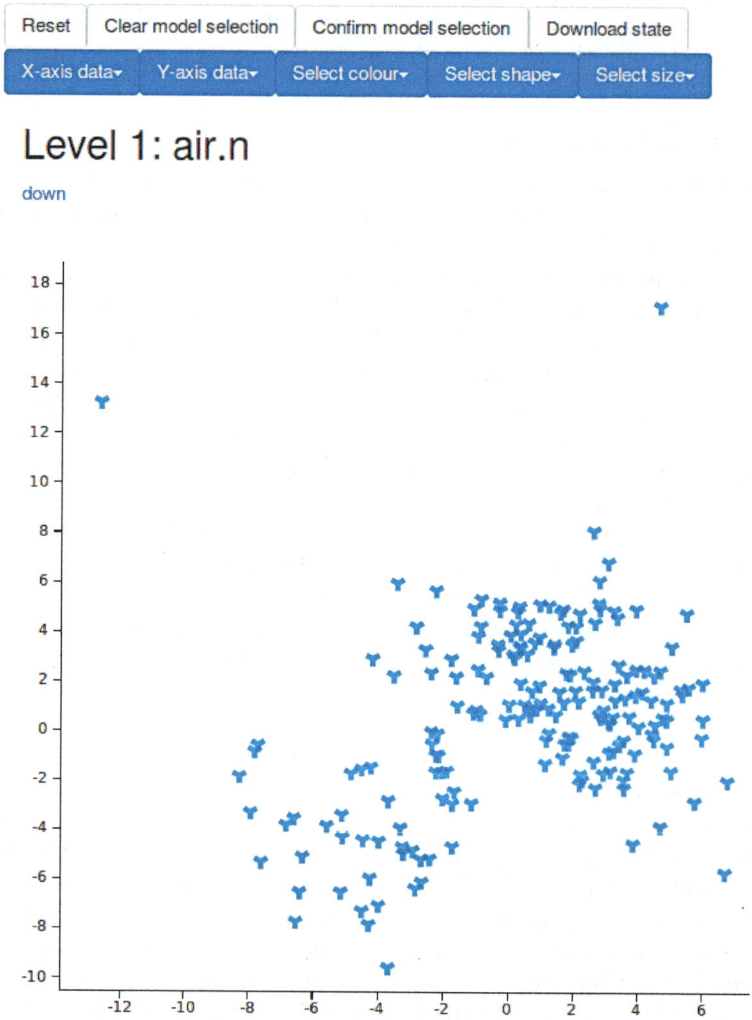

FIGURE 1 Level 1: basic scatterplot view of different models.

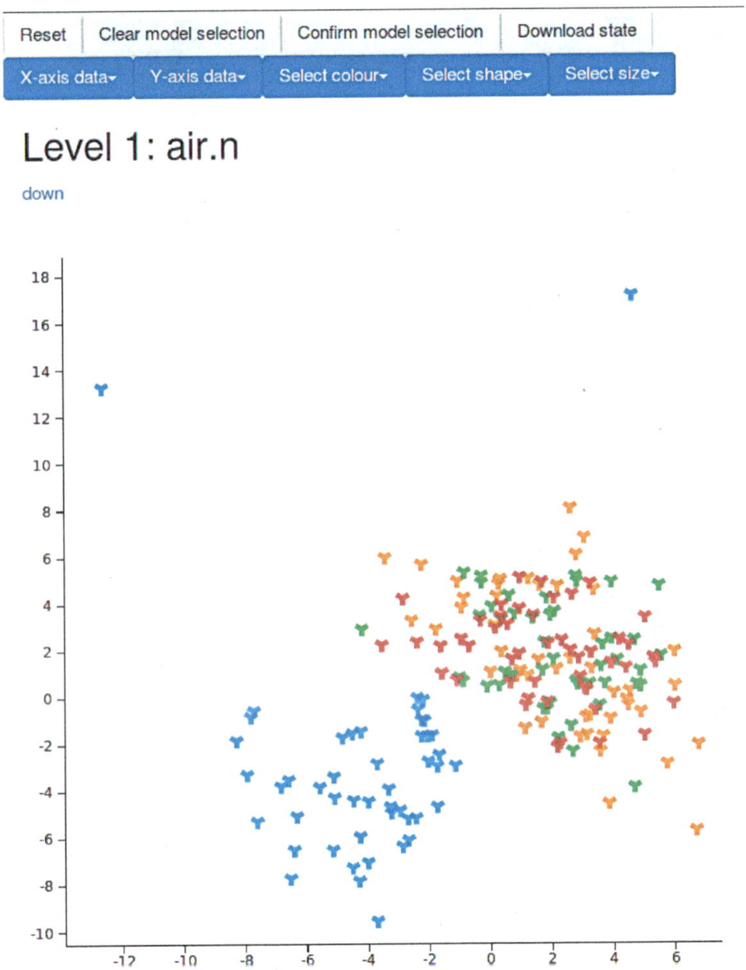

FIGURE 2 Level 1: scatterplot models color-coded for first-order weighting.

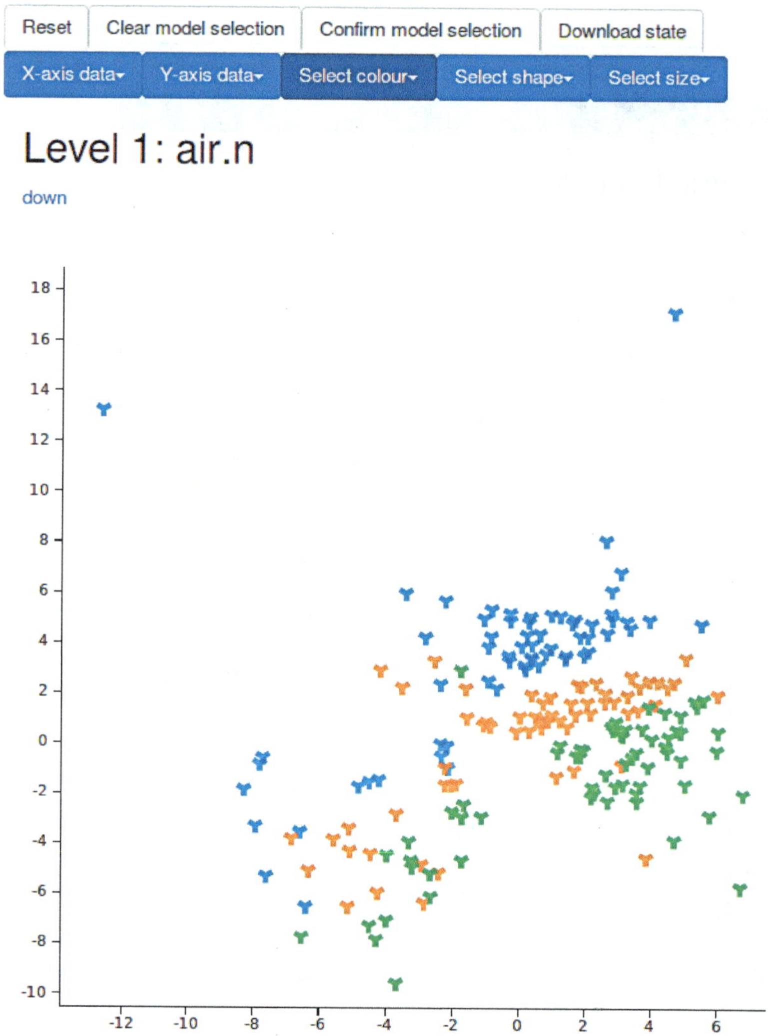

FIGURE 3 Level 1: scatterplot models color-coded for context window.

conclusions, but it might give a clue about which models are similar to each other and which are not. Repeating the color coding for first-order context window (the number of words left and right of the target that are taken into consideration) in Figure 3, we can easily see that the three window sizes (coded as L10-R10, L20-R20 and L40-R40) reveal a pattern that makes them quite separable. Actually, two patterns have become visible, namely both the previously described first-order weighting and the window size form a pattern now. At this point, it would be useful to code both features visually: the first one with color, the second with shape. Even though shape is one of the more suitable (Bertin 1967, Mackinlay 1986) and, in the case of a scatterplot, usable visual variables to encode nominal data, it does not provide the clearest visual distinction. Zooming in on the weighted models as in Figure 4 shows indeed that the wyes, crosses and diamonds, which code the window are separated in the y-dimension of the plot. This pattern however is slightly obfuscated by the first-order weighting vs. non-weighting pattern which has been coded with four categories (NONE, BNC2-2pospmi, BNC4-4pospmi and BNC7-7pospmi) rather than a binary variable (weighted vs. non-weighted). The next step in a Visual Analytics interactive process between model and visualization could be to add this binary distinction to the data frame, which creates a new pattern that more clearly distinguishes the separation, as we can see in Figure 5.

Keep in mind that the main goal of this first level is to get some insight into how dozens of models relate to each other without having to inspect them individually at a more detailed level right away. The next step is to select the models for a comparison at Level 2, the scatterplot matrix. Hovering over the glyphs reveals the model's name, in which by convention of the tool, the used parameter settings are encoded. Models can be selected or deselected in an intuitive way by simply clicking them. The useful selection of models is limited to 9, which fit the 3x3 scatterplot matrix at Level 2, and the order of selection is maintained. Models that are selected beyond the limit of the 9 available positions will remain hidden until a slot in the scatterplot matrix opens by deselecting a previously selected model.

Below the plot, the parameters space used to create the different models is shown in a table (see Figure 6) as an alternative way to access this list of parameters more directly. The columns can be sorted and the table is searchable through the search box at the top, allowing to filter the models by keyword. Furthermore, models can be selected by either clicking the relevant glyph in the scatterplot or the corresponding table row. The table provides a more direct way of accessing

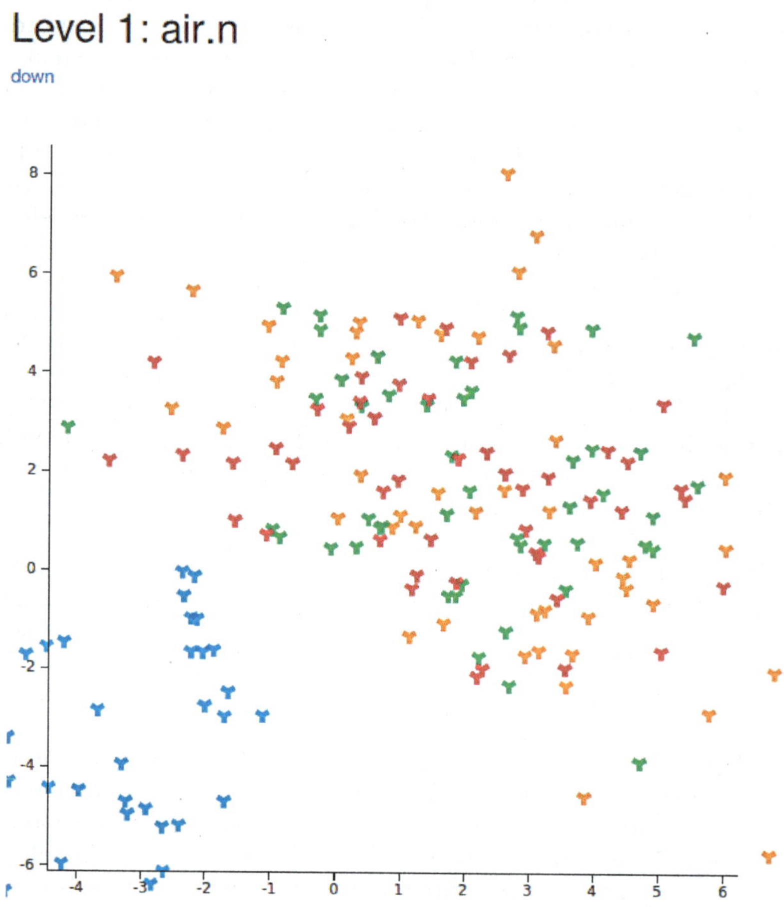

FIGURE 4 Level 1: zooming on the first-order weighted tokens.

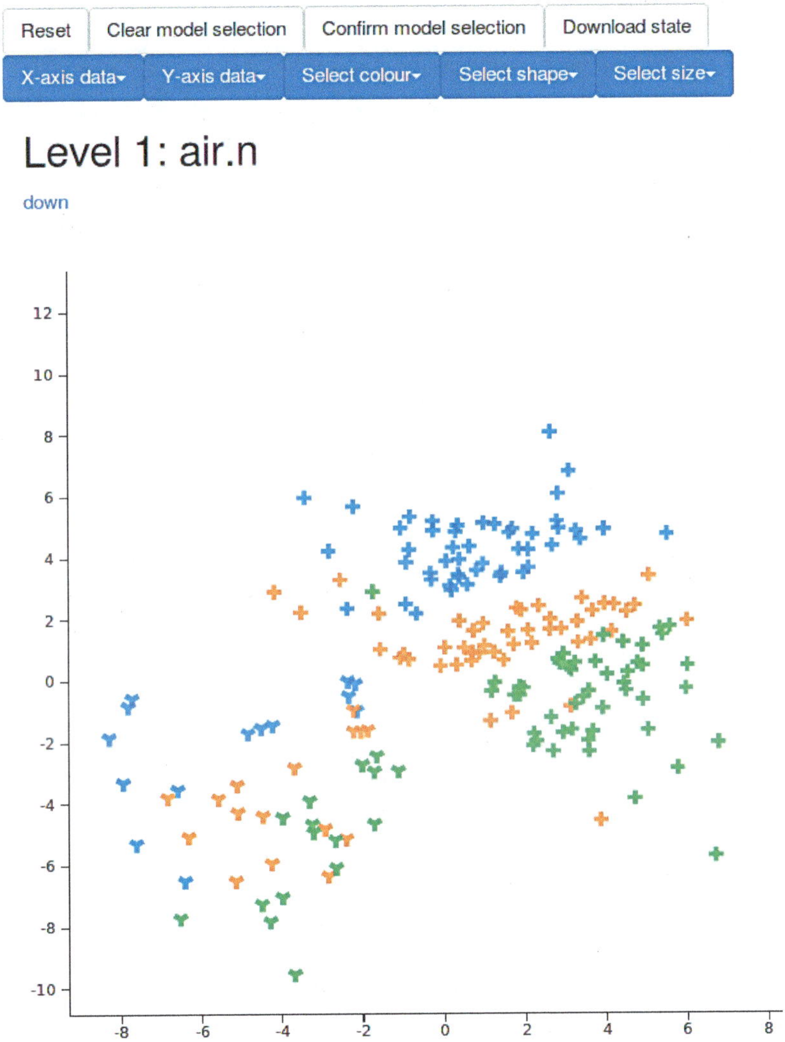

FIGURE 5 Level 1: binary coded first-order weighting.

Show 10 entries Search:

ID	weighted	first-order weighting	context window size	second-order window size	second-order scheme	MDS stress	Same Class Path ratio
air.n.10-10.weightsBNC-2-2pospmi.10-10.diceM	yes	BNC-2-2pospmi	L10-R10	L10-R10	diceM	23.17	0.306712555
air.n.10-10.weightsBNC-2-2pospmi.10-10.LLR	yes	BNC-2-2pospmi	L10-R10	L10-R10	LLR	27.46	0.370938665
air.n.10-10.weightsBNC-2-2pospmi.10-10.pospmi	yes	BNC-2-2pospmi	L10-R10	L10-R10	pospmi	22.7	0.251978716
air.n.10-10.weightsBNC-2-2pospmi.10-10.tScore	yes	BNC-2-2pospmi	L10-R10	L10-R10	tScore	25.05	0.340232128
air.n.10-10.weightsBNC-2-2pospmi.2-2.diceM	yes	BNC-2-2pospmi	L10-R10	L2-R2	diceM	26.85	0.315310208
air.n.10-10.weightsBNC-2-2pospmi.2-2.LLR	yes	BNC-2-2pospmi	L10-R10	L2-R2	LLR	31.55	0.382858357
air.n.10-10.weightsBNC-2-2pospmi.2-2.pospmi	yes	BNC-2-2pospmi	L10-R10	L2-R2	pospmi	26.14	0.232464029
air.n.10-10.weightsBNC-2-2pospmi.2-2.tScore	yes	BNC-2-2pospmi	L10-R10	L2-R2	tScore	28.35	0.325643366
air.n.10-10.weightsBNC-2-2pospmi.4-4.diceM	yes	BNC-2-2pospmi	L10-R10	L4-R4	diceM	24.97	0.294405543
air.n.10-10.weightsBNC-2-2pospmi.4-4.LLR	yes	BNC-2-2pospmi	L10-R10	L4-R4	LLR	29.76	0.403132174

Showing 1 to 10 of 192 entries

FIGURE 6 Level 1: Table with available models and their parameters.

the parameter space that is traversed over the different models. For the case study, we described the parameter space in details. However, this process might not always be straightforward. This way, we avoid having to browse through the menus or individual glyphs to get a gist of what data is actually represented in this overarching Procrustes model of distributional models.

Once a selection of models has been made, there are two ways to proceed to the next (second) level, the scatterplot matrix. The easiest option is using the button "Confirm selection" which saves the selection and loads the second level of the visualization. The alternative is to use the hyperlink "down" (in light blue) just below the title of the plot. These links, "up" and "down" are repeated throughout the three levels, providing a fast and intuitive way to move between levels.

9.5 Second Level: Model Comparison

In the second level the selected models from Level 1 show their actual content (the tokens), each model occupying one cell of the scatterplot matrix. In other words: the glyphs are no longer representing models, visualized as wyes on the first level, but rather a set of tokens that is kept constant over the different models in order to compare them. The menus at the top are similar to the first level, but the most powerful functionality of this visualization type lies in the so-called brushing

TABLE 2 Parameter table: "air.n" selected models.

1'order		10L-10R				20L-20R				40L-40R			
	weight	none	ppmi			none	ppmi			none	ppmi		
2'ord.	scheme		2L-2R	4L-4R	7L-7R		2L-2R	4L-4R	7L-7R		2L-2R	4L-4R	7L-7R
2L-2R	dice	001	017	033	049	065	081	097	113	129	145	161	177
	LLR	002	018	034	050	066	082	098	114	130	146	162	178
	ppmi	003	019	035	051	067	083	099	115	131	147	163	179
	tscore	004	020	036	052	068	084	100	116	132	148	164	180
4L-4R	dice	005	021	037	053	069	085	101	117	133	149	165	181
	LLR	006	022	038	054	070	086	102	118	134	150	166	182
	ppmi	007	023	039	055	071	087	103	119	135	151	167	183
	tscore	008	024	040	056	072	088	104	120	136	152	168	184
7L-7R	dice	009	025	041	057	073	089	105	121	137	153	169	185
	LLR	010	026	042	058	074	090	106	122	138	154	170	186
	ppmi	011	027	043	059	075	091	107	123	139	155	171	187
	tscore	012	028	044	060	076	092	108	124	140	156	172	188
10L-10R	dice	013	029	045	061	077	093	109	125	141	157	173	189
	LLR	014	030	046	062	078	094	110	126	142	158	174	190
	ppm	015	031	047	063	079	095	111	127	143	159	175	191
	tscore	016	032	048	064	080	096	112	128	144	160	176	192

and linking functionality (Cleveland and McGill 1988, Buja et al. 1991) which we implemented here. Brushing and linking allows the user to select an area of interest by dragging over it with the cursor, while simultaneously seeing the selection made in all the other cells. The brush is enabled by selecting the radio button "brush" above the plot. The brush allows to draw a rectangle of any size by dragging the cursor in in the desired direction over an area with tokens. In combination with color (or shape) coding the glyphs according to their sense label, this brush function provides a powerful tool to study how the location of closely positioned tokens compares to the rest of the selected models. These selections are stored and maintained throughout Level 2 and 3, meaning one can seamlessly switch between these two levels while adding and/or removing tokens from the selection. In the scatterplot matrix with different models, the information is already dense. Therefore we only display the sense label, which only occupies little space. We would recommend to switch back and forth between Level 2 and 3 in order to further inspect and adapt the selection.

Suppose we have selected the nine models in Level 1 for "air.n" as shown in Figure 7 in their numerical order: #087, #091, #095, #103, #107, #111, #115, #123 and #127 as highlighted in Table 2. Not coincidentally, these models are very similar to each other in terms of parameter settings; they all have a context window of 20-20 and use pospmi for both the first-order weighting and the second-order scheme. The only varied parameter here is the size of the first-order weights

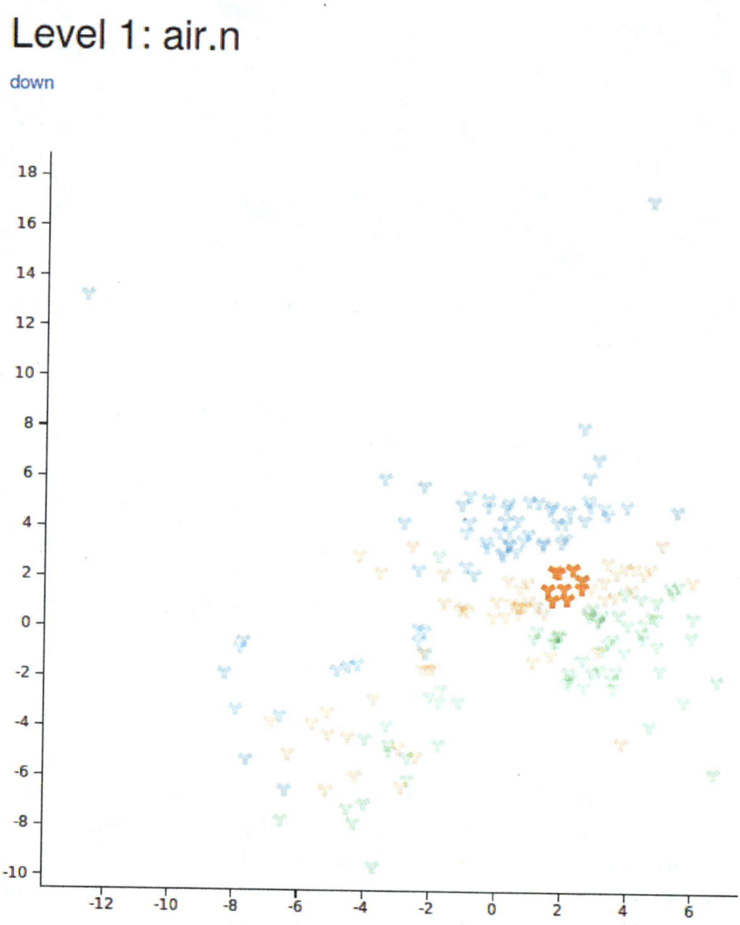

FIGURE 7 Level 1: scatterplot with nine selected models.

window. The visual encoding on the first level allows to easily select models from the same category. Admittedly, at first this might not look like the most interesting selection for comparison. By keeping all but one parameter constant however, we can narrow down the visual space that needs to be explored and start selecting precisely those parameters that generate the visually most interesting model. In Figure 8 we can see the nine models, each wrapped in a cell and ordered according to ID.[8] After color coding the glyphs according to sense, a diffuse pattern emerges which is not equally clear in all plots, even though the pattern looks (except for some rotation) in all cells quite similar. Roughly speaking, we could say that the blue dots (coded as label.4) form a cloud near the origin of the plot while the red and purple ones (label.1 and label.5) aggregate more in the periphery as if the model is distinguishing them as very different from the blue ones. At this point, it would be the right moment to take a closer look at individual models and inspect the tokens they contain.

9.6 Third Level: Individual Model Inspection

The third and lowest level is again a scatterplot where each individual model can be inspected in detail, as if it were a zoomed-in version of the scatterplot matrix. The third level provides a very similar interface to the first, but at this level the glyphs represent tokens rather than models. These tokens reveal their full context (in this case the three sentences from the SemEval task, with the target word in the middle sentence) on a mouseover gesture (hovering the cursor over the glyph) in a so-called tooltip, a small window that appears next to the respective token. Below the context snippet in the tooltip, the metadata encoded in the data frame for that token are also shown. Click selection works in the same way as on the other levels: click on a token to select and deselect it. However, at this point the aim of the selection, which is saved at each change, is to be able to see the details (and thus changes) throughout the different models. As all models contain exactly the same tokens, these selections are stored in memory to switch easily between Level 2 and 3.

After returning to the selection we have made in the previous levels, we can now go over them and look at the actual tokens, see whether their labels are correct and ultimately decide whether the groupings make sense. We take a look at one of the "air.n" models that we se-

[8]For the sake of simplicity, we manually reordered the models according to their ID. Under normal circumstances, the scatterplot uses the order of selection from Level 1 and displays them in a natural left-to-right and top-to-bottom order.

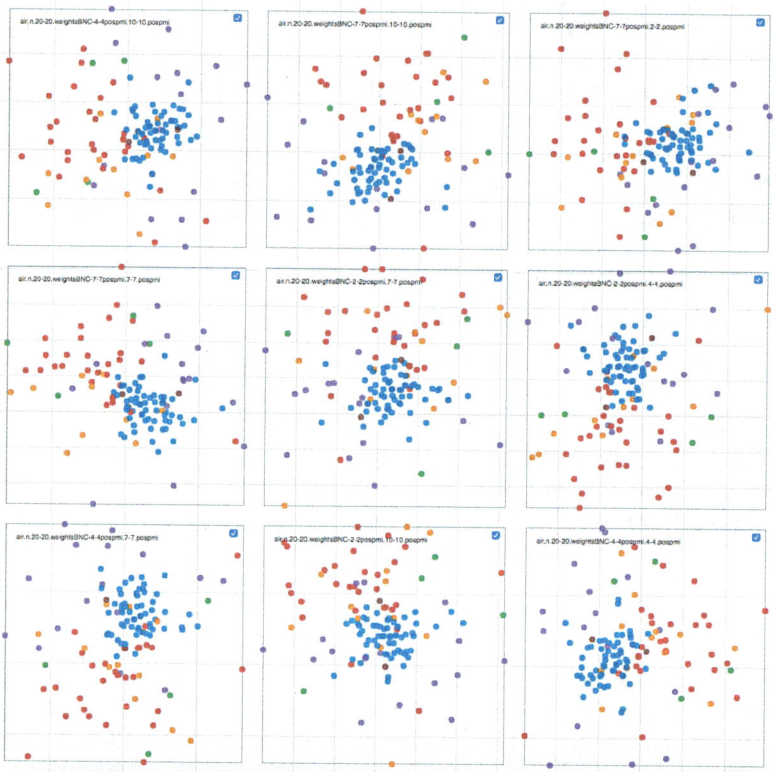

FIGURE 8 Level 2: scatterplot matrix with the previously selected models.

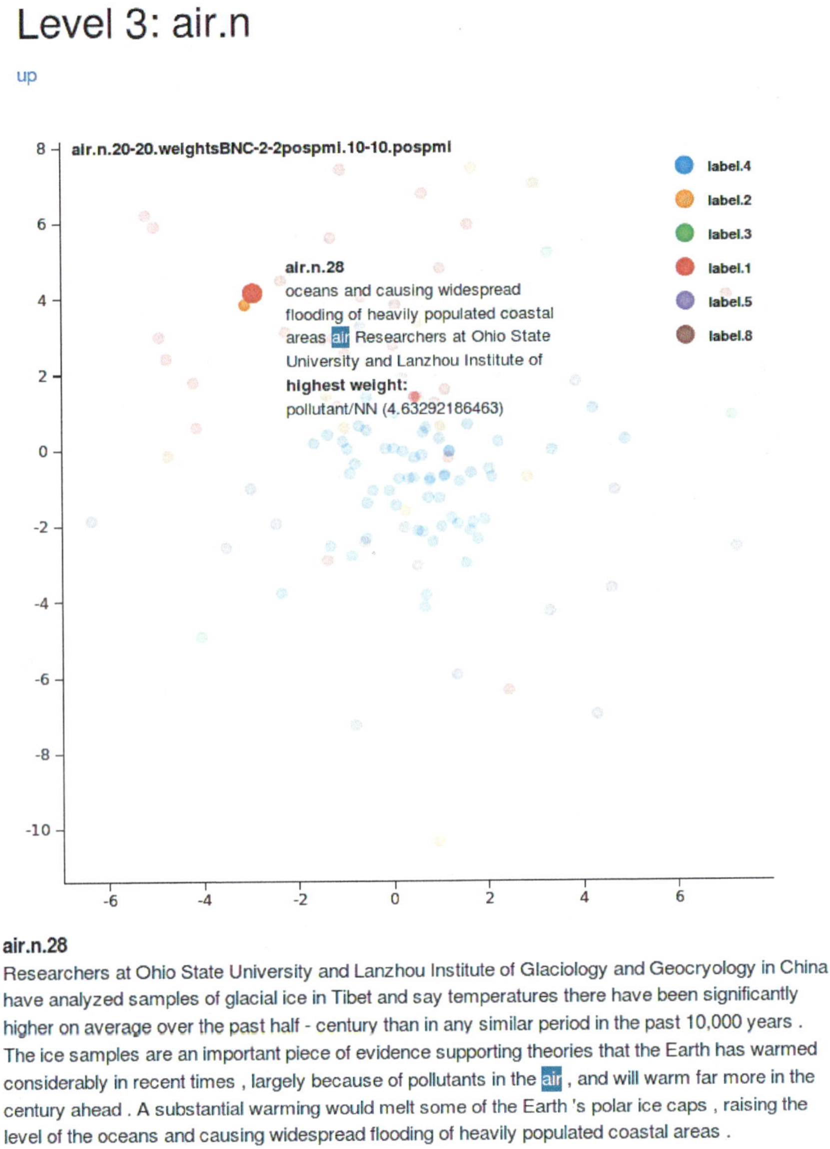

FIGURE 9 Level 3: air.n model #095 with active tooltip on token air.n.28.

lected at Level 1 and inspected at Level 2, namely #095 alias "air.n.20-20.weightsBNC-2-2pospmi.10-10.pospm", the top right model in Level 2. In Figure 9 the individual model is color-coded in the same way as in Level 2. When hovering over token "air.n.28", a small context snippet appears, selecting the token by clicking shows the entire context below the plot. The tooltip also shows the highest weighted context word within the context window, in this case *pollutants* (weighted 4.63). Now we can ask the question whether the surrounding tokens are indeed semantically related to this one as most of them (but one, which is coincidentally the closest token to air.n.28) have been tagged with the same sense label. At this point however, we might learn more about the semantics that have been captured by this specific model by looking at those tokens which are so-called outliers, meaning they have a different sense label compared to the surrounding tokens. "air.n.73" is such a token; it is the closest token to "air.n.28", but has a different label. The context snippet is shown in Figure 10. In this case, the highest weighted context word is *tropical* (weighted 1.36). One could argue that *pollutant* is indeed a more informative context word for the meaning of *air* than *tropical*. This also helps to understand why these tokens are misclassified in the plot; there are no (other) informative context words used in the model, despite the large (20-20) context window. In this case, the informative context word is actually *rainbow*, but that context word is apparently not decisive in this particular model. This exploration could continue by investigating whether this is also the case in all the other models.

After observing cases where no informative context words are present, and as a result, tokens can not be automatically disambiguated by the model, we decided that weight values are something we want to code visually. In our case study, we have provided two options to visualize the impact of the first-order weights: sum of weights and maximum weight. In previous experiments, we found that if either value is relatively low, the token will probably be misclassified and should consequently not even be considered when evaluating a model. After all, only information that is (implicitly) present in the training data can be used by the model and this model should not necessarily be penalized for this. In Figure 11 we can indeed see that some of the tokens have a relatively low weight. This mechanism could also work in the other direction: a context word with a relatively high weight could also lead to misclassification error, so it might be interesting to consider both sides.

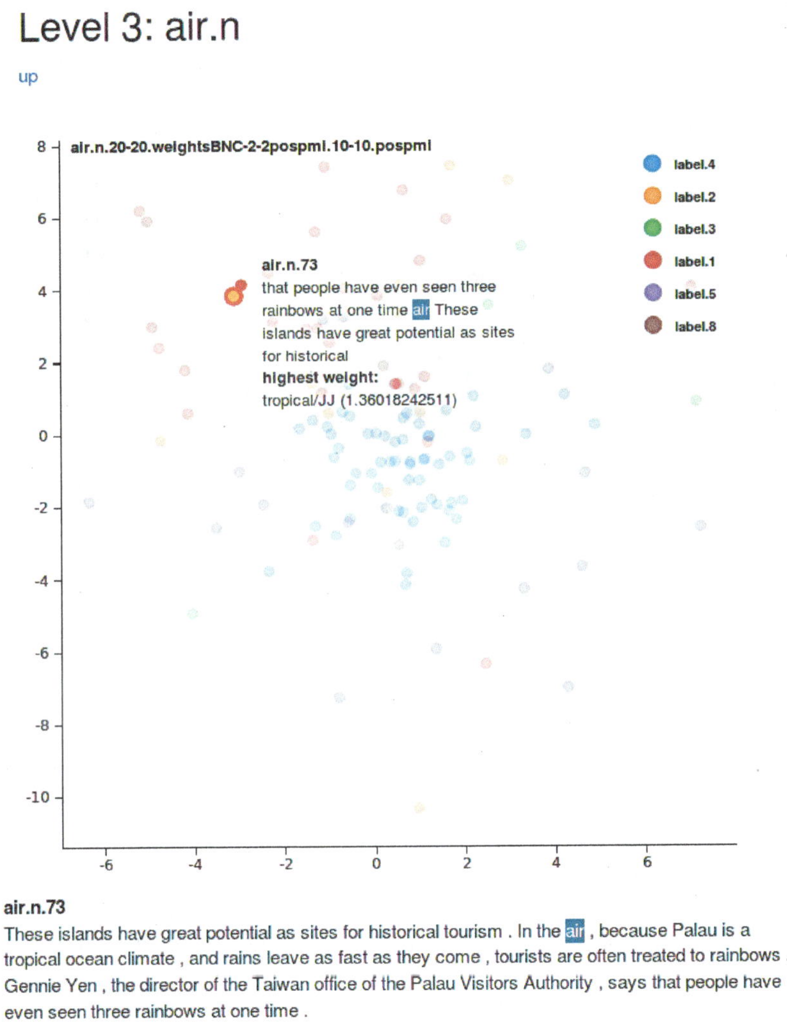

FIGURE 10 Level 3: air.n.73 highlighted with tooltip.

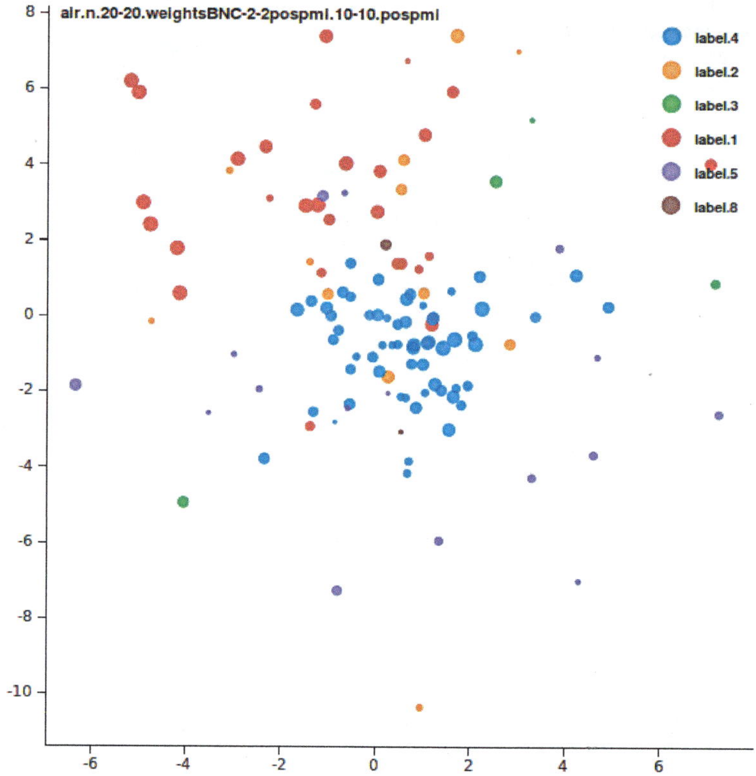

FIGURE 11 Level 3: glyph size representing maximum weighted context word value.

9.7 General Discussion and Conclusions

To wrap up, we created a multilayer Visual Analytics tool with a twofold goal. At first, we aimed at a new, visual approach to task-based modeling that can complement the more traditional one of evaluating a model's performance against a gold standard in terms of precision and recall or F-score. Second, when the modeling is unsupervised and not task-based, a statistical-mathematical evaluation of a model is simply not possible. This is exactly the situation where Visual Analytics can make a difference. Next, we created a tool that allows us to explore the variation in a large number of parameter combinations and making this process more scalable, within the limits of what both the human brain and an average modern-day computer screen can capture in a single view. The tool allows to select and deselect models in a 2D scatterplot on the first level. On the second level, the goal is to verify whether the models are indeed as (dis)similar as the aggregated view on Level 1 suggests and quickly spot potentially interesting patterns that are worth reviewing in Level 3. Although this approach is not exhaustive in the sense that countless extensions are imaginable, we tried to create a visual framework where a fairly large number of distinct, yet comparable models can be plugged in without overcrowding the visual space and thus make it cognitively tractable to interpret and interact with. By adding an extra variable to the models data frame to visualize the difference between weighted and unweighted rather than showing the weighting options in all their details, we have also illustrated that Visual Analytics should not be a static interpretation of the data. By adding this variable, we were able to reveal a pattern that was not visible before. To reach its full potential, it should be a process or rather an interaction between the user and the data. However, one should keep in mind that this tool is not meant to hand over to the end user, but is merely restricted to a research context where the user has full control over the modeling.

A challenge we briefly touched upon before, but in general consider beyond the scope of this study, is the role of the dimension reduction algorithm. Even though it is a crucial step in the pipeline to get from corpus frequency data to 2D coordinates, it is the one that rarely receives much attention. The reason for this is probably similar to why an intrinsic analysis of a distributional model is rarely done: dimension reduction, in this case Non-metric Multidimensional Scaling (NMDS), is a black box algorithm as well: we feed it data, but have little clue about how the algorithm spatially orders the data and how this process can be influenced to provide different and preferably better results. In our case study, we have only been looking at so-called stress-levels as a diagnostic for the NMDS performance. The dimension reduction in this case provides another diagnostic or goodness-of-fit test though, namely a so-called Shepard plot (Everitt and Howell 2005:p. 1830), which visually represents how well the distance between points is preserved in the output. Although it could be interesting to integrate this in our visualization at Level 2 and 3, it remains an open question how the user should handle such a goodness-of-fit model while visually inspecting the token space. As this question relates to dimension reduction techniques proper rather than visualization techniques, it is beyond the scope of this study. Furthermore, we used NMDS as a dimension reduction algorithm, but lately the distributional semantics community has embraced a new algorithm, dubbed t-Distributed Stochastic Neighbor Embedding (t-SNE) (Van der Maaten and Hinton 2008) which supposedly performs better with larger data sets. It is the de facto standard algorithm to visualize large-scale so-called Word Embeddings, deep learning models or recurrent neural networks for word sense representation.[9] In response, we experimented with this algorithm but got unsatisfactory results; not even a gist of a pattern, but seemingly random distributions of glyphs in a circle around the origin. On top of this, the repeated NMDS algorithm we have been using is in any case faster and more robust for a medium sample size.

Finally, this tool was created in response to the authors' own research needs. During the development process, emphasis was put on the reusability by keeping the assumptions about the data frame to the bare minimum. The tool was built in JavaScript and both the case study itself as well as the code are shared online. Therefore it can be used and fairly easily adapted by other researchers who are facing similar research questions. Future improvements to the tool, however, should be user-driven. The study by Chuang et al. (2012), for instance, provides an example of how such a user evaluation of a visualization can be done, in this case a visualization of topic modeling to structure Stanford PhD thesis subjects. In comparison, we face an additional challenge with our tool, namely that the parameter optimization highly depends on the individual research question that the user would like to answer. It is rather unlikely that a general case study can be constructed which is ready to use for research purposes by other researchers. Consequently, to perform such an evaluation we do not need just users, but for researchers who are willing to plug their own data into our tool. How this

---

[9]See for instance Google's word2vec (Mikolov et al. 2010) and Stanford NLP Group's GloVe (Pennington et al. 2014).

can be done in practice, remains to be seen, but we have conceived this visualization tool with the flexibility to achieve this goal in mind.

References

Baroni, Marco, Georgiana Dinu, and Germán Kruszewski. 2014. Don't count, predict! A systematic comparison of context-counting vs. context-predicting semantic vectors. In *Proceedings of the 52nd Annual Meeting of the Association for Computational Linguistics, Volume 1: Long Papers*, pages 238–247.

Baroni, Marco and Alessandro Lenci. 2011. How we BLESSed distributional semantic evaluation. In *Proceedings of the Workshop on Geometrical Models of Natural Language Semantics*, pages 1–10.

Bertin, Jacques. 1967. *Sémiologie graphique*. Paris: Mouton/Gauthier-Villars.

Brody, Samuel and Mirella Lapata. 2009. Bayesian word sense induction. In *Proceedings of the 12th Conference of the European Chapter of the Association for Computational Linguistics*, pages 103–111.

Buja, Andreas, John Alan McDonald, John Michalak, and Werner Stuetzle. 1991. Interactive data visualization using focusing and linking. In G. M. Nielson and L. Rosenblum, eds., *Proceedings of the 2nd Conference on Visualization '91*, pages 156–163.

Bullinaria, John A. and Joseph P. Levy. 2007. Extracting semantic representations from word co-occurrence statistics: A computational study. *Behavior Research Methods* 39(3):510–526.

Cao, Nan, Jimeng Sun, Yu-Ru Lin, David Gotz, Shixia Liu, and Huamin Qu. 2010. Facetatlas: Multifaceted visualization for rich text corpora. *IEEE Transactions on Visualization and Computer Graphics* 16(6):1172–1181.

Chuang, Jason, Daniel Ramage, Christopher Manning, and Jeffrey Heer. 2012. Interpretation and trust: Designing model-driven visualizations for text analysis. In *Proceedings of the SIGCHI Conference on Human Factors in Computing Systems*, pages 443–452.

Cleveland, William C. and Marylyn E. McGill, eds. 1988. *Dynamic Graphics for Statistics*. Pacific Grove, CA: Wadsworth, Inc.

Dunning, Ted. 1993. Accurate methods for the statistics of surprise and coincidence. *Computational Linguistics* 19(1):61–74.

Everitt, Brian S. and David C. Howell, eds. 2005. *Encyclopedia of Statistics in Behavioral Science*. Hoboken, NJ: Wiley.

Heimerl, Florian, Steffen Koch, Harald Bosch, and Thomas Ertl. 2012. Visual classifier training for text document retrieval. *IEEE Transactions on Visualization and Computer Graphics* 18(12):2839–2848.

Heylen, Kris, Thomas Wielfaert, Dirk Speelman, and Dirk Geeraerts. 2015. Monitoring polysemy: Word space models as a tool for large-scale lexical semantic analysis. *Lingua* 157:153–172.

Hovy, Eduard, Mitchell Marcus, Martha Palmer, Lance Ramshaw, and Ralph Weischedel. 2006. OntoNotes: The 90% solution. In *Proceedings of the Human Language Technology Conference of the NAACL, Companion Volume: Short Papers*, pages 57–60.

Jurafsky, Dan and James H. Martin. 2018. Speech and language processing. Draft of 3rd edition, available at `https://web.stanford.edu/~jurafsky/slp3/`.

Keim, Daniel A., Florian Mansmann, and Jim Thomas. 2010. Visual analytics: How much visualization and how much analytics? *ACM SIGKDD Explorations Newsletter* 11(2):5–8.

Kruskal, Joseph B. 1964. Multidimensional scaling by optimizing goodness of fit to a nonmetric hypothesis. *Psychometrika* 29(1):1–27.

Lapesa, Gabriella and Stefan Evert. 2014. A large scale evaluation of distributional semantic models: Parameters, interactions and model selection. *Transactions of the Association for Computational Linguistics* 2:531–545.

Lau, Jey Han, Paul Cook, Diana McCarthy, David Newman, and Timothy Baldwin. 2012. Word sense induction for novel sense detection. In *Proceedings of the 13th Conference of the European Chapter of the Association for Computational Linguistics*, pages 591–601.

Le, Tuan M. V. and Hady W. Lauw. 2016. Semantic visualization with neighborhood graph regularization. *Journal of Artificial Intelligence Research* 55:1091–1133.

Mackinlay, Jock. 1986. Automating the design of graphical presentations of relational information. *ACM Transactions On Graphics* 5(2):110–141.

Manandhar, Suresh, Ioannis P. Klapaftis, Dmitriy Dligach, and Sameer S. Pradhan. 2010. Semeval-2010 task 14: Word sense induction & disambiguation. In *Proceedings of the 5th International Workshop on Semantic Evaluation*, pages 63–68.

Mardia, Kantilal Varichand, John T. Kent, and John M. Bibby. 1980. *Multivariate Analysis*. New York: Academic Press.

Mikolov, Tomas, Martin Karafiát, Lukas Burget, Jan Cernockỳ, and Sanjeev Khudanpur. 2010. Recurrent neural network based language model. In *Proceedings of the 11th Annual Conference of the International Speech Communication Association*, pages 1045–1048.

Miller, George A. 1995. Wordnet: a lexical database for english. *Communications of the ACM* 38(11):39–41.

Niwa, Yoshiki and Yoshihiko Nitta. 1994. Co-occurrence vectors from corpora vs. distance vectors from dictionaries. In *Proceedings of the 15th Conference on Computational Linguistics - Volume 1*, pages 304–309.

Pennington, Jeffrey, Richard Socher, and Christopher D. Manning. 2014. Glove: Global vectors for word representation. In *Proceedings of the 2014 Conference on Empirical Methods in Natural Language Processing*, pages 1532–1543.

Peres-Neto, Pedro R. and Donald A. Jackson. 2001. How well do multivariate data sets match? The advantages of a Procrustean superimposition approach over the Mantel test. *Oecologia* 129(2):169–178.

Rapp, Reinhard. 2003. Word sense discovery based on sense descriptor dissimilarity. In *Proceedings of the Ninth Machine Translation Summit*, pages 315–322.

Schütze, Hinrich. 1998. Automatic word sense discrimination. *Computational Linguistics* 24(1):97–123.

Shneiderman, Ben. 1996. The eyes have it: A task by data type taxonomy for information visualizations. In *Proceedings of the IEEE Symposium on Visual Languages*, pages 336–343.

Turney, Peter D. and Patrick Pantel. 2010. From frequency to meaning: Vector space models of semantics. *Journal of Artificial Intelligence Research* 37:141–188.

Van der Maaten, Laurens and Geoffrey Hinton. 2008. Visualizing data using t-sne. *Journal of Machine Learning Research* 9:2579–2605.

Wynne, Martin. 1996. A post-editor's guide to claws7 tagging. Tech. rep., University Centre for Computer Corpus Research on Language, University of Lancaster.

Zhao, Jian, Fanny Chevalier, Christopher Collins, and Ravin Balakrishnan. 2012. Facilitating discourse analysis with interactive visualization. *IEEE Transactions on Visualization and Computer Graphics* 18(12):2639–2648.

Index